P🐾W Across My He🐾rt

Rescues and Other Stories of Animals Who Have Touched My Life

Debi P🐾ce

s🐾eetgrassbooks
an imprint of Farcountry Press

ISBN: 978-1-59152-291-1

© 2021 by Debi Pace

Cover art by John Nelson.
Book design by Steph Lehmann.

For more information or to order extra copies of this book call Farcountry Press toll free at (800) 821-3874.

sweetgrassbooks
an imprint of Farcountry Press

Produced by Sweetgrass Books; PO Box 5630, Helena, MT 59604; (800) 821-3874; www.sweetgrassbooks.com.

 Produced and printed in the United States of America.

24   23   22   21   1   2   3   4

Dedic♥tion

Dedicated to all the quiet heroes of animal rescue.
To those who give unselfishly of their time, money,
energy, and sanity to help animals in need.
*You **ARE** making a difference!*

Contents

Acknowledgments

*T*here are so many people to acknowledge, but first I would like to say thank you to all the animals who gave me their companionship, trust, and friendship. Their lives have been interwoven with mine since I first jumped headlong into animal rescue. These animals have enriched my life in so many ways and made me a better human.

I would like to thank my wonderful friend and first editor, Nancy Anderson. She provided great insight and ideas on how to enhance my stories as well as correcting tons of grammar errors. Nancy is also involved in animal rescue. I met her at the Camp Collie Rescue, so she understood much of what I was trying to convey. She is a dear friend and was a pleasure to work with.

I would like to thank my dear friend, John Nelson, for his amazing front-cover artwork. John and his kitty, Brandy, are best furry friends in our Senior for Senior Program. His artistic talent has made my book a showpiece.

I want to thank Mitch Telson. Mitch was involved with the Camp Collie rescue and drove many miles from California to help care for the dogs and cats. I remember meeting him while he was volunteering in Montana. However, it wasn't until his wife, Jeffyne, published her first book, also on animal rescue, that I contacted him for guidance. He willingly answered many of my questions and pointed me in the right direction. He was very gracious to allow me to learn from his mistakes. Without Mitch, I may have given up on publishing this book.

Mainly, I would like to thank the good Lord for the strength He gave me to do the work called "Animal Rescue." God gave me a double dose of compassion for animals, which I have often called both a blessing and a curse. I know there is no way I could have done any of this work without His help. Especially during Camp Collie, I often wondered how I would find the time and energy to continue, but God provided. I know that it was never through my strength but through His. One of my favorite Bible verses which has helped me continue this work through the difficult times is *Philippians 4:13 "I can do all things through Christ who strengthens me."* I have found myself saying this verse when the trials of animal rescue seemed impossible and over-whelming. The Lord has been my anchor.

God also opened so many doors for me as I put my stories to paper. While the book seemed to write itself, I was clueless on how to get it into print, published, and in a sellable form. Often the doors He opened for me were ones I didn't even realize were there. Since I had never done anything like this before I was running blind, but every time I was close to giving up, I felt His gentle nudge, another obstacle fell, and I continued. I feel lucky to be so blessed! 🐾🐾

Introduction

Writing a book about animals has been a dream of mine for many years. I started this book about fifteen years ago soon after the Camp Collie saga began, by writing short stories about the dogs, cats, and people I met. Writing was a way to hold onto the experiences of that amazing rescue. I never wanted to forget about the animals and the people that changed and touched my life in such a profound way. Writing has also helped me to deal with the emotional roller coaster that was then and is still now a large part of "animal rescue."

These are the stories of many of the creatures who have shared their lives with me through rescue. Some of the animals written about in *PawPrints* were with me for a long time and some, unfortunately, for only a short while, but they all left their paw prints on my heart. Many of the animals who have touched my life have stories that are too short to write more than a paragraph or two about, but I felt compelled to mention them. There are also countless animals not included but they still left their lasting mark on me. I truly believe all of these precious creatures were in my life for a reason and I want to celebrate them. Animals make our lives richer; the blessings in my life from these animals have been immeasurable!

The stories I have included before each of the chapters are what I call "asides" about some of the animals who have passed through my doors and my heart. Not all stories about rescue are sad and I wanted to convey to readers the joy and silliness we often experience while working with animals. 🐱🐈

– Chapter 1 –
Rescue is a Lifestyle

These are stories of my experiences in animal rescue. What started as a way to help animals has become my passion and my lifestyle.

I have always had a love for animals. Wherever I have lived, I have helped at the local shelter or humane society with fund raising and other events. However, there was always this deeper calling to help in a more hands-on way with abused or abandoned animals given up as a lost cause. They are the ones I gravitate towards; I want to share my heart and home with the overlooked ones. In hindsight, someone should have told me to "watch what I wish for" because I am knee deep (sometimes literally) in animals, especially dogs, that have used up their chances and have nowhere else to turn. I like to think of my home as the "Kennel of Last Resort."

Animal rescue work has turned from something nice to a fire that feeds my soul. I say that in a good way, since helping animals has been in my heart since I was a little kid. As long as I can remember, I have tried to help animals in need. Whether birds with broken wings or stray cats in need of food, I have ached to help them become whole again. Now as an adult with more resources, I am able to do my small part to make a difference in the lives of the animals who cross my path. I have always volunteered to bake brownies or help with rummage sales to raise money for the local shelter, but I knew there would someday be an opportunity to do a lot more. I just never really knew what the "a lot more" consisted of. That was until a huge dog confiscation took place near my home in the winter of 2002.

Not long after reading a story in the local paper about a very large dog seizure in northern Montana and becoming heavily involved with caring for the animals, I began to define myself as working in "Animal Rescue." The confiscation of animals consisted of dogs, mostly Collies, a handful of other breeds, and several cats. The animals temporarily lived in the small town of Shelby, Montana while the courts decided what to do about them and their owners. The dogs and cats stayed for nine months in several makeshift shelters set up to care for them solely with donations and the help of volunteers. It was a huge undertaking and a constant rollercoaster of emotions, especially for the people who worked with and fell in love with these animals. I went to Shelby to help care for them after serious internal debate. I figured it would just be for the day and ended up becoming involved with them until the adoption of the last cat and dog many months later.

The US Border Patrol stopped a semi-truck of 172 purebred Collies, about a dozen cats, and a few other dogs while crossing the US/Canadian border on a cold October night. The animals were confiscated and the owners arrested. The truck carrying these animals had been on the road for over a week. The dogs and cats had been crammed into small carriers and wooden crates traveling from Alaska to their new home in Arizona. The owners wanted to move their breeding facility to a more populated location. The animals had lived on little to no food and water during their trip. They were in extremely poor physical condition and living in their own waste. Once confiscated, the officers transported the dogs and cats to the Shelby fairgrounds and a frantic request went out to the local residents asking for money, food, supplies, and mainly volunteers to help care for them. Shelby is a very small town in northern Montana with limited resources. Taking care of this large number of animals, especially during the winter, was a burden, but the community stepped up to the challenge. The residents of Shelby and the surrounding communities jumped in to assist in countless ways to help these sick and starving dogs and cats, not knowing how long it would last or the amount of work entailed. Without the local citizen's willingness to help, the story may not have had a good ending.

I read about this story in the *Great Falls Tribune* and was sickened that anyone could treat animals this badly. I knew I should go to Shelby to help but was scared of what I would find, knowing my heart would break. Two weeks after the confiscation of the animals, I made the seventy-five-mile one-way trip to Shelby and my heart did break, many times, but I also felt a sense of incredible peace settle over me when I told the people in charge that I would be back the following weekend. I came back every Saturday and Sunday as well as all holidays to help with the dogs and cats until the two cruelty trials (the first trial ended in a hung jury so a second trial was conducted) ended and we began the process of finding homes for our four-legged friends.

One of the clever volunteers named the animals' temporary fairground home "Camp Collie" and this name stuck. Many of the dogs at Camp Collie had no human socialization and any previous contact with people appeared to have been a negative experience. These fearful and untrusting dogs were the ones I felt I could help. I have absolutely no formal dog training skills, but I knew in my heart that with love and patience they would come around. Happily, they did. In time, even the most un-socialized dogs seemed to respond to the love and care of the volunteers. That is when I realized that I had a calling to animal rescue.

As I think back to my nine months working with the dogs and cats at Camp Collie, I understood that this event jump-started my lifetime yearning to help animals on a large scale. The confiscation and the need to care for these animals was my headlong plunge into animal rescue. While I was relieved on the day we could finally adopt them all out to loving homes, I was sorry to end this amazing time of my life. For the first time, I felt like I was doing what I had been born to do. It was nice to get a rest, but I did not want this to be the end of my animal rescue work. I was hooked! The following spring there was another large dog seizure in Montana where I found myself again becoming involved. The three months of caring for these dogs ended with most of them going back to their owners. Despite this sad ending, I knew that I had to follow my heart and not give up helping those without a voice.

Rescue is a lifestyle and everyone I work with helping animals in need says the same thing. It is always hard to describe to "normal" people what drives us to continue despite the all-too-common despair and heartache we experience. Many who get into rescue work quickly burn out and give up, going back to their lives. While they truly love animals and want to help, the sacrifices and heartbreak are often too much. To me it does not feel like a sacrifice. I love what I get to do. Seeing the face of a once-scared dog or cat relax and give me his trust is an amazing experience. It is especially wonderful to have a foster animal who comes into our rescue program sick, undernourished, or abused be cared for until he or she heals. Volunteers work hard to match them with a person or family who will love them for the remainder of their lives. We see it often and it is what gives all of us the strength to continue. Watching that dog or cat interact with their new family is the best "Thank You" imaginable. We are so lucky in that we get to see these small miracles over and over again.

Rescue is also hard physical work and seldom leaves time for other fun stuff. Vacations will rarely happen for me since caring for my pack is not something I can ask another person to take on for even a few short days. In addition, some of my rescued dogs are not friendly with people they don't know. During an unexpected overnight trip to pick up a Collie in need I asked a friend who was also involved in dog rescue to stop at my house and feed my critters. She ended up badly bitten. The dog who bit her was terrified of anyone other than me from the abuses in his past. When she tried to get him into his kennel, he freaked out and bit from fear. That was the last time I spent a night away from home.

Even though I don't often take vacations, occasionally I need to board one or more of my dogs, which is never easy. I use a wonderful boarding facility whose owners are supportive of rescue. (Nancy and Kathy, the owners of the boarding kennel, would often make room for a dog or two who needed a safe place and never charged the rescue group for taking up space in their facility.) Both gals also taught obedience classes and had houses full of their own rescued dogs, so they understood my dogs' occasional "quirks."

Once when I had to be away for a few days, I had to leave my dogs at their facility. I assumed my large Lab-Pitt mix, Baxter, would be happy with them for the two days I would be gone. Before he came to live with me, Baxter had been found abandoned on the streets of an Indian reservation. He was a tiny puppy, about eight to ten weeks old, and had never gotten over his separation anxiety. As long as I am around, he is Mr. Tough Guy, but the minute I leave him with strangers, he is terrified.

All dogs staying at the boarding facility are given daily play times in the outside fenced yards. Baxter took this opportunity to hunt me down by trying to go through the six-foot chain link fence. Luckily, the kennel workers saw him trying to make his great escape and stopped him. Baxter also remodeled the inside kennel where he was housed with another of my dogs. I asked to have him kenneled with his girlfriend, Taylor. I figured Taylor would help keep him company and distract him from the fact that he was in a strange place *without his mom*. (I am sure that my being away for two days and leaving him at the boarding facility left permanent scars on his psyche, but I had no choice.)

Well, good old Baxter managed to remove the chain link gate to his kennel several times during his stay in his frantic efforts to find me. After two days and many attempted escapes, the damaged kennel gate was beyond repair. When I came to pick him up, all I saw were bungie cords and rope holding together the remains of the gate. I was embarrassed and offered to pay for the ruined gate. I never tried to board Baxter again after that fiasco. I guess I will have to take him with me the next time I go anywhere. Kinda hard to pack a seventy-five-pound mutt in a suitcase, but I will figure something out.

Rescue is a passion and a lifestyle, and I wouldn't have it any other way. All of my dogs and cats have been saved from a difficult life. Most have suffered some level of mistreatment and neglect. They have come to share their life with me, but I feel like I have gotten the better end of the deal.

Animal rescue also becomes your social life; at least that's how most of us in rescue feel. My friends are all involved in some aspect of helping animals. Most of us are single and while there are a few married couples, the unexpected nature of rescue would tend to wear on a relationship. I never know in the morning if another homeless animal will be coming home with me. We rarely get any warning but most people in rescue are used to the unexpected. A call for help will come in and it is hard to say no, knowing that it can be life or death for an animal in need.

I got a call recently that a bunch of people on Facebook were freaking out over a dog running loose in my community of Vaughn. People spotted the dog on the state highway as well as the interstate. He was so terrified that he wouldn't come to anyone. Sadly, it was inevitable that a vehicle would hit this very frightened dog. A gal called the Pet Paw-see Animal Rescue to see if we had a large dog trap, which we do. The following day I got the trap and set it at the dog's last known hangout, an old abandoned house next to the dump where he was seen looking for food. I also asked this gal to post a message on Facebook to all concerned about the dog. If I was to help him, everyone had to leave the poor animal alone. The dog was terrified of all the goodhearted people who were chasing after him. People trying to catch the dog had nearly run him over with their own vehicles in their efforts to "help" him.

I set the trap with some canned dog food and checked it several times that day, with no luck. We never leave a trap set up for a long time; we don't want a terrified animal to be caught and then left in it. Therefore, at night I just left the trap tied open with the food dish near the front so the dog could easily eat and get used to being around the trap. The traps we use are humane and don't hurt the animals. When we are ready to trap a dog or cat, we place the food on a pressure plate at the back of the trap. When the animal enters it to eat the food the gate comes down. It has to be scary for the animal when he realizes he can't get out, so we want to limit their time in the trap.

I never saw the dog but heard he was a small reddish Boxer cross. I continued to check the trap and leave food for the dog but soon realized that other animals were eating it. One morning after I had tied the trap open for the night, I checked, and a young raccoon had gotten himself locked in it. He had chewed through the cord that held the trap open and the gate closed on him. I gently put the trap on its side and opened the gate to let him free. He looked happy to be free, but I am sure he missed the meals he had been getting all week. By this time, no one had seen the dog in days, so I brought the trap home. The dog was long gone, and I hoped was safe. I told the people on Facebook to keep me posted if anyone saw him again.

A few weeks later, I got a call that the dog was back at the old abandoned house. I immediately brought the trap back out to the house but didn't set it, I left it tied open with canned food near the entry. This way the dog could get the food while feeling safe about being near the trap. I checked the trap often and after driving away from the house one afternoon, I finally spotted the dog walking tentatively towards the trap. From a distance, I could see he was quite thin, but I was also very excited to know that he most likely was getting some good food into him rather than letting the raccoons eat it all.

Every day I moved the dish of food a little further towards the back of the trap until one night I set it. Excited to see if I got lucky, I went home and waited until the sun went down. When I came back to the site, I saw a dark shape in the trap. After so many weeks of driving around looking for this poor dog, I had finally caught him. Except it wasn't a dog! It was a very unhappy hissing cat. Darn! The cat was going postal, but I did not want to let her out. For a second I thought about opening the trap to free the cat but knowing it was a female, I couldn't let her go. (We never pass up the chance to spay or neuter an animal once we catch them. Since she was a tortoiseshell kitty, which are usually female, I couldn't release her knowing she would likely reproduce.) But I was desperate to catch this poor dog before he got hit by a car and did not want to wait another night. Reluctantly, I ended up taking the cat home and figured I would get her spayed and released the next day. Once she calmed down, I realized she was tame and was able to get her into a wire cage with food, water, litter, and a bed for the night. She was actually very friendly, and I was glad I did not release her. (Nellie, the trapped kitty, ended up in the Pet Paw-see's adoption program and found her *purrfect* home with a lovely couple and a very nice Golden Retriever.)

By this time, it was very dark out and the area where the dog hung out was creepy, so I did not want to spend much time there. (I had long believed there were illegal pharmaceutical exchanges taking place at this old house and wasn't excited about being there late at night.) Nevertheless, I wanted this Boxer badly, so I brought the trap out again, tied it open, and placed another bowl of food in the trap. I got up very early the next morning and spotted the dog sneaking around the side of the house. He had gotten the food from the previous night, but I doubted he would turn down an extra breakfast. So, I put another bowl of canned food in the trap and set it. I left with my fingers crossed and an hour later went back. The dog was in the trap, growling, and very scared. Hallelujah! A friend helped me get the dog and the trap into my pickup and to a vet.

It turned out that the dog was female and an absolute sweetheart. Once my friend Jo Anne and I got her out of the trap, she laid down on the floor of the vet clinic and enjoyed belly rubs. She was nothing but skin and bones with a terribly rough, dry coat. We named her Tess. She learned her new name quickly and appeared to be between one and two years old. In addition, she was very well behaved. After a vet check and spay surgery, Tess went into a foster home to heal from her misadventure. She loved taking walks, being groomed, and of course food and more food! With a bath and good nutrition, she turned into a gorgeous dog with a lovely red coat.

We will never know where she came from and why she was out running for weeks or maybe even months. No one was searching for her. We checked the animal shelter as well as the local pet Lost and Found and Facebook; no one was missing a wonderful young Boxer. She appeared to be a purebred Boxer but since her tail and ears were un-docked, everyone assumed she was a mixed breed.

It took a few weeks to find the perfect home for Tess, but we finally found a single man who loved the outdoors, hiking, and running. When he met Tess, they bonded, and we know he will give her a lifetime of love. Great endings like Tess's are why we work so hard.

We never get tired of hearing how happy our rescued animals are in their new homes. This gives us the strength to go on to help the next homeless dog or cat.

Tess took a little while to find her perfect home but not because people were not interested in her. Many people inquired about adopting her. We try hard to match the right person/family with an animal depending on the animal's age, activity level, and health issues. Many people are angry when we tell them the dog or cat they are considering may not fit their lifestyle. If we have a dog for adoption, we insist the potential owners have a secure fenced backyard and someone who will give the dog the activity and exercise that he or she needs to be content. There is nothing worse than seeing an active dog left outside on a chain because the owners are too busy and don't have the time to give the dog what it needs. (Unfortunately, the excitement of adopting a new pet often wears off once their daily care becomes WORK!) Likewise, with an older or special needs cat or dog we want the potential owners to understand how to provide quality of life to the animal. They also need to understand that a special needs animal often requires more vet visits.

The Pet Paw-see, one of the rescue groups I am involved in, has weekly adoption events at both Petco and Pet Smart. We are fortunate to be able to house some of our cats in the kitty habitats at both stores. Our group requires all potential adopters fill out an application, which is just the first step in the adoption process. Our goal is never to get rid of animals; it is to match cats and dogs with families where both humans and animals benefit. It has to be a positive adoption, or it will not work, and the animal will be returned or worse. With dogs, we always do home checks to make sure the yard is secure which in itself angers many. Some people feel they are good pet owners and that we should know that by some sort of telepathy.

Unfortunately, we are lied to a lot. I had one very nice woman come into Petco one day during an adoption event to meet one of my puppies. She said all the right things and told me she had a fenced yard. She sounded like the perfect home for Pearl. That was until her husband came in a bit later to see the dog and started swearing at me because I told him I needed a fenced yard (which he didn't have) and would do a home check. Apparently, his wife forgot to warn him that she had already told me their yard was fenced. (The couple really needed to get their stories straight. Lucky for Pearl they did not talk with each other before meeting with me, but I would have discovered their lies when I did the home check.) He called me many choice words while I walked away. I am done and I end the conversation whenever anyone gets nasty or snarky. A friend of mine once told me "You can't play tug-of-war if you don't pick up the end of the rope." I prefer not to pick up the end of the rope and engage in conversations with openly hostile people, so I generally walk away. Also, since we are guests in Petco and Pet Smart, it's not a great idea to start a shouting match with a customer.

Many people often talk their way out of adopting an animal, like this angry man, and we let them do their own damage. They love to tell us their wild and sad stories of what happened to their previous pets. This makes the refusal much easier for us. Their attitude about rescue and poor treatment of their other pets often disqualifies them for one of ours. On the other hand, we love to talk with the people who understand that these cats and dogs are a commitment for the rest of their lives; they are not disposable when times get tough or the work become too much. We do appreciate that sometimes events in a person's life become unmanageable and they must give the animal back to us. We always take them back no matter how long it has been since the adoption. The good adopters tell us how much they welcome our process and don't mind the questions. The bad ones, well they just go away mad!

One of the questions we ask on our adoption applications is if the potential new owners have other animals now or have had them in the past. We also like to know what happened to any previous pets. It is amazing how many of these people tell us they moved and had to give the animal "to a good home". I guess what is even more amazing is that there are so many cities and towns in the U.S. that do not allow pets. (Ok, I am being sarcastic, but we get that "moving and can't keep the dog/cat" excuse often and I have yet to hear the name of an actual municipality that forbids cats and dogs.) I want to ask if they took their 42-inch TV, work-out equipment, and their kids with them when they moved. Those are sometimes harder to move than a cat or dog in a carrier. (Well the 42-inch TV is certainly hard to pack but I doubt many people kick the TV to the curb as the moving van pulls away.) This excuse seems entirely rational and logical to them and it angers those of us in rescue. You don't dump a family member because it is inconvenient to drive a few days with an unhappy animal in his carrier. Your pets come with you without question, otherwise we feel the owners don't have a clue about commitment when adopting. We generally deny these people and sadly, we score negative points from the public as well as get another round of nasty attacks on Facebook. Oh well, we do it for the animals!

On the other hand, we do meet people who have transported their animals all over the world when they move. I live near an Air Force town where many people relocate every few years. The good ones realize their animals are a part of their family and don't hesitate to bring them to their next duty station. Unfortunately, these people are often few and far between. We have seen over and over that it is easier to dump the animals they have and find news ones in their new town. Our animal shelter is full of them.

An example of an animal who has lived in many homes (six that I know about) and has been dumped quite a few times is Meka. Years ago, I took in a very large Alaskan Malamute who needed lots of activity. She loved everyone but had all the finesse of a semi-truck.

This large, hairy mutt loved to get face-to-face with new people because she knew they wanted her to give them a big wet kiss. Meka would knock a person over and stand on his or her chest to make sure a potential adopter understood just how friendly a dog she was. This made her not too great for a family with young children or small adults. Meka needed a secure yard since she was also an escape artist and needed someone who was committed to running her every day. Many people who wanted to adopt her either lived in apartments or had no fenced yards. Unfortunately, some who wanted to adopt her were elderly and had mobility issues. We try to be polite and not insult people, but it is hard because when someone sees an animal they want they don't take "No" for an answer. Very few people understand what the needs of an animal are and how badly we want to match them up with the perfect person. Rarely are we able to convince someone that maybe a Chihuahua or Yorkie is a better fit for apartment living than a 70-pound hairball like Meka. Typically they go away angry and then blast us on social media. We are used to it, but it tends to wear us down, and eventually we lose good volunteers.

We had a similar experience recently when a lovely elderly woman and her daughter were in Petco looking at our tiny kittens during our weekend adoption events. This woman was so sweet and gentle with our babies. She held each kitten while she showered him or her with kisses. She would have made a great pet owner, but she was 97 years old and she wanted a kitten. As nicely as possible, we told her that we don't adopt young animals to elderly people because it is our experience the cat will eventually be dumped at a shelter or have to be re-homed. We tried to interest her in the Pet Paw-see *Senior for Senior Program* where we match a mature cat with an older adult. We have numerous cats in retirement homes and assisted living apartments, which has been a blessing for both the people and our older cats. The Pet Paw-see will take care of all medical expenses, bring the animal to the vet when needed, and then take the cat back into our adoption program if the person passes or can no longer take care of him or her anymore. This provides a wonderful companion to an older person, often on a fixed income, who will not have to worry about what happens to the animal when they are gone. (Many of the cats in our *Senior for Senior Program* are older, stable, mellow cats and if returned to us they seem to adjust more easily than a young kitty.)

Unfortunately, the woman's daughter wouldn't take "No" for an answer, she insisted on getting a kitten for her mother. We told her cats can live 15 to 20 years and while it is sad to say it, this lovely elderly woman would likely not be around that long. When asked who would care for the kitty when her mother was no longer able, she angrily told us, "I will just give the cat back to you". Wrong answer! We need to get people to understand that pets are not disposable. They have feelings and bond with their people. Dumping an animal at a shelter or even giving one away to a "good home" is confusing and they mourn the loss. Sometimes the animal never recovers. Many get depressed, refuse to eat, and eventually die. Sadly, too many re-homed cats exhibit bad habits like peeing outside their litter box. We deal with many animals who have to be re-homed and it is always heartbreaking.

When we first started the Pet Paw-see, we thought nothing of adopting young kittens to older people until we heard of some of unfortunate accidents. One kitten chewed through their person's tube to his oxygen tank. Another elderly man broke a hip as the kitten tried to rub up against him and got between his feet, causing him to fall. In addition, kittens have NO scratch inhibitions. They will run up your leg in a moment's notice and leave claw marks the entire length. They also can be very bitey and hurt an older person with fragile skin. Not so great for people on blood thinners!

We also don't adopt tiny kittens or puppies to families with young children. Some little kids can be rough with young animals, and while not meaning to hurt them, can injure or kill a small kitten or puppy. A while back, we had a family with several kids come into Petco to adopt a kitten. They found one they were interested in and asked a volunteer about the adoption process. She told the parents about our process and then asked the mom the age of the youngest child. Mom immediately said he was six years old. The little boy piped up and said, "I'm not six, I'm four and a half." So much for teaching your kids not to lie. This family went away mad at us when they did not get the kitten; they should have set better examples for their kids. We find that the children are often honest while the parents are often not. Our volunteers have learned, the hard way, to tailor our adoptions to match the adoptive person or family's lifestyle. Sometimes we have a great person or family inquire about a cat or dog, but we feel this may not be "the one" for them, so we gently steer them to another more suitable pet. However, we make few friends in the process.

Unfortunately, swearing and yelling at the volunteers seems to be the norm. Denying an application resulted in the potential assault on one volunteer. She had to file a police report because the person she denied threatened her with bodily harm. He described in gory detail what he wanted to do with her when he found her. Another volunteer was in a local parking lot when someone started pelting her car with rocks. She quickly got out of there but recognized it was a woman whose application we had previously denied. At that point, we KNOW it was the right decision to deny these people. With some people, we will try to find them a more suitable animal but for many we don't feel they will make good responsible pet owners. We all hate this part of rescue. It causes many to burn out and quit. Most people in rescue are volunteers and have better things to do than be subjected to yelling or swearing. No volunteer deserves physical threats.

Many people who see us at adoption events make comments like "How many did you get rid of today?" That is the exact opposite of how we feel; getting rid of an animal is never our goal. The attitude I see often is that some people feel they are doing us a favor by taking an animal off our hands. We need people to understand that an adoption entails watching a part of our heart walk out the door. We love these animals and want to feel like we gave them the best chance at a great life. Each one is special to us. Getting RID of them is never our goal.

Another issue is the adoption fee we charge. It is very inexpensive to adopt from us. A cat is $80 and a dog $100. All of our animals get at least one vet check, spay or neuter, all vaccines up to date, worming, flea and tick prevention, micro chipping, and the cats are tested for FIV/FeLV. That adds up to hundreds of dollars for each animal in our program. And that's for the healthy animals. Often, we take in animals who need surgery, wound care, blood work, amputations, x-rays, and many other medical procedures. We never pass the costs on to the new owners.

If we were in a real business and trying to make a profit, we would likely close down before our first year. Yet we try to tell people what we put into each animal and only ask for this small amount to help us with our bills. I am amazed at how many angrily tell us they can get a "free cat" from the newspapers or Craig's List. They snarkily tell us they would never spend that much on a pet. That is one way to talk themselves out of one of our foster animals. I think some figure if they get mad and yell loud enough at us, we will relent and give them a cat or dog because they appear to be such wonderful responsible pet-owners. NOT!!! Other people try to play "Let's Make a Deal." They give us a million reasons why we should give them the cat or dog for free or at least at a reduced rate. That is never a good idea since by that time we know they have absolutely no idea of what rescue involves. We are not running a used car lot; we are trying to give our precious fosters the best chance we can at a loving *furrever* home. Our feeling is that if someone cannot afford the little we ask for the adoption fee, it is unlikely the new owners will be able to provide the vet care needed down the road.

Recently during one of our Saturday Petco adoptathons, a woman who had filled out an application on a cat the day before, loudly told all of the volunteers and customers within hearing distance "I am not leaving this store until I get my cat"! She assumed since she had completed the paperwork the cat named Mani was automatically hers. In her mind, she was a great home for this kitty but her very pushy attitude ended with us rejecting the application. This woman's rude manner and "eye-roll" after a volunteer tried to explain our adoption process resulted in us turning down her application for one of our animals. If she had been a little patient and less obnoxious, she may have been able to adopt this kitty, but her belligerent, bulldozer demeanor kept us from approving the application. (This was a sweet, friendly kitty and she had a few other people interested in adopting her. So it was no hardship to reject this woman's application and adopt Mani to another "more pleasant" person.)

None of us is a paid employee. Since we are all volunteers with families, pets, and jobs, it sometimes takes a day or two for us to review and approve an application. We call property owners if the person is renting and do all we can to make sure our precious animal is going to a good *furrever* home. Most people don't understand what we do or why an application is even necessary. Many of the public think that adopting an animal is like picking out a pair of shoes or blouse from a clothes rack. They point to a cat or dog and we hand him or her over, no questions asked. I actually had someone do that to me once over a puppy I was fostering. He was looking at two dogs during an adoption event, pointed to mine and said, "I'll take that one." I felt like he was picking out a chocolate donut at the bakery. He had not interacted with, petted or touched either dog. His nonchalant attitude towards the puppy made me doubt this would be a lifetime commitment.

I denied his application. (I want to see a potential adopter get on the ground to hug and play with the puppy, not make a hurried decision like this guy.)

When people learn the adoption process is not as simple as pointing to one that may work and taking him or her home, they pass their annoyance on to the volunteers. Some even go so far as to complain to the store manager when we reject an application. Luckily, the managers of both Petco and Pet Smart are supportive and understand our rescue group always has the final say on who adopts one of our animals.

Sadly, many of us go home dejected and some never come back after an afternoon of rudeness and disparaging remarks. There are easier ways to spend a day off and we fully understand. I hear the same comments from people who volunteer in other animal rescue groups. Something I hear frequently and have said myself during stressful times is "I do it for the animals, not for the people." The public, many of whom make terrible pet owners, often beat down the volunteers with their attacks. The only times I have considered quitting rescue are over some of the people I have had to deal with, never because of the animals.

On the other hand, we meet some amazing people, and this is what keeps us coming back for more. We greatly appreciate the people who give us donations, large or small. We get handmade blankets and toys for the animals, supplies, food, and many other items that we either use or donate to the local Neighbors in Need Program for low income families. Many people write us nice cards or letters and we get many photos of our former foster animals with stories of how happy they are in their new homes. Some people just come up to us and give us a hug or a word of encouragement. That is what feeds our souls and gives us the strength to continue this work. We could never do it without the people who support our group and our animals. All of us in rescue are very grateful to those who help in numerous ways.

A little kindness from the public goes a long way in helping volunteers continue in rescue rather than leaving for a saner lifestyle.

Those of us in animal rescue also try very hard to support each other. The volunteers in our group have a variety of skills and talents and we all have strong feelings on how we should run our group. I think this is typical of most non-profit groups of any size. This passion for helping animals is in our blood. In addition, while the volunteers have various means and methods of doing rescue, we try to encourage each other especially when things don't go well or we lose an animal. I know all of the members in the Pet Paw-see as well as in fellow rescue groups offer help to each other when needed. This is critical to keeping volunteers from burning out and quitting. It is always encouraging to know there are others out there who understand our frustration. Feeling as though you are the only person in the world holding your fingers (and toes) in the dike can be overwhelming.

While we live in a rural state with more cows than humans, we have a network of fellow animal rescuers throughout Montana who jump in to help during emergencies. Large seizures of animals, fires, floods, and other catastrophes have brought out the absolute best in many of the residents of our state.

A few years ago, one of the organizations that flies animals to safe shelters and rescue groups throughout the country made an emergency landing in northern Montana due to engine trouble. They were flying across the state and had to land at a small rural airport north of where I live with a plane full of dogs. (Most rural "airports" in Montana are just dirt or gravel airstrips where the pilot has to make a few low passes over the runway to chase the livestock and antelope off before they actually land their aircraft.) The pilot, handlers, and dogs were stuck until they got the parts needed for repairs, so they sent out a plea for help in housing and maybe even transporting the dogs to their next location.

I called one of the gals who was requesting help and told her we could find temporary lodging for the animals until their plane was repaired. The boarding facility I used had offered their kennels for the dogs free of charge. The plane had landed less than 100 miles away, which in Montana was "close by." I knew it would be no problem to round up enough vehicles to take the dogs to the boarding facility in Great Falls.

By the time I had gotten in touch with her, the plane was almost air-worthy again. Before we hung up, she mentioned how amazed she was at the overwhelming response from state rescue groups and local residents. It made me feel good to hear so many people were willing to help animals in need. That is what all of us in animal rescue long to hear; I have been lucky enough to experience it numerous times. My current "lifestyle" may not be normal to most people, but it has become a blessing to me in so many ways. 🐾🐾

D uring the Camp Collie saga, many people who volunteered wrote about their experiences with the dogs and cats and posted them on the American Working Collie Association (AWCA) website. People from all over the country were interested in this rescue and were concerned about how the dogs and cats were faring.

The stories also generated much-needed donations to care for the animals. Since this was a criminal case with the dogs and cats as "evidence" they had to be guarded day and night. The cost for security as well as supplies, rent, and medical care added up quickly for so many animals.

After following the numerous stories posted on the website about the dogs and cats, many people drove or flew to Montana from all parts of the U.S. and Canada to adopt them. Some of the potential adopters had picked out the animal they wanted to adopt long before ever arriving at Camp Collie. We even had one family from Florida, drive to Montana to adopt two of the dogs. They had followed their stories and wanted these wonderful Collies for their very own.

– Chapter 2 –

BC

My encounter with BC was a story I had to get onto paper and share with the followers of the Collies. BC's sad face was branded on my soul from the first day I met him. There was something in his eyes that connected me to him, even though at the time I didn't recognize it. No matter how I tried, I couldn't forget this scared but remarkable dog!

My Camp Collie experience is the story of many amazing dogs, cats, and people. BC is at the center of my story but there are countless stories that started on a very cold Halloween, October 31, 2002, night.

I first read about the semi-truckload of almost 200 sick, filthy, starved animals on a beautiful Sunday morning three days after a U.S. customs agent at the Montana/Canadian border in Sweetgrass, Montana, stopped the truck. I was sickened over their inhumane treatment after seeing the newspaper photos and reading about the condition of the animals. The animals were confiscated and taken to the fairgrounds in Shelby, Montana for food, water, and medical care. (The cats, sick dogs, and mothers with nursing puppies lived in the heated Search and Rescue building in Shelby. I wouldn't meet them or work with them for several weeks.) I followed the story in the *Great Falls Tribune* over the next week and read about the dozens of volunteers and businesses who had donated their time and resources to help these animals. It was heart-warming to hear of the compassion of so many.

I couldn't get the plight of the animals out of my mind and finally called the Shelby sheriff's office to see how I could help. The officer who answered the phone said they didn't need food, but they did need money and volunteers. I immediately sent a check, but my inner voice wouldn't let me forget about the animals. I found myself going up to Shelby the second week of November, terrified of what I would see and how it would affect me. I never envisioned how it would change my life.

Nervously I filled out the information sheet for the security guard at the entry gate of the Shelby Fairgrounds. The temporary dog kennels had been dubbed "Camp Collie." The security guard handed me a list of dos and don'ts with regard to working with the dogs. The guard also warned that the dogs had giardia and that all of the volunteers had to wear latex gloves when handling them. Bleach pans had been set up in the parking area for the volunteers to step into before leaving in order to keep from bringing the giardia home to family members or other pets.

After parking my truck, I looked off in the distance where I could see people walking the dogs and thought, "This doesn't seem too bad!" I was so wrong. I had read they were purebred Collies and my first glimpse of them up-close was heartbreaking. They were filthy, matted, and so thin that despite their heavy coats you could easily see the extent of their emaciation. However, what was most disturbing was the look in their eyes. They had a shell-shocked expression. The spark of joy that seems inherent in most dogs was gone in these poor creatures. There was something else very disturbing about the dogs, but it took me weeks to realize what it was. None of the dogs, except for the very young puppies, wagged their tails. If the tail of a dog is its emotional barometer, then these dogs had given up any hope of a better life.

I remember saying a quick prayer and then asking someone what I should do. That's when I met BC. A volunteer handed me the leash of a cowering, terrified dog and asked me if I could get him to walk. The poor dog was crouching down, shaking, and trying to get as far away from me as possible. His eyes and body language spoke volumes about how he felt about people. The note on his pen said #47, BITE CASE: CAUTION. (That is how he got his name at Camp Collie; BC was short for "Bite Case" or more like "Basket Case.") I learned later that he, like some of the other dogs, had bitten the officers while they tried to unload the truck on Halloween. BC was a filthy, ragged, very scared dog and my heart broke for him. I knew that whatever caused him to bite wasn't meanness; it was fear. His eyes were full of terror and distrust. I spoke quietly to him to try to gain his trust, but he acted more like a wild animal at the end of the leash than a domestic dog. The look in his eyes told me how traumatized and frightened he was. I knew it did not get there during the long truck ride. He had never bonded with humans, and the presence of so many people was more than this poor animal could handle. I soon realized he didn't want to walk, and I wasn't going to force this frantic creature. After having no luck trying to coax him, I put BC back in his pen and went to walk another dog.

Most of the dogs seemed to enjoy the outing in the fresh air but couldn't walk too far; they were still very sick and weak. Despite their poor health, they were responding to the kind volunteers. The older puppies were the happiest of the sad lot. There were fourteen of them housed in two horse stalls and they acted exactly as puppies are supposed to act. The puppies immediately "attacked" with licks and nips, anyone brave enough to go into their stalls. They were thin and sick with giardia, but abuse and neglect had not destroyed their natural exuberance. People were here to play with them, and they were going to enjoy every minute of it. I think seeing the puppies gave me strength that first day at Camp Collie.

I walked the dogs with the other volunteers until they had all been outside for some exercise and then left for the long drive home. Before I left for the day, I spent some time with another dog that had "Caution" written on his stall. He was a tall, thin, red sable and while he was very shy, he allowed me to put a leash on him. When I got him outside for a walk around the fairground racetrack, he started to prance. My heart broke that moment. This sad animal showed me that underneath his filthy, matted coat, the Collie was a proud, noble dog. I know he was trying to tell me that there was still hope for him and his pack-mates. BC and other dogs like him stayed on my mind long after I left that day. I knew I had to keep coming back to help with the animals. To turn my back on them wasn't an option.

The quick organization for the day-to-day caring of these animals was amazing. There was a system for feeding and watering, cleaning their stalls, and for walking the dogs. Animals had a number assigned to them when they were unloaded from the truck. Tacked to the front of their stalls was an index card with their number and health information. Many of the index cards had information about the poor health of the dogs: bad teeth, bleeding gums, bloody diarrhea, underweight, wounds, injured paw etc. The pitiful list of aliments seemed endless and my heart broke reading them. Some signs said, "Bite Case Caution," "Very Timid and Scared Dog," or "Injured Dog, Don't Walk."

The volunteers improvised collars for the dogs out of long plastic cable ties. Each dog's collar had a piece of duct tape with the dog's number written on it. (Over time, the volunteers were able to distinguish each dog by their markings, but in the beginning, they all looked alike.)

By the third week, a large army tent had been set up as a wash station. That little bit of comfort was greatly appreciated by the volunteers who until then had been doing this job outside in the very cold Montana winter. Two huge water barrels with heating elements gave us hot water for washing the dishes after their twice-a-day feedings.

A generous rancher had donated a water truck to supply water for washing and watering the dogs because there was no running water available at the fairgrounds. It was heartwarming to see several of the horse stalls completely filled with bags of donated dog food and dog treats. There were plastic bowls and buckets of every size, hurriedly scrounged from garages and kitchens to help provide food and water for so many animals. I talked to one Shelby resident about that first night and she told me that everyone just started calling friends when the word got out about a truck loaded with sick, starving dogs and cats. The people and businesses of Shelby heard of the plight of these animals and did everything in their power to help.

During the following week, I felt overwhelmed after my first day at Camp Collie and knew in my heart that I had to help these wonderful dogs in any way I could. Waiting for the week to pass so I could make the 75-mile trip back to the fairgrounds in Shelby seemed to take forever. My thoughts were continuously with the animals during those long days and I often wondered how they were doing. It was November, the temperature was dropping every night into the teens or single digits, and I worried about them being cold in the horse stalls. Some of the stalls housed from two to six dogs so I knew those animals could huddle for warmth and comfort. Other dogs labeled "biters" lived alone. I thought of those dogs often. My thoughts went back to the frightened eyes of #47, the first dog I had met at the fairgrounds. He was alone in his stall and I hoped that maybe someone had made some progress with him during the week.

Early the following Saturday morning I got up, threw together a lunch, and raced to Camp Collie to see the dogs. Feeding time was over by the time I arrived so I grabbed some leashes and started walking. It was very easy to walk three or four dogs at a time. They were still very weak and although it was apparent that they were not leash trained, they did not have the energy to pull or fight the leash.

The dogs seemed content to be out of their stalls and some were starting to beg for attention. Sadly, leashing some of the dogs caused noticeable fear; no amount of quiet talk would convince them of our good intentions. The panic and terror in their eyes told a story of their lives until now and it was a constant battle to keep from breaking down and crying.

While I was walking, I noticed someone in #47's stall. The dog, named BC, had the same terrified look on his face as he had the weekend before. A woman was trying to pet him and talk nicely to him, but nothing seemed to help. I remember walking away and thinking there were others I could possibly help but he seemed beyond my capabilities. I visited my prancing friend again and took him out of his stall for a spin around the track. While he seemed to enjoy the fresh air, he did not want any physical contact; petting was out of the question. I found this true of many of the dogs. They enjoyed each other's company, but humans were either something to be feared or ignored. The dogs seemed to lack the ability to connect with people.

Over the weeks, I would try to spend time with BC and the other dogs like him that were distrustful of people. Many of them were coming around but it did not seem to be making any difference to #47. BC still hated anyone to be close to him. At one point in my weekend visits to Camp Collie, I started to ignore him, figuring he was a lost cause. I doubted there was anything I could do to help this poor dog. So many of the other dogs were responding to the kindness and love of the volunteers. In addition, there was so much work to do. I thought I could rationalize not trying to help him. However, I couldn't forget about him. The terrified look in his eyes haunted my dreams.

No one would walk BC; he was too frantic at the end of the leash. I did see people trying to spend time with him in his pen, petting him and trying to gain his trust. BC got as far as possible from them and just trembled, hoping they would go away and leave him alone.

Despite his fear of humans, I knew he had to get outside for some exercise and fresh air. The Collies loved to play with each other and burn off energy in several large fenced exercise runs next to the barns. I wanted so badly to get him out there but was afraid we wouldn't be able to catch him again. I remember the first day I was able to get BC into one of these dog runs. I put a leash on this very wary dog and led him outside. After taking the leash off, he raced down the pen doing something that was foreign to him. He was having fun. BC ran, jumped, and played with the other Collie in the run, wagging his tail, and rejoicing in just how wonderful it was to be a dog. All the volunteers stopped to watch his surprising accomplishment. We had never seen BC act this way. The transformation was amazing! BC was a new dog! After that, I vowed to get him out in the run as much as possible. I also asked the gals who took care of the dogs on weekdays to take him outside to play. It did wonders for his attitude and helped to drain away some of his anxiety.

During the months of December and January, the wonderful Collie groomers who were in Shelby to bathe and groom the dogs and cats, transformed the filthy, matted animals into gleaming, proud creatures. The AWCA paid professional groomers to come to Shelby from Colorado to take care of their awful coats. The groomers set up washing and drying stations in the Shelby Search and Rescue Building to clean up the dogs and cats. The grooming took place indoors since winter was upon us and it was too cold for us to do this work in the barns. While the dogs were badly matted with their own excrement, straw, and other debris, shaving them was not an option. It was winter and Montana winters are not kind. These dogs needed to retain as much of their coats as possible to keep them warm in the cold fairground stables.

I watched each week to see if BC had had his "spa day" and was saddened to see that his coat was still a mess. I knew the groomers would be gone soon and wondered if they would be willing to take a chance on him. He was a handful and I figured they did not want to stress him out. Therefore, it was a surprise when they asked me if I would stay with him while being groomed. I was so touched the groomers asked me to help and looked forward to spending some time with BC.

He did great! After some initial apprehension, he seemed to understand that we were trying to help him, so he relaxed and trusted us. The bathing, drying, and brushing process was very time intensive since his coat was in such bad condition, but he tolerated it better than any of us would have imagined. The groomers had set up deep tubs filled with warm water. The dogs had to soak in them covered in a doggie conditioner while we worked the mats out with our hands. This process often took hours for the rough-coated Collies but was the only way to preserve their coats. Once we got the mats out, they were shampooed, rinsed, blow-dried and brushed. Unfortunately, the coat on BC's belly was badly matted close to his skin and couldn't be brushed without hurting him. Clipping was the only way to remove his heavy mats. Nevertheless, the groomers and I were concerned about how he would respond to the noise and vibration of the clippers. Well he astounded us! He not only allowed us to clip the mats on his belly; he fell asleep in my arms as I held him. Every few minutes he would raise his head, look around peacefully, and then close his eyes as if to say, "Let me know when you're done, I'm trying to catch some ZZZZZZ's." It still brings tears to my eyes when I realize the enormous leap of faith BC took to do this. I have always known dogs were amazing, forgiving creatures, but BC really reinforced this lesson.

Since that weekend, BC continued to make great progress. Many of the volunteers had a special place in their hearts for this dog and tried to spend time with him. When we went up to his pen instead of cowering, he came to the front and sniffed. I even saw him wag his tail.

Amazingly, the heartbreaking look of fear was gone from his eyes. A few weeks earlier, he had confidently walked up to me and licked my hand. Did he smell the remnants of the peanut butter sandwich I had for lunch? Maybe, but I like to think he was telling me we were friends.

BC has taught me so much about trust. I know that if I had been through what he had been through, trust wouldn't be an option. The volunteers all continued to spend time with him and the other dogs that needed extra TLC. I know it worked; BC is the proof.

P.S. Oh yeah! BC is no longer short for "Bite Case," it now stands for *"Beautiful Collie"!!!* 🐾🐾

My menagerie of small, furry, rescued animals included Bob the Bunny, and his three little piggy (guinea pigs) friends: Rueben, Triscuit, & Jelly Bean. These critters enjoyed each other's company and loved their outside kennel during the warm months. The kennel is covered to keep out the birds of prey that frequent the area and is surrounded by a sturdy fence to keep out the dogs. They have plenty of places to hide and lots of sunny spots for napping.

Bob the Bunny was found on a road after being hit by a car. The kind person that spotted him took him to a vet clinic where they had to amputate one of his badly damaged back legs. I heard about this sweet little bunny and adopted him. Bob's injury did not seem to prevent him from enjoying life. His favorite sunning spot was on the top level of the cat tree in his habitat. Climbing with only three legs didn't seem to hinder him. He enjoyed life with me for many years before hopping up the Rainbow Bridge.

I have always had an affection for guinea pigs since I got my first one at age sixteen. If I know of a guinea pig in need of help, I will always try to give him or her a safe place to call home. Rueben, Triscuit, & Jelly Bean are guinea pigs I took in from homes who did not want them anymore. They were such cute little critters, easy to care for and lots of fun to watch.

Both bunnies and piggies are easy keepers for homes without a fenced yard for a dog or for homes with family members who may be allergic to cats. Think of adopting one of these fun critters. Most shelters have both species looking for good homes. These little guys were a delightful addition to my family.

– Chapter 3 –
Home at Last

During the long weeks of the Camp Collie rescue, many friends asked if I would consider adopting BC. I would not allow myself to hope, afraid of jinxing the process. When it finally happened, it was a dream come true.

The day had finally arrived. It was a day I had tried hard not to dream of, but it was always in the back of my mind. Through all the emotional ups and downs of the last eight months, through two court trials, and constantly thinking and worrying about the Camp Collie animals, today I was signing the adoption papers for BC and taking him to his *furrever* home. I was terrified! I did not have a clue how I was going to get this fragile, damaged dog to trust me and feel safe in his new home. My biggest fear was that I would do something to put that frightened look back in his eyes.

He had made such improvements at Camp Collie. When I was near his kennel, he would jump up and down and wag his tail to show how happy he was to see me. As I worked near his pen, I would catch him watching me with those big, beautiful, brown eyes that seemed to say, "Please come over and talk to me, I would like to be your friend." He was also getting good on a leash and I did not want to ruin his progress.

I knew the only way I could get him to feel safe and happy in his new home was with the help of my other furry, four-legged friends. I was counting on my three Cocker Spaniels to help me convince BC that he was in a good place and could relax. Sophie met him first and wanted to play. Libby Loo looked at him, sniffed and said "Mom did it again! She brought home another critter. Well as long as he doesn't eat my food, maybe we can be friends." Finally, Dylan, my young Cocker Spaniel/Border Collie just looked scared as this very large dog poked him with his nose. BC was a total gentleman with them all and was just interested in being friends. After lots of sniffing, BC settled down in his new kennel and seemed to realize my home was an ok place to live.

I spent time with him after work each day trying to entice him with bits of steak and chicken to come to me. He would take the food out of my hand but was still very wary. Everything was ok as long as I did not try to pet him. One night not long after I brought him home, I was outside in the yard throwing the ball for Dylan when BC started jumping up and down, tossing his toys in the air. He saw another dog having fun and wanted to play too, so I let him out of his kennel. He chased after Dylan and the ball, not really understanding the game but loving it, nonetheless.

Then came the zoomies!! BC and Dylan would run around my yard as fast as possible and zoom in and out of trees, the garden, and my other two dogs. BC's legs were twice as long as Dylan's and sometimes he would just run right over the top of his new little friend. BC thought this was great fun and Dylan seemed to forgive the big dog for his clumsiness. It was wonderful to see BC experiencing and enjoying his new world. He ran and played like a young puppy and smiled that wonderful Collie smile that I had seen so often with the Camp Collie dogs.

While he did not let me pet him, he had no qualms about sneaking up on me and nipping me in the back of my legs. His herding instinct was very strong, and I guessed that since he had no sheep or cattle to herd, I was the next best thing. In addition, after he "got" me he would give me the funniest look as if to say, "I'm not afraid of you. I just want to play." This was likely the only way he knew how to get my attention.

Every day there was progress. He came in the house, but stairs were still a mystery to him. He adjusted to the sounds of the TV, but the other household noises like the phone scared him. Not surprisingly, like most dogs, he understood the cookie jar contained tasty treats. Over time, he felt confident enough to take one from my hand. BC also learned about the toy basket I kept in the living room. He liked to rummage around until he found the toy he wanted and then prance around the house with it in his mouth. When he let me, I was able to stroke his nose with one finger but petting him was still out of the question. He was just not ready for that yet.

It took time, but I had time and patience. In addition, my other dogs were the tools I used to teach BC that his new world was safe and forever. I looked forward to the time when I would wake in the night to fight a Collie for a corner of the blanket and my half of the pillow. I didn't know if my bed was big enough for three Cocker Spaniels and a Collie, but I hoped to find out.

I felt so blessed to see this fragile dog that had been through things I didn't ever want to know about grant me his trust. I will never forget that first day I saw him, filthy and petrified, cowering in his stall at the barn in Shelby. That mental picture was always in the back of my mind and I never actually thought of him as a beautiful dog. One evening as I watched him zoom around the yard with my Cocker Spaniels while the setting sun turned his coat to shades of red and gold, it finally struck me that BC really was a very ***Beautiful Collie!***

P ip was another Collie from the Camp Collie rescue. He was
an extremely shy and fearful dog, adopted to a lovely gal from
California named Kathy. The volunteers had always thought BC and Pip
were brothers. The two dogs seemed to have a strong bond and looked alike.
(I am sure this sounds odd, as most of the collies looked alike. But, these
two dogs were identical in personality and looks.) Because of this, I kept in
contact with Kathy over the years to hear how Pip was adjusting to his new
life. Kathy did wonders with Pip, even teaching him agility.

Through the years of corresponding with Kathy, I had hoped that she and
I could someday meet with our two Camp Collie dogs. We wanted to give
Pip and BC a chance to visit with each other again, even for just one weekend. Southern California and Montana may as well have been on opposite
ends of the earth. Sadly, I knew neither of us could feasibly make the trip with
our dogs.

I got a sad email one day and read that unfortunately, Kathy was
fighting cancer. Her health began failing after having had Pip for over
eight years. Friends of hers, also involved in the Camp Collie rescue, asked
me if I would consider taking Pip into my home. I was saddened at the
terrible news about Kathy but gladly took Pip to live with BC, Mr. Winnie
(my other Camp Collie dog), and me.

Instead of a weekend Pip and BC got almost two years together. After
getting Pip, it took no time at all for the two dogs to become re-acquainted.
Pip and BC immediately remembered each other after all that time
apart and were inseparable for the rest of their lives.

– Chapter 4 –
Community Cats

Feral cats have a very difficult life. Through education we would like to see people show them the compassion they deserve and not treat them as nuisances or evil. They are truly intelligent, amazing animals.

Until recently, I called them "feral cats." However, that has such a miserable connotation and brings to mind a ratty-looking, thin, dirty, shifty-eyed cat that would sooner rip your liver out than come near you. That is until I started working with a rescue group that tried to help them. I first worked with feral kittens for a rescue group alled CLAWS located in Bozeman, Montana. The gal that founded the non-profit organization would trap, spay/neuter, socialize, and then place the kittens in suitable homes. I was surprised at how beautiful these tiny feral kittens were. Many were thin and sick, but they were every color and coat type as the typical domestic cat. In addition, since they were very small, they were relatively easy to tame. Lots of hands-on TLC usually changed a hissing, spitting ball of fluff into a purring little angel in no time. I enjoyed working with these babies in the hopes that maybe some of their lives would be better. Unfortunately, many were sick and did not make it, but we tried our best to help them and grieved over the ones we lost.

The two groups I am involved in now, the Pet Paw-see and Humane Society of Cascade County (HSCC), do a lot of Trap, Neuter, and Release (TNR) for feral cat colonies. Many kind-hearted people feed and shelter these cats, but few can afford the cost to alter them. Both groups have worked hard to use TNR at several cat colonies and have been successful in many areas of the county. Some of the caregivers who watch over these cat colonies report few if any new litters, which is the result we all work hard to achieve. When we do hear of newcomer cats to a colony our volunteers immediately organize to trap them to be spayed or neutered and vaccinated.

Undoubtedly, the biggest issue we recognize is to educate to change people's attitudes towards feral cats. The word "feral" implies the cats are evil, mean, or dangerous. They aren't. These cats are just trying their best to survive and want to avoid people at all costs. Feral cats are smart. They have a healthy fear of humans mainly because many humans want them dead and gone.

The first step in educating people is to change the language we use. Jackson Galaxy from the TV show *My Cat from Hell* calls them "community cats" and we have taken that label to use in the Pet Paw-see's TNR program. It is a much more friendly term than "feral." These are cats who through no fault of their own have been abandoned, dumped, or kicked out of their homes and have learned how to survive in a dangerous world. Community cats living in a colony are similar to one large extended family. Many have been born to mother cats who were abandoned, especially if their owner discovered she was about to have a litter of kittens. (Too many unfortunate females are dumped when their owner realizes she will soon have a litter of kittens. It is the same as kicking your teenage daughter out when you find out she is pregnant. Not very nice!)

Numerous people wrongly assume a cat who has been living indoors with a family and eating kitty kibbles will automatically be able to hunt for food if dumped out in the country. That is completely incorrect. Many cats who suddenly find themselves homeless end up starving to death, hit by cars, or killed by predators. If they have lived the easy life of a house cat, they are not likely to revert back to their wild origins. The Pet Paw-see gets many calls to help pregnant cats or moms with newly born kittens. These babies, if not brought into a home when they are small, will become feral whether or not their moms started out as tame or feral.

Feral or "community cats" are smart and resourceful and while the adults will likely never become tame, they can learn to trust their caregivers. Many of the volunteers in the Pet Paw-see and HSCC feed and care for community cats. Over time, they will tolerate our presence as long as we don't try to grab them.

When I am feeding community cats at my house, I just talk to them quietly while I place their food down. Over time, they begin to show some semblance of trust. Many cats who live on my property will wait at the foot of the porch steps until I put the food out. When I go back inside my house, they walk up the steps to enjoy their meal. They no longer run at the sight of me opening the door. It is pretty rewarding to see them relax, even just a little bit. They learn that I will not harm them and know they have found a safe haven. Many of us have small cathouses stuffed with straw or blankets to give them some comfort during the cold months. The Pet Paw-see rescue group also builds kitty houses to give to people who care for community cats. Even an old doghouse converts into a comfortable cat shelter. My vet saves me the large Styrofoam containers that medications are shipped in which I convert to cat shelters. A small hole cut in the side and the interior filled with straw makes a warm dry haven for cats. This is a lifesaver during our cold Montana winters.

While many people in our county call us to trap and remove community/feral cats, many just call for help with TNR and/or food. They know each cat by color or marking and by their different personalities. Many caregivers name the cats and are concerned for them. We are more than happy to help in any way we can to give these animals some quality of life.

We live in an agricultural community where sadly cats, especially feral cats, are highly expendable. The Pet Paw-see and the HSCC have been working hard to educate people and help these amazing animals live better lives. They are so worth the effort and deserve better treatment than most receive. We hope through education and TNR we can change people's hearts and attitudes towards these wonderful cats. 🐱🐱

*A*fter helping care for the Camp Collie dogs each Saturday, I would drive to the Search and Rescue Building in Shelby to care for the cats and some of the young or sick dogs housed in that facility. Rudy, one of the rescued kitties, was feline leukemia virus (FeLV) positive but was the sweetest and friendliest of all the cats. (Most of the cats were Siamese and were a bit on the snarky side.) He was a beat up old barn cat with a battle-scarred face and was the ONLY animal in the entire group of dogs and cats that had been previously neutered.

Not knowing a lot about FeLV, we did not want him to mingle with any of the other kitties for fear of transmitting the disease to them. Rudy would patiently wait for someone to clean his kennel and then enjoyed cuddling with us. He was always the last cat to come out for social time, but he didn't act slighted. He loved everyone and had a large fan club at Camp Collie.

The volunteers at Camp Collie were afraid that once we had permission to adopt the animals, old Rudy would be put down because of his FeLV diagnosis. I knew he might not have a many days left but wanted to give him whatever time and attention I could, so I gladly adopted him. He fit in very well with my household of eccentrics and made himself right at home. Rudy had no fear of dogs and we all suspected that he had lived in the kennels with the Collies while in Alaska.

Sadly, Rudy did not live with me very long. After only eighteen months, he crossed the Rainbow Bridge to join his feline and canine friends. Even non-cat people fell in love with this old boy and mourned his passing. I sure miss him and hold a very special place in my heart for this sweet kitty.

Chapter 5

Very Special Needs Animals

I n the past, many special needs animals have been put down. We all need to understand that they can live happy, quality-filled lives if given the chance.

Special needs animals are dogs and cats who are often labeled "unadoptable" due to either physical or emotional problems. Often animals are born with birth defects or injured in an accident and require medical care either for a short time or sometimes for the remainder of their lives. Some of the animals in our rescue program were abandoned, neglected, or harmed by humans and it takes them a while to learn to trust again. Some don't look pretty from their disability, but they are all precious to our volunteers and we strive to give them the care and love they need to have quality-filled lives.

We get many animals who need amputations, and while it horrifies us to think about going through life without a limb, these animals bounce back very quickly. Unfortunately trapping is legal in our state so we see many cats who have lost a leg or need to have one amputated due to trapping.

One such cat came to us right before the holidays several years ago. The caretaker for Max's colony noticed a cat in terrible condition, likely from trapping. Max was taken to a vet who determined that his badly damaged back leg was unable be saved so it was amputated. He healed from his ordeal and went back to live in his colony. Max lived with his old friends until one day the caregiver noticed that Max had been shot in the face, so he was brought back to the vet for care. The vet removed the shotgun pellets from his face and told his caregiver that he was completely blind and was likely deaf. The caregiver for these community cats left Max with the vet hoping they could find a home for a blind, deaf, three-legged cat. He knew this animal could not live outside with so many predators. Max's chances of survival would have been extremely slim.

Max was a young kitty, about one year old, and super friendly. He lived at the clinic until the vet's receptionist called the Pet Paw-see for help finding him a home. We gladly took in this wonderful cat, determined to make up for his tough start in life.

A visit to our vet told us that the pressure in one of his eyes was very high and he was likely in significant pain from being shot. He had the blind eye removed and after a recuperation time, Max came to one of our adoption events. He was sweet, playful, and acted as if he didn't have a care in the world. Max charmed everyone who came to meet him; he wasn't going to let a streak of bad luck sour his outlook on life. During this time, a volunteer in our group and her husband fell in love with Max and took him home to see if he got along with their other kitties. He fit in well and we all knew that Max was meant to live with them. By that time, we determined that his other eye was also causing him significant pain. Sadly, a third major surgery removed his remaining eye. He seemed to sail through his very tough surgeries and was excited to get home to live with his new mom, dad and sibling cats. Max is a very happy kitty now and despite his handicaps, he plays fetch with his toys and loves his new family. He has even gotten some of his hearing back and is enjoying the life of a very spoiled kitty. We are so happy to have been able to help this cat get the second chance he deserved.

Both the Pet Paw-see and HSCC have also taken in many other special needs animals. The Pet Paw-see has had several kittens with cerebellar hypoplasia (CH). This is similar to human cerebral palsy. Kittens with CH are born with very jerky movements. They suffer from tremors and fall down often. These cats have trouble with coordination but are not in pain. The kittens we have taken in with CH have from very mild to more pronounced issues with mobility. However, they are kittens and don't know there is anything wrong. They still play, chase, wrestle with their friends, and have a wonderful time. Anyone adopting one of these special friends has to learn the limitations of their particular cat but with minor adjustments can give a CH kitty a great life. Some of these cats cannot climb stairs well and need assistance but many do quite well. They often are not able to run or jump quickly enough to get out of the way of a dog or young child, so we are very careful when adopting a CH cat to anyone. We want to make sure they understand the cat's limitations and can provide him or her a safe environment. They are worth the trouble and extra precautions needed to ensure quality of life for these special babies.

I have taken in numerous blind foster dogs over the years and have even had some of mine go blind from old age. Most dogs seem to adjust to gradual blindness and do just fine. When people ask if it is hard for a blind dog, I just tell them "They don't have to hold down a job, write a check, or drive a car so being blind is just an inconvenience." Once they know the obstacles in their house and yard, they can negotiate easily.

I had one old dog named Harriet years ago who was blind when I took her in from a puppy mill. Harriet had been blind for so long that her eyes had atrophied and shriveled up into their sockets, but she didn't let anything stop her. She would go out the doggie door, make a left, and do her perimeter patrol of my back yard. Harriet walked along the entire fence line until she got back to her doggie door and to her warm comfy crate for a nap. I was so amazed at her ability to navigate the back yard that I asked my vet if she could see even a little bit of light. He told me she couldn't see a thing. It was as if she had no eyes. Despite this handicap, nothing stopped her from living her life as she wanted. Harriet was a feisty little Cocker Spaniel who gave me many years of love. If you asked her, she would have told you that eyes were a luxury and she was fine without them.

I had one dog, another Cocker Spaniel, who went blind overnight. When I rescued him, Riley had a painful, blind eye. The only option for Riley was to remove his bad eye. After healing from the surgery, he went about his life as a happy little dog. Having only one good eye did not seem to slow him down. One day as I was getting ready for work, I noticed that Riley was acting strangely. He was bumping into the walls and furniture and seemed to be extremely anxious. After a few minutes of watching him, I realized he couldn't see. I rushed him to the vet who told me that Riley was blind and although rare, blindness can sometimes come on suddenly. My heart broke for my sweet little dog as he tried to figure out how to live life again. It took him a while to adjust to not seeing. I don't know who it was harder on, him or me. We both adjusted and I made sure he felt safe in his new world. Riley has been blind for about seven years now and as long as he can find his food and his couch, he is happy.

Addie was a blind dog who I fostered until finding her a home. Addie had been living at our local shelter for a long time where no one appeared to be interested in her. I told the manager that I could foster her if no one else wanted her. After several months at the shelter with no luck, they allowed me to take her into the Pet Paw-see. Addie stayed with me for about a month until she found a wonderful family. This very lovable hound mix now has her own boy as her *furrever* friend and constant companion.

Cody's person passed away suddenly and his buddies were worried about what would become of their friend's blind Husky mix. The poor dog was still living at his person's house while friends took turns going over there every day to feed him. Cody had been left outside in the back yard and was very confused wondering why his pal never came home. The Pet Paw-see took him into our foster program, and I adopted him to a great couple. It was wonderful to hear his new owner tell me how blessed he and his wife felt to have found such a special dog.

Helen was a puppy rescued from an Indian reservation along with her two siblings. While all the rescued puppies were thin and ragged-looking, Helen was worse than her sister and brother. At first, it appeared that the larger puppies were hogging all the food, keeping her from getting any. A vet visit revealed she wasn't getting the correct amount of nutrients because she had something called mega esophagus (ME). I had never heard of this before but learned it can happen in humans, cats, dogs, and horses. The esophagus works as a muscle, pushing the food down the throat when we swallow. Animals with ME tend to throw up their food because of the failure of the esophagus to push the food into the stomach, thus they do not get the nutrients they need. Poor Helen wanted to eat but couldn't and she looked terrible. The only choice was to either put her down or figure out a way to let the food get into her stomach by gravity.

One of the owners of the pet boarding facility where she was living did some research on ME and learned that dogs with this problem benefit from a sort of chair they sit in to eat while the food travels by gravity to their stomach. Nancy and Kathy from the boarding kennel found a template and built her a chair. They also taught her how to sit and eat, and then stay in the chair for about thirty minutes to allow the food to get to her stomach. The chair looks something like a high chair for a young child. It sounded like quite the ordeal, especially for a puppy, but she learned well and started to gain weight. After a short time, Helen went to a foster home where she continued to do well. It took a while but eventually she found her perfect family who understood her very special needs. For the rest of her life, Helen has to eat sitting in this chair or a similar one, but can enjoy a happy life like any other dog.

The animals with emotional needs are often more difficult to place than the ones with physical disabilities. They often take longer to heal and trust again. Some dogs are so fearful that if you raise your hand to scratch your nose, they run for cover and pee on themselves. Those precious dogs take extra time, love, and a lot of patience but we have seen some amazing outcomes. Chili Dawg, whose story is later in this book, is one example of a fearful, abused young puppy, who over time came to trust me.

BC is also another example of a terrified dog who was rehabilitated enough to become one of my education dogs. (The Pet Paw-see volunteers give presentations at the local schools on humane education. Once BC learned that I would not hurt him, he relaxed and joined me at these events. And he loved the attention from the kids.) BC had lived his life in a puppy mill and had little to no positive human interaction. It took time but he turned around and eventually learned that I was his friend. Once he relaxed, his silly personality came out and he spent his remaining years as a happy and playful Collie.

It seems that emotionally damaged cats are sometimes even harder than dogs to rehabilitate. Once humans have harmed them, they do not want to trust people again; they act more like feral cats than domesticated ones. These poor animals will lash out and spit at anyone who tries to help; they only know survival.

Lily was a momma cat who I fostered along with her three babies. She was not feral but did not want ANY human interaction. Someone saw a man dumping her out of a vehicle, and Lily found a barn nearby where she had four kittens, one of whom died. We have no doubt that she was treated roughly at her former home and learned that people were cruel and not to be trusted. It took a long while for her to come around, but she now lives with a wonderful family who loves her. Her three remaining babies were so young when taken into my house that they never had a problem with socialization. The Pet Paw-see found homes for them when they were old enough to leave their momma.

The Pet Paw-see has shown that it is possible to help special needs dogs and cats live good lives. Many potential adoptive homes are looking for a special needs animal to become a part of their family. Luckily the people who do take a chance on adopting a special needs animal realize their love and compassion will be returned ten-fold over the lifetime of that pet. The joy of seeing an animal with issues, whether it is a cat with three legs or a fearful, neglected dog, turn around and enjoy life is a feeling that is beyond words. While it isn't easy and often takes time, it does happen with the right *furrever* family. We have seen it happen many times with our rescued animals. Special needs animals often don't know there is anything wrong with them, but they do know they are ***very special*** to us! 🐾🐱

Rambo and Rocky were born to a feral momma, but they were lucky enough to find the Pet Paw-see. These precious kitties came to live with me along with their other two siblings while still young enough to tame down, which they did. (If a feral kitten weighs about one pound or less, they can often be tamed down relatively quickly. Once they get bigger and older, they become less easy to domesticate.)

Rambo and Rocky were littermates who luckily were adopted to the same home. Their new dad wanted kittens that would grow up together. Watch what you wish for! I forgot to tell him that two kittens are not double the trouble; they are more like quadruple the trouble. Even if I told him, I have no doubt he would still have adopted both.

A little while after their adoption, these babies moved with their new dad to Arizona. Several years ago, Rocky and Rambo's dad was visiting family in Montana and stopped in the Petco store where we were doing adoptions. He told me the two kitties are happy adult cats, living with a new puppy and teaching the pup how to live in a cat's world. Good luck puppy! 🐱🐶

– Chapter 6 –
Little Miracle

*T*hose of us in rescue celebrate even the smallest miracle!

The Pet Paw-see was still a very young rescue group when Kate, one of the volunteers, learned of a feral momma and her five tiny kittens living in a barn where she stabled her horses. Also living near the barn was a family of wild foxes. Momma cat was obviously streetwise and knew how to avoid the foxes, but her babies were too small and slow to escape if a fox spotted them. Other creatures common in this area were coyotes, owls, and hawks. Sadly, kittens make an easy-to-catch meal for these predators.

What made the situation even worse was that one of the babies appeared to be extremely deformed. All four of her tiny legs were crooked. She had to drag herself along any way she could to keep up with momma and her siblings. She typically lagged far behind her family as they journeyed throughout the pasture in search of food. Kate watched day after day as this family tried to survive and was especially worried for the little handicapped baby. She was desperate to help the kittens and tried for weeks to save them from what looked like an unavoidable fate, especially the little deformed kitty. Luckily, she was able to trap four of the kittens and bring them into our foster program. Kate also trapped the momma cat to have her spayed and vaccinated. After momma cat's vet visit, Kate released her back to her barn home.

The two girls, Autumn and Spice, tamed down quickly but the two boys, known as the "Hell No Brothers," would always be wild. (They were named after their foster mom said "Hell no! They won't let me touch them!") The tiny kitten who struggled to keep up with her family, Little Miracle, was the last of the family to be trapped and brought to safety. She may have had physical problems, but she was good at evading the trap.

A vet visit and x-rays showed the extent of her deformities. All of her tiny limbs were twisted and there was nothing medically that could help her. However, other than those issues, she seemed to be a healthy, happy little kitten and thrived in her foster home. It was a miracle this special needs kitty had survived so many obstacles. "Miracle" was the perfect name for her, and she quickly became a favorite of the volunteers. Everyone who came to our adoption events wanted to hold her and was amazed at hearing her story. She was a beautiful gold and gray tabby like her two sisters, Autumn and Spice. Autumn had found her *furrever* home with members of the Pet Paw-see. Spice's foster mom adopted her. The Hell No Brothers, Fred and Floyd, were too wild to adopt out and ended up living with their foster mom, while little Miracle waited and waited.

Miracle loved the attention she got from her many fans, but it seemed no one was interested in giving her a *furrever* home. I think most people were afraid of future expensive vet bills and of the probability that she wouldn't live too long. Our group has a hard enough time finding good homes for the healthy animals; the ones with special needs sometimes take quite a bit longer. The foster moms and dads often end up adopting many of our special needs animals after trying unsuccessfully for months and sometimes years to find a person or family to love them.

After realizing that finding Miracle a permanent home where she could get the care she needed wasn't likely going to happen, one of our volunteers wrote to the Best Friends Animal Society in Kanab, Utah, to see if they would accept her into their facility. (Best Friends Animal Society is world famous for their work in animal rescue and welfare. They have a large complex in Utah where they take in many animals from puppy mills to natural disasters. Best Friends is often the first rescue group at a site in the event of a hurricane, flood or fire to assist the community with helping displaced animals. They also partner with small rescues such as the Pet Paw-see and will accept animals that are often harder for these smaller groups to place in their communities.)

It was bittersweet when she was accepted and driven to Utah, but we knew it was the best outcome for this precious little girl. This took place may years ago and the latest news of our special needs kitten was that she was doing well. We don't know if she still lives at Best Friends or was adopted but we know this organization could offer her more than our small rescue group could hope for our Little Miracle! 🐾🐾

Most of Foxy's history is unknown to us. She was found running stray and was taken in by a rescue group that helps Indian reservation dogs find good homes. Her first home after being rescued was to a family who promised to keep her furrever. Sadly, it seems that "furrever" has an expiration date. She lived with her people until they decided they did not want her anymore. Unfortunately, once again, Foxy found herself homeless and ended up back at the same rescue.

Knowing I have a passion for Collies, I received a call to help this special dog. That was no hardship for me as Foxy was a sweet, well-behaved dog that got along with everyone in my menagerie. The uncertainty in her young life didn't seem to have left her emotionally damaged; she was a very happy Collie.

Foxy enjoyed her weekend outings to Petco for our adoption events, meeting and greeting the public. It only took a few weeks before her people found her. It was love at first sight for her new mom and dad. Even their resident Collie fell in "like" with her and b grudgingly allowed Foxy into his pack. Foxy now lives the life of leisure with another rescued Collie and is the queen of the house!

– Chapter 7 –
Saving the Best for Last

And then there were two!

It was almost the last weekend of Camp Collie and we still had a few dogs who had not found their *furrever* homes. Some people from around the country associated with other Collie rescue groups had planned to take any remaining dogs after our last day at the building. The first six months the dogs and cats lived at the fairgrounds in Shelby, but the town of Shelby needed their fairgrounds back, (and moving the dogs to a more populated area would hopefully give us more volunteers.) A small army of volunteers using their vehicles transported the animals to Great Falls for the last three months of their stay. During these last months, they lived in a large warehouse modified to hold dog kennels, a quiet cat area, washroom, and supply room.

We hoped to adopt them all before we closed the doors for the last time, but it looked like we would have a couple of stragglers left. The building lease was up, and we did not want to pay another month to kennel just a few dogs. Additionally, the volunteers were tired and looked forward to relaxing. Leaving that last weekend was bittersweet. We were happy the dogs and cats were in their own homes, loved, and spoiled rotten, but we would miss their happy faces and the comradery of friends made over the long nine-month saga.

As we got closer and closer to the last day, I gave a lot of thought to taking one of the overlooked Collies. I had already adopted BC from Camp Collie as well as one of the cats, named Rudy. The gorgeous Collies (they were all beautiful, but some were spectacular, they knew it, and liked to strut their stuff) had all gone to homes weeks before, as well as the puppies and all of the cats. The remaining dogs were mainly older but still deserved to find great homes. I told the gals in charge of adoptions that if the dogs were not all adopted, I would take one of the smooth tri-colored males. The dog I was considering, number 168, did not have a name. Excitedly, the last Saturday of the rescue I anxiously drove into town to see if "my" Collie was still available. He was good-naturedly waiting in his kennel for me to take him home. I asked him if he wanted to live with me and if he had any preferences for his new name. He told me that he was already packed and that he had always been partial to Winston. I liked it too and signed the paperwork to adopt Winston or Mr. Winnie. He joined BC and Rudy at our happy homestead.

That left only one more Collie dog without a home, a dog named Watson. Watson was an older, smooth, tri-colored dog with the top of one of his ears torn off. He was a rugged boy with a silly personality and that sweet Collie charm. I called my good friend Jan, told her that her dog was waiting, and she had better get over to Camp Collie right away to pick him up! Jan had worked with the Collies the entire time and we had become close friends. She adopted one of the cats but wasn't interested in adding another dog to her household, especially one who required so much grooming. However, Watson was a smooth-coated Collie! Once she heard that, her husband, Jim, told her to pick him up. I was outside walking Watson when I saw her drive into Camp Collie with her son, Kalen. They were both excited to meet their new dog and take him home to meet Jim and the rest of the family. All of us at Camp Collie that last day were so happy to see him finally get his *furrever* home, especially since he went to one of the hard-working volunteers. Watson, renamed Don Diego de la Vega (after Zorro), fit in well with his canine and feline brothers and sisters. He quickly became a happy, spoiled daddy's dog for the final years of his life.

Jan and Jim lived on a farm where their dogs had acres to run and explore. They would often ask to pet-sit Winnie, as he and Diego seemed to have a special bond. Winnie would "go to camp" at least two weeks each summer to spend time with his pal Diego. It was wonderful to see these once neglected dogs enjoying life. Even after Diego crossed the Rainbow Bridge, Winnie still spent time each summer at "camp." Jim and Jan were his second family and when he visited them, I knew he was well cared for and spoiled rotten.

Being last always seemed to fit Mr. Winnie. As well as being one of the last to find a home, he was one of the last dogs off the truck that terrible Halloween night. I would envision him waiting patiently for the rescue people to get him out of his cramped, filthy cage and bring him to a stall with clean straw, food, and water. (The dogs were each given numbers since they would be evidence in a cruelty trial. Winnie, #168, was one of the last of about 178 dogs rescued that night.) He was a very mellow dog, kind of a couch potato, never pushy, and he always tried to please his person. After over ten years of having this special dog in my life his heart was failing and it was time to say goodbye. I held Mr. Winnie for the final time and whispered in his ear that we always *Save the Best for Last!* 🐱🐶

*D*riving down the road one day, I saw two hitchhikers throw something into the ditch. It looked like it could have been a tiny kitten, but I wasn't sure, it may have just been trash. It really bothered me, and I couldn't continue driving without going back to look so I turned the car around and stopped in the general vicinity of where they threw their "trash."

It was a very cold rainy November day and a kitten wouldn't likely survive long in that awful weather. I remember searching and seeing nothing, so I figured I had seen them throw out some fast-food wrappers. As I was heading back to my vehicle, I saw a tiny orange and white kitten streak out onto the highway. Luckily, I grabbed her before she was hurt or killed, and took her home. She was only about eight weeks old, dirty, skinny, scared, and she had ear mites. I cleaned her up, fed her, made her comfortable, and then left for work. My plan was to bring her to the animal shelter the next day since I already had two cats and did not want another one. By the next morning, she had made friends with my two dogs and acted as though she found herself a home.

Not surprisingly, Willie never made it to the shelter; she lived with me for fourteen wonderful years. She was a sociable girl who loved to talk and follow me around the house. We would have long conversations about how life was treating her. She often told me how lucky she was; she finally had her furrever person. Willie never mentioned how she ended up on a scary highway, alone and hungry but I suspect someone dumped her there. I am forever grateful that I saw those two guys throw their "garbage" out that day and glad that I stopped to pick it up.

– Chapter 8 –
Collie Olympics

I wrote this not long after adopting my second Camp Collie dog, Winston. BC and Mr. Winnie were wildly running, jumping, and playing while my three Cockers just tried to stay out of their way. I even saw one of the Collies leap over a Cocker Spaniel as he raced around the yard. It looked like a couple of athletes practicing for the Olympic Games, which inspired me to write this.

WE ARE PROUD TO ANNOUNCE THE UPCOMING FIRST ANNUAL COLLIE SUMMER GAMES

Similar to the Olympic Games for humans, Collies have often inquired about creating something comparable, tailored to their particular talents. The following events are planned for this new and exciting Collie gathering. The details announcing time and place are coming soon!

✿ TRACK AND FIELD EVENTS ✿

✿ **Footrace and Obstacle Course**—This is a favorite of Collies and their handlers. The idea is to race at breakneck speed around the back yard to see how many obstacles the Collie can jump over or go through.

Music accompanies this exciting event. Collies receive points on their choreography as well as the type and size of obstacles they use in their program. This is both a singles and pairs event. The pairs event is especially exciting since two Collies must synchronize their moves. The participants in this competition must train many hours to perfect their talents.

🐾 **High Jump**—This event is very similar to the human event where the athlete jumps over a bar, raised incrementally until there is only one person left. In the Collie version of this sport, instead of a bar, Cocker Spaniels of various heights are used. The Collie must run at high speed towards the little dog, jump over, and clear the Cocker Spaniel. If he succeeds, a taller Cocker Spaniel is used until only one Collie is left as the winner. The Collie who cannot only jump over the Cocker Spaniel but leaves the little dog intact scores extra points. Handlers please warn your Collies that fighting with the Cocker Spaniel will result in immediate disqualification, even if the little dog starts it!

🐾 **Food Bowl Toss**—This event involves starting with a full bowl of food, eating it as fast as possible, and then tossing the empty dish high into the air. Not only do speed and distance earn points, but the Collie will also score higher for the number of flips the dish does while airborne. Most Collies love practicing for this event but feel they can only keep in world-class shape if they also train for the Footrace and Obstacle Course event. A fat Collie is a slow Collie! This is an individual event although the judges are considering making it a pairs event at the request of many Collies and their handlers.

🐾 **Grab and Go**—This event requires the Collie to not only be extremely athletic but to be able to think fast on his feet. It involves taking objects from the house, through the doggie door, and hiding them in the back yard. The Collies who score the highest are the ones who show the most ingenuity in the objects they choose. The dog accumulates points for the most unique item they can find and hide. Items such as computer keyboards, remote controls, and binoculars score high points for originality. Other objects such as Collie toys and handlers shoes score a bit lower since almost any Collie can grab and hide them. Collies must also negotiate the doggie door with their prizes and points are given for the degree of difficulty in cramming each item through the door. (Collies will lose points if the dog damages the item during the cramming process.) The length of time required for the judges to find the objects is also a big part of the total score and of course, speed is a factor since this event does fall under the Track and Field portion of the Collie Games. All in all, this event is not for the amateur Collie. Practice for this event should only occur under the watchful eye of a trained professional handler.

HANDLERS PLEASE WARN YOUR COLLIES THEY MAY ONLY USE INANIMATE OBJECTS FOR THIS EVENT. IF A COLLIE IS CAUGHT TRYING TO GRAB AND HIDE A SMALL FURRY MAMMAL, SUCH AS A CAT OR A BUNNY, HE WILL BE IMMEDIATELY DISQUALIFIED!

(I don't like to brag, but a certain beautiful rough sable, I won't mention names, has been perfecting his art and will be an odds-on favorite during the Games.)

🐾 **Full Body Slam**—This is a pairs event. The Collie must give much consideration when choosing a partner for this sporting competition. Each Collie must face his partner from opposite ends of the field. At the sound of the starting gun, the Collies race at approximately Mach III towards each other and before impact, (if they have perfected their routine) rise up on their hind legs and slam into each other. Judges give the highest scores to the Collies who are able to remain standing and conscious. The Collie team also gets points for the loudest and most original sound effects emanating from the Collies.

(Children in the audience seem to like that part the best.) The Collie's timing must be perfect otherwise one or both end up cartwheeling across the yard. A warning to all spectators, this sport is not for the faint of heart!

🐾 **100-Meter Tree Chew**—This exciting event requires the Collie to run toward a small diameter tree, chew it off at approximately four inches from the ground and then race to the finish line with the tree in his teeth. This event may be for single athletes or the Collies are able to pair up for a relay race. The relay race requires the first Collie to chew the tree off at the base and then pass it on to his partner. Unfortunately, many times the starting Collie has a hard time giving up the tree to his partner so you will often see two Collie dogs running in tandem to the finish. Speed is an important factor in deciding the winner of this event, although judges will often give points to Collies who can complete the race in unison.

🐾 WATER EVENTS 🐾

🐾 **Synchronized Swimming**—In this event, both the Collie and his trusted handler compete for their place on the podium. The event calls for the Collie and his person to swim a set distance out into a river or pond. At some point in the swim the Collie must climb on the handler's back and stay there until the handler swims them both safely back to shore. The Collie will lose points if the handler drowns or needs CPR at any time during the event. Although the person must be in top physical condition to compete in this event the Collies must be agile enough to hang on since the handler is generally fighting for his life and would like nothing more than to remove the large wet Collie dog from his back. Teams who qualify for this event must learn to trust each other completely.

🐾 **Water Dish Drag and Dump**—This event is becoming very popular with Collie athletes everywhere. The event starts with a full doggie dish of water. The Collie must use his front feet to drag the dish as far as he can without spilling. When he gets it to the finish line, he turns it over and jumps up and down in the water. The water dish must be in a completely inverted position to score the highest points.

(A certain Collie dog in my house claims the only time he has to practice his technique for the Water Dish Drag and Dump Event is during the midnight hours. It took a few mornings of walking through an inch of water on my kitchen floor to appreciate the kind of talent needed for this event. In fact, as I am writing this article my very dedicated Collie dog is in the kitchen dragging the water dish across the floor into the living room. Practice, practice, practice, that's what it takes to be a champion!!!)

🐾 **Mud Dog Event**—It is best to practice this event immediately after the Water Dish Drag and Dump Event and works best with rough-coated rather than smooth-coated Collies. The Collie dog must get his feet and belly as wet as possible and then find some nice soft dirt to play in. When the athlete feels he has absorbed as much mud as he can carry, he enters a room preferably with white or off-white walls. The Collies who accumulate the most points are those who are able to distribute mud onto as many objects as possible during the time allotted. The Collie earns extra points if he is able to deposit mud on the ceiling or at the least, as high up on the walls as possible. The judges are discussing whether to include points for choreography. After all, the Collies put in many long, grueling hours practicing this event and feel that footwork is as important as speed and proper mud dispersal. The merits of artistic creativity versus technical ability will most likely create some heated debates among both the athletes and judges of this event.

Well, all you Collies and Collie owners out there, doesn't this sound like fun? The organizers of the First Annual Collie Summer Games are excited to sponsor this gathering and hope the response is positive from the Collie Community. The sponsors are already looking ahead and planning for a winter version for those cold weather-loving Collies. How does the Collie Ice Slalom sound? This event will most likely be a handler and Collie team event. The Collie who scores the most points will be the one who is able to pull his handler over, around, and through obstacles on ice-covered terrain at breakneck speeds. This event will take great strength and finesse on the part of the Collie. The handler must just be able to hang on for dear life. This is only one of many exciting winter sports for our competitive Collies.

We hope Collies everywhere will start training in earnest for these events. I personally know of two very special Collies who are working hard at perfecting their sport.

So, all you Collies out there, pick an event or two and

Let the Games Begin!!! 🐕🐕

*O*ggie was a very old, crippled Border Collie when I took him home to live with me. A friend, Renee, saved him from a high-kill shelter in Idaho several years before. Oggie was in bad condition and scheduled to be put down when she spotted him at the shelter. He happily moved to Montana where he lived with her family until Renee's living situation changed and she could no longer care for him. Knowing he was old and wouldn't easily find a good home, I took him into my house and heart for his remaining time.

Oggie was a delightful old boy. Even though he was arthritic, he still enjoyed life. His job (all Border Collies need jobs no matter their age) was to follow me around as I did chores and protect me from danger. He did a spectacular job keeping me safe! I never once under his watch, stubbed a toe, hit my finger with a hammer, or got abducted by aliens, all thanks to Oggie.

Every night before I went to sleep, he would come up to me and put his head next to my pillow so I could tell him what a special boy he was and how glad I was to have him in my life. After petting his nose for a bit, he would lay down on his bed, next to mine, and go to sleep. I told him the same thing the last time I held him after he had passed. I felt so lucky to have had the love of this wonderful old boy until his last day. Oggie gave me much more than I gave him.

— Chapter 9 —
Train Wreck Sally

I had recently lost several older dogs and wanted to give a homeless golden oldie a chance at a few more good years, when I heard of Sally waiting at the shelter for her furrever person.

Sally was a typical un-adoptable dog who ended up at our local shelter when her person passed away. She was an old, fat, arthritic, black lab mix with a snarky attitude and a large cancerous tumor on her mouth. Otherwise, she was perfect. I had heard of her, and from the sounds of it, there was little chance she would be adopted, so I adopted her. I have a soft spot in my heart (and head) for the un-adoptable ones. When I went to the shelter to get her, the shelter workers asked if I wanted to meet her first; she wasn't all that attractive. I told them it didn't matter; I would adopt her no matter what she looked like. Well she lived up to my expectations; she was an ancient train-wreck-of-a-dog. She had old dog warts and bumps all over her body, a graying muzzle, cataracts, and an awful-looking tumor that protruded from her bottom jaw. The tumor was inoperable since to remove it meant that she would lose most of her bottom jaw. In addition, by its shape and appearance, the tumor was likely cancer. I fell in love instantly and took Sally home.

Sally did great at my house and fit in quickly. She loved her walks but wasn't interested in interacting with the other dogs. She was used to living with an elderly gentleman, and my house is kind of noisy at times. Sally found her safe places to hang out where she wouldn't be harassed and seemed to enjoy her new home. The couch was hers as well as a few other locations she had staked out. And because of her sometimes snarky personality the other dogs left her alone. If another dog entered her space, Sally let him or her know how she felt about the intrusion.

After having her for a few weeks, I brought her to the vet and asked him to remove as much of the tumor as possible and for a dental cleaning. The vet was able to remove a good portion of the tumor, which allowed her to eat better, but he said it would grow back, which it did. Eating wasn't really Sally's problem; anything not nailed down was hers. When she got a treat, she would snarl if the other dogs even looked her way. I avoided her at these times, too. Sometimes you have to pick your battles and taking a treat away from Sally was a battle I knew I would lose, along with a few fingers!

When medicating my dogs, I typically give them their pills mixed in peanut butter. I make them sit and be nice while they politely lick it off my finger. Not Sally! Sally would about bite my arm off. I NEVER let her eat it off my fingers. I would put the peanut butter and pill on a spoon and stand back. She would grab the spoon and I would have to wrestle it away from her. A friend of mine calls these dogs "Land Sharks," which described Sally perfectly. They will bite off your arm to get a morsel of food and Sally was anything but gentle when food was involved.

Actually, Sally was kind of sweet and affectionate when she wanted to be. She loved to wear her warm coats and sweaters since winters here are very cold. I would settle her into her bed on chilly nights and tuck a blanket around her. When she could no longer navigate the stairs,

I made sure she was comfy on the couch instead of trying to get her to climb with her old, tired legs. In her own way, she conveyed how much she appreciated me taking care of her. The only time she showed any real aggression was during bath time. She would growl and snap but only for show. She never bit me and after a while, she tolerated bathing. I think she liked the rub down after her shampoo and rinse. Sally also loved all kinds of fruit and vegetables, mainly apples, carrots, and melons. She once stole a bunch of bananas out of my fruit basket and ate every one before I realized what she had done. If anyone, myself included, ever came near Sally while she was munching on her produce she would growl and show her not-so-pearly-whites. It wasn't a pretty sight, but I indulged her since I knew her time with me was growing short and I wanted to spoil her a bit.

As with all my old animals, I know each day is a gift. Their health can take a turn for the worse quickly. When a dog or cat stops eating, I know something is wrong. Since Sally lived to eat, I knew she was failing when one day in August 2016 she refused anything I tried to tempt her with, even her favorites. I brought her to the vet fearing the worst and wasn't surprised when he called me to say she had only about one quarter of her kidney function left. I told him I would be right over and sadly left work, knowing I would have to say goodbye to my train-wreck girl. However, when I got to the clinic, instead of putting her down, he said he wanted to try something. There was a chance it would not work but I was willing to postpone what I figured was the inevitable. The vet put her on a type of prescription dog food that supports the kidneys. He told me if she would eat some, it might bring her back from the brink. I brought Sally home, hopeful for a little more time with her.

Surprisingly, she liked the food and started to eat as she had previously done. Once again, food became her best friend. Happily, after a few days, she began acting like her old snarky self. About six weeks later I brought her back to the vet for some follow-up bloodwork and was told her kidneys were functioning in the "high normal" range. The vet and I were both very happy to see those results. Usually with kidney failure there is not much that can be done and it's more humane to put the animal down. I was so glad he was willing to give both of us a chance at more time together. The prescription dog food was able to give me one more year with this cantankerous, old, train-wreck-of-a-dog.

When I first adopted Sally, I figured she was about ten to twelve years old and had only about one year or two left. Sally lived with me for three and a half years, which is a lot longer than I had imagined. Up until her last days, she loved to take her walks and eat as if she was never going to see food again. However, I knew it was time to say goodbye when once again she started to refuse food, even chicken and hamburger. Her time with me was suddenly over when I came home from work one night and saw that she was in distress. Sally was a special girl. I miss her and am glad I took the chance on bringing this snarky, old train-wreck-of-a-dog into my life.

*L*ex E Loo, a tiny black and white Cocker Spaniel, had gone from one home to another over a very short time, four homes in two months. She ended up living at a vet clinic until the HSCC could find her a permanent home or at least a foster home. Lex E was so terrified when I first saw her that I didn't know if she was adoptable. When I came up to her cage, she vibrated with fear but once I got her outside for a walk, she relaxed a bit and enjoyed the fresh air.

Ms. Lex E had a habit of biting people, which was likely due to the uncertainty and constant change in her young life. Most potential adopters chalked that up to meanness. I quickly realized she wasn't mean. But even if she really was mean, that never stopped me from helping an animal in need and Lex E Loo qualified as "in need". The terrified look in her beautiful eyes told me how scared she was. Life had not been easy for this misunderstood little dog.

I adopted Lex E Loo and enjoyed every minute of her company. She never showed me any aggression and was just an amiable little Cocker. She took her responsibility to be my best friend seriously and never left my side. Lex E showed me nothing but love during the years I had her. Little Lex E Loo left me for the Rainbow Bridge and is terribly missed!

– Chapter 10 –
The Summer of the Puppies

The Indian reservations in Montana are often overrun with dogs and unwanted litters. I felt compelled to help by taking in a litter or two. Be careful what you wish for!

One summer I took in some puppies from a rescue group that tries to help stray dogs living on a nearby Indian reservation. The gal from this rescue group had taken in numerous litters and was overloaded so I agreed to take about five to six puppies into the Pet Paw-see foster program. I only had one foster dog at this time, and I thought some puppies would be fun. Well the five to six turned into two litters totaling nine young puppies. Seven puppies from the first litter were about six weeks old and the other litter of two pups were about eight weeks old. It was the end of May so I knew they would be safe and comfortable in the outside kennel I built for them. With a comfy, straw-filled igloo doghouse, plenty of room to run, and tons of toys, I didn't think it would be too much work for me. I picked the nine babies up one afternoon and brought them to my house. They looked to be in fairly good condition and were quite sociable, friendly little pups. And soooo cute!!

While I was at work, they spent their days in a large enclosure with plenty of sun, shade, water, food, and toys. It had been a while since I had puppies so I had forgotten how much young puppies could eat and poop. I was afraid to do the math; five to six times a day times nine puppies is a very large number. I felt like the man in the circus who follows the elephant with a bucket and shovel. All I seemed to do each morning and night was clean up after the puppies. It was endless! But at least the messes were not in my house.

When I let them out of their enclosure, they were hysterical to watch and were such a delightful group of happy little dogs. I loved sitting in the grass with them as they played, wrestled, and romped around the yard. There was nothing better after a tough day at work than to tickle little tummies and watch how they interacted with each other. It was easy to see which pups were the shy, timid ones and which would be adventurous, Alpha-type dogs. I took me over a week to sort them by sex and even longer to name them. There were six females and three males, and I wanted to see their different personalities before naming them.

They did not have any specific breed identifiers but were such nice little guys and gals I doubted I would have any trouble finding them homes. I brought them to the vet for worming and just waited until they were a bit older to be able to show them to potential adopters. The seven in the younger of the two litters needed their first puppy shots before they were able to come to Petco for an adoption event. The two older pups had their first set of shots, were spayed, and were good to go. They caused a riot when I brought them to their first adoptathon. People coming into the store to buy bird food decided on the spot they couldn't leave without a puppy. There were people lined up to adopt them, but unfortunately, many applicants were not suitable. After my first day at Petco with the two puppies, I was exhausted. This wasn't because of the work caring for the puppies but because of the people who thought they would die if they didn't get a puppy right away, even if they only came in for bird food. It gave me a glimpse of what my summer of adoptions would be like. I was used to taking in one to two foster dogs at a time and while many of them attracted lots of attention, nothing generates interest like a puppy.

Like kittens, we don't adopt puppies to families with very young children, typically under six years old. It can be dangerous for both the animal and children. Puppies like to gnaw on everything, even if it's a human limb. Their needle-sharp teeth are painful and could hurt a young child. In addition, we don't like anyone to make a snap decision to adopt. This is a lifetime commitment, and puppies—as cute as they are—can be a LOT of work. These babies were not housebroken, pooped/peed all over the place, and chewed everything in their path. If you are not prepared mentally and have not puppy-proofed your house, the damage can be overwhelming even from only one tiny puppy.

I never let the puppies stay in my house unsupervised. I would take only one or two inside at a time to teach them about life in the civilized world and then try to keep them from destroying everything within sight. They chewed several power cords, the couch, the dining room table leg, tons of shoes, the corner of a wall, and numerous other things. While I was running after one puppy, the other would be doing the maximum destruction possible. I knew the house was a dangerous place to leave them for long because of the damage they could cause, but never did I think they could destroy my backyard. After all, I have my own pack of hairy mutts, so I felt my backyard was very dog safe. Not so!

Unfortunately, I learned the hard way that you should NEVER plant a garden that you hope to harvest from if you have a pack of marauding puppies. They demolished most of my tomato, pepper, and herb plants, several pots of flowers, and the worst damage was to the seedlings I planted that summer. Those little home wreckers chewed down four small trees I had planted less than a week before. It was depressing to see my plants ruined, but I was able to salvage some of the seedlings and moved them out of reach of the tiny terrors. My potato plants seemed to be safe until later in the summer when the potatoes started to mature. They must have smelled the spuds because I would find many small potatoes strewn around the yard with numerous teeth marks in them. The puppies would dig them up, chew for a bit, get bored, and then scatter them in the grass. When one puppy was into something, they all decided they couldn't pass up on the fun. However, despite them being little wrecking machines, I loved every minute they lived with me. The puppies were such fun and while it was sad to say goodbye, I felt good they had all gone to great homes. It took almost six months to adopt all the puppies out and by that time, the weather was turning into winter. I couldn't imagine the harm they would do to my house if I had to take them inside during the cold months. I miss the little monsters but will always smile when I remember the *Summer of the Puppies* and I would do it again in a heartbeat!

I ended up keeping one of the puppies, named Pearl. She was the shyest and most timid of the bunch. Pearl was the last puppy up for adoption, and I worried how I would find the right home for her because of how sensitive she was. She trusted me but would go belly-up or hide whenever anyone else tried to pet her. I finally found a wonderful family who fell in love and wanted to adopt her, so I let them try Pearl for the day. A few hours later they called and told me that she had bitten their son and the mom so they felt they couldn't keep her. This was a nice home, with another rescued dog, and I knew it would be great for her. However, she was so terrified when I left her with her new family that she hid, and when they tried to get her out from behind the couch, she bit them. So much for this adoption.

The potential adopters were a great family with a very gentle ten-year old boy, but I couldn't leave her there knowing she would likely bite again out of fear. So, I took her back, did the paperwork to adopt Pearl, and once again become a Foster Failure. It's okay because Pearl is the sweetest and most amiable of all my dogs. She is a perfect little lady on a leash and just wants to make her mom happy. I don't regret keeping her and figure that was her plan all along. She is a wonderful lovable little dog who tells me every day how happy she is to have gone from an unwanted mutt living on the reservation to a loving home. 🐾🐾

Bailey seems to be a common name for dogs and cats. I have met quite a few over the years and even named one of my cats Bailey. He was a beautiful soft buff kitty, the color of Irish Crème liquor. He showed up in my driveway as a tiny kitten one cold afternoon and stayed for about thirteen years.

My first foster dog named Bailey was being beaten by her angry owner when a fellow animal rescue friend, Gloria, saw the mistreatment and got the dog away from her abuser. After Gloria "got" the dog to safety, she needed a place for her to stay so she came to my house. This sweet girl ended up living with me for a few weeks until her adoption. Bailey was a playful, energetic dog who just needed obedience work to become a well-behaved family member. She found a home that could give her the training she needed as well as love and patience.

My second foster dog named Bailey was a beautiful black lab mix who became homeless when his owners divorced. There was nothing wrong with this wonderful dog; he was just unlucky enough to be "unwanted" when his mom and dad parted ways. Bailey escorted me to our weekly Petco events and eventually found a happy home with a member of the Pet Paw-see.

– Chapter 11 –
Visions of the Iditarod

***N**ever let anyone squash your dreams!*

I was running with one of my Coyote/Husky "puppies," Bugg Z, hoping to burn off some of his endless energy when I realized it was a losing battle. There was no way that I could possibly run far enough or fast enough to tire him out. That's when I got the great idea of harnessing Bugg Z and having him pull me on a sled. I figured if he did most of the work, maybe I could get him (and me) to sleep at night.

Not knowing anything about training sled dogs, my first question to my dog-owner friends was "How do you get a Husky to stop?" I envisioned being pulled for miles over icy ground by a manic Husky dog. Well, none of them had a clue, but most had the same reaction to my plan; they told me I was insane! After one of my dear friends stopped laughing, she suggested that I try to teach him to pull me on one of those round plastic kiddie sleds. At least then I would be closer to the ground and less likely to break anything if, or rather when, I fell off. That sounded like a wonderful idea, so I devised a harness system, which attached to my new "sled" and looked forward to my first training session with Bugg Z.

We had gotten a lot of snow that week, and the day was beautiful for a dog sled trek. Mr. Bugg Z knew something fun was about to happen and he willingly allowed me to harness him to his sled. While the other dogs crowded around to sniff at the harness and the sled, my Collie, Winston, knew exactly what to do. He sat down in the sled and waited for the wild ride to start. I knew that if I were to make any progress with training it would have to be away from the rest of the pack. So, I took Bugg Z to the snow-packed road out in front of my house, sat in the sled, and yelled, "Run, Bugg Z run! Feel the wind in your ears. You're a sled dog now!"

All my visions of tearing through the countryside on a crisp winter day came to a crashing halt when my "sled dog" did exactly what he thought would make me happy. He came over to me, crawled into my lap, and covered me with wet dog kisses. I hugged him back and quickly came up with "Plan B." I figured maybe I was expecting too much for our first sledding adventure, but I wasn't going to give up. I needed something heavy in his sled to get him used to the idea and the feel of pulling a weight. The 40-pound bag of kitty litter fit the bill. Bugg Z quickly figured out what his role was supposed to be and after getting used to something chasing him, he had a blast. I had to run next to him the entire time, but he did great and seemed to love it. I'm sure we were quite the sight, a large Husky dog pulling a purple, plastic sled with a sack of kitty litter around the neighborhood with his favorite human to keep him company. My plan was to add gradually more weight until he could eventually pull me. Well my dreams of running in the Iditarod never happened, but that's okay. More than anything, I love the bond of trust and mutual respect formed when I work with one of my dogs. Bugg Z showed me that he was happy to try something new and exciting, and that makes him a winner! 🐾🐾

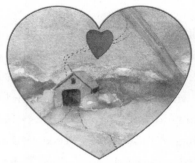

A friend and member of the Pet Paw-see named Gloria was involved in rescue for many years before we became a non-profit organization. She had a good relationship with our local shelter and would often take animals out of the shelter for adoption. She had a long list of potential homes and was great at matching dogs to the purrfect family. Gloria had lived her entire life in Great Falls, so she knew the good as well as the bad pet-owners. Once we met and became friends, I would take some of the larger dogs and foster them until she could find them homes.

Dakota, a rambunctious Collie mix, was just another dog at the shelter waiting for his person to find him. After being there quite a long time, Gloria asked me to foster him. He was a wonderful, friendly dog who loved playing with my pack and didn't bother the kitties. Luckily, it didn't take long to find him a purrfect home with a wonderful family.

Many people don't like to visit shelters because it's too depressing. If the animal is in a home environment as a foster pet, he is more likely to be relaxed and to allow his "inner beauty" shine through. This was the case with Dakota.

Chapter 12

Ten Reasons Why Pet Owners Should Never Put Up a Christmas Tree

*L*ike most pet owners, I have had to learn the hard way!

1. The cost of emergency vet care is not proportional to the size of the broken ornament imbedded in your dog's paw.

2. Even the smallest Christmas tree ornament becomes a dangerous missile when your Labrador's tail propels it towards your face.

3. Unless you have pink carpet, never hang candy canes on your tree. No matter how much you scrub, pink doggie drool always leaves a stain.

4. Small packages under the tree will eventually be found buried in the back yard.

5. Those little metal ornament holders really stand out in an x-ray.

6. If, like me, you poop scoop at night holding a flashlight, you learn quickly that tinsel is reflective.

7. The cat is only interested in the ornament at the very top of the tree.

8. Beautifully wrapped packages make wonderful scratching posts.

❖ **9.**   Garland is not a pretty sight after it has been partially digested.

❖ **10.** And, the 10th best reason why dog owners should never put up a Christmas tree:

"Thanks Mom! You finally got us an indoor toilet!!!"

Wolfie came to me from the local animal shelter where he wasn't generating any interest. He was a large, active boy with too much energy for a small kennel. Since he had spent so much time cooped up, he went crazy when any shelter worker took him out to visit with a potential adopter. This is a sad fact of many shelter dogs. They are often great dogs and make wonderful pets, but a possible adopters' first impression is of a wild, untamed animal who will be nothing but a headache if adopted.

Unfortunately, most people want to adopt an obedient "Lassie" and won't take the time or make the effort to rehabilitate or train a dog to have manners. So, these dogs are passed by over and over again. Wolfie was one of those dogs. He was actually a very affectionate, nice dog who needed a good amount of interaction and exercise, but he wasn't a bad dog.

Once I got him into my home and wore off some of his energy, he was reasonably well mannered and willing to please his person. Still, I didn't get a lot of interest in him at the Pet Paw-see adoption events. However, those of us in rescue like to say there is a family or person for every animal and Wolfie's family finally found him. He went to live with a single dad and his very own boy. It was the purrfect home for this rambunctious dog.

– Chapter 13 –
Thanks for Giving

This Thanksgiving was one of the more memorable holidays I have ever experienced. A terrible event brought out the best in so many people.

By Thanksgiving 2002, the dogs had been at Camp Collie only a few weeks. I had been up to Shelby to help a few times and was worried there wouldn't be enough volunteers on Thanksgiving Day to take care of the dogs. So, I got up early, threw together a peanut butter and jelly sandwich, grabbed a bottle of water, and arrived at Camp Collie just as the sun was coming up. It was a beautiful but very cold morning. Besides the security guard, I was the only one there at that early hour. Shortly after I had gotten to the fairgrounds, another gal arrived, and we started the job of washing up the doggie bowls from the night before. The dogs lived in the horse stalls and the washing took place in a large army tent, donated by a generous rancher. A water truck provided water, which was heated in large 55-gallon barrels so that we didn't have to use freezing water to wash the bowls. While the other volunteer collected dirty food dishes, I washed and washed and washed. It didn't take too long for many other volunteers to arrive and quickly pitch in. All had felt the same as I had; there wouldn't be enough help since it was a holiday. So many people showed up to help that morning that by

11:30 all the dogs had eaten, were watered, and walked. By noon, there were only a handful of us left, and since I had made no plans for the day, I decided to stay to keep walking the dogs and then help with their afternoon feeding. It had warmed up a bit and turned into a perfect sunny Montana winter day.

At noon, I decided to take a break and, as I walked back to my truck to eat lunch, a gal told me about woman in town who had cooked an entire turkey dinner for the volunteers. She insisted I join them for the meal. I remember looking at my clothes thinking there was no way I was going to someone's house looking like that and only wondered what I smelled like, but she wouldn't take no for an answer. It actually wasn't too difficult to persuade me to go. My peanut butter sandwich wasn't that exciting. Turkey with all the trimmings sounded wonderful. Happily, I went with five other volunteers to eat dinner at the home of this lovely, generous lady. When we got to her house, all she could talk about was how thankful she was for the volunteers who had worked the past month to help the animals. She was physically unable to work with the dogs but wanted so badly to do something, so she stuffed us full of turkey, dressing, and pie. When we left her house, she insisted on sending back plates of food for others at Camp Collie. I still remember sitting on the floor in her living room with five strangers eating this wonderful meal and feeling so grateful and lucky. Not just for the meal, but for the compassion and generosity of so many.

I realized at that point that there were really two stories in the Camp Collie saga. The main story was about the dogs and cats, how they were treated, and what was going to happen to them. The other one was about the people whose hearts were touched by the plight of these animals and who had decided to help in any way they could. This woman was just one example. Some people couldn't work with the animals for a variety of reasons, but they still felt compelled to do whatever they could. I saw this many times during the remaining eight months we cared for the dogs and cats.

Generous donations came in from people from all over the U.S. and Canada. The monetary donations were necessary, and we could not have taken care of so many animals without their generosity. However, I think what touched me the most were the other ways people willingly helped. Many people in Shelby opened their doors to volunteers from out of town who had come to work with the animals. They offered total strangers a spare room and cooked them meals after a long, cold day of hard work. After leaving the fairgrounds barn where the dogs lived, I would often stop in town for a bite to eat before the 75-mile drive back home. I never paid for a meal. So many times when I went up to the counter to pay, I heard that another customer had taken care of my bill. (What gave me away? Was it the smell of my clothes and the straw in my hair?)

Many businesses in Shelby and the surrounding area offered items or services to help with the animals. Often baked goodies would show up at Camp Collie for the volunteers. For Valentine's Day, the volunteers received a beautiful bouquet of flowers thanking everyone for their hard work. I remember crying after reading some of the cards and letters sent by people from all over the U.S. and Canada with their prayers and thanks. This generosity and thoughtfulness made such a difference especially to those of us who became so emotionally involved with the fate of these creatures. All of the volunteers greatly appreciated everyone who followed the story and tried to help in various ways. These kind gestures gave us strength when things seemed overwhelming.

Even though Camp Collie is over and we pray that nothing like that ever happens again, I will always cherish these memories and thank God that I was able to be a part of this. The people I met are truly some of the best I've known. Camp Collie was one of my most heartbreaking and heartwarming experiences and it profoundly changed my life. 🐾

Mercedes, another Collie mix, was a shelter dog saved by Gloria. She looked almost exactly like a previous dog I had fostered named Bailey. They were identical from the color of their coats down to their double dewclaws.

Mercedes was a sweetie of a dog who only stayed with me a short time until her family saw her on the Pet Paw-see website and had to adopt her. She moved into a home with two boys, a cat, and a bunny. The last time we heard, she was doing great!

Oliver, a flame-point Siamese, found locked inside an abandoned vehicle, was rescued by a friend and brought to a vet for care. Sadly, Oliver tested positive for feline leukemia. I adopted him and loved him for the short time he had left. Oliver told me every day how thankful he was for food and shelter. I told him that I was the lucky one, to have had his company, however brief.

– Chapter 14 –

R&R

*T*hese boys are brothers in spirit!

Years ago, the president of the American Working Collie Association (AWCA) asked me if I was able to assist any Collies in need in Montana. The AWCA also offered help with medical bills for any of the dogs I took into my home. I said I would be happy to help because I love the breed. I was also glad to partner with the AWCA because I was impressed with how quickly they jumped in with money and supplies to save the Camp Collie animals. (Even though there were cats and several other dog breeds besides Collies in this animal seizure, the AWCA had no problem paying for their care.) The AWCA stuck it out until the last dog and cat was adopted. They were also committed to helping any animals that were returned or needed additional medical care for the rest of their lives. It was a pleasure to be a part of an organization that did so much good.

Collies are not a popular dog in Montana despite their long coat and natural instincts for herding. (I mentioned earlier that I had never seen a Collie until I got involved in the large seizure of mostly Collies in October 2002.) Since saying "yes" to the AWCA president's request, I have only taken in a handful of Collies. Typically, when I foster a Collie, I will find suitable homes for the dog through one of the two rescue groups that I volunteer with: the Pet Paw-see or the Humane Society of Cascade County (HSCC). This has worked well since both rescues have websites, adoption applications, and contracts for any Collies I take into my home.

I passed my contact information on to other rescue organizations and shelters in the state, so it is never a surprise when I get a request to help a Collie. I got a call one day from a small rescue saying they had found a purebred Collie running stray and brought him to their facility. He hadn't been claimed, so the gal who called asked if I could foster him and find him a home. I picked up the Collie and immediately saw he was a mix, not a purebred dog. No problem, I had the room and happily took him in. He was very skittish and fearful, with no manners, skinny, and a matted coat. Oh boy, I thought, another impossible-to-place dog!

He was found in a rural area of Montana with widely spaced ranches and homesteads and had likely been fending for himself for a while. My guess was that he came from a ranch but wasn't a very good herding dog (he was probably afraid of the livestock), so his owners turned him loose to sink or swim. Unfortunately, that happens much too often in Montana. If the animal doesn't earn his keep, he is put down or left somewhere on his own to live or die.

First, a vet visit was in order. The vet checked him out and said he was young (about 2 years old) and healthy, just thin. I wanted to have him groomed so I made an appointment to clean up his terrible-looking coat. The groomer took all day with him, and when she was done with his bathing, clipping, and brushing, he was a gorgeous dog! He definitely had Collie in him along with some other breed, maybe German Shepherd or an Alaskan breed, both very common in Montana.

He was a sweet, goofy boy who loved to go for rides in my truck, so he earned the name Ryder, and it seemed to fit him. However, poor Ryder was afraid of his own shadow; he was extremely nervous and unsure of himself. He acted as if someone was always out to get him.

Ryder had no doggie confidence and anything new scared him to death. Being in a strange home with other dogs pushed him way past his comfort zone so my first task was to help him gain some self-assurance.

Actually, my FIRST task was to keep him from marking the walls of my house. It was evident that he had not spent much time, if any, in a house. He wanted to lift his leg on everything, inside or outside, peeing whenever and wherever the mood stuck. So, Job Number 1: he had to be potty trained. Job Number 2: he had to learn appropriate doggie manners, like keeping off the kitchen counters. Becoming a "civilized" dog was critical, because while I love dogs, I also like having a clean house and do not want to live in a kennel. Luckily, it was summer, and I was able to keep him outside for a good part of the day. I left him in his own enclosure with food, water, toys, and a comfy doghouse. I wanted Ryder to feel safe while he adjusted to his new temporary home. Besides, I was tired of washing my walls. I felt sad for this dog and wondered what had made him so wary of the world. Despite all his fears, Ryder and I bonded quickly when he decided that I was his person. I could tell that he really wanted to be a good dog and please me; he just had no idea how. Peeing on the walls, however, was not helping!

After a few weeks of working with him, Ryder was showing positive signs that our time together was paying off. He started to learn some manners and relaxed around my pack and me. Nevertheless, his body language screamed out to the other dogs how unsure he felt. Knowing that most dogs are opportunistic creatures, I knew my pack would take full advantage of him if they could. Therefore, I was careful not to leave him alone with any of the pushier dogs that would bully this timid, nervous dog.

The first Saturday that I took Ryder to Petco for an adoption event was an adventure, to say the least. I am not sure who was more exhausted when we finally were done for the day, him or me. He was frantic in this busy, noisy store. In addition, the worst part was there were CATS in the store. (It was the Pet Paw-see's weekly adoption event where we have many cages set up for our kitties.) He acted as if he had never been around them, so we took it slowly. I kept him away from the cages displaying our kitties, which was fine for him and fine for the cats. None of the cats was too impressed with Ryder and his long snout. I did not want one of them to claw his nose; it would have sent his snail-slow progress into a downward spiral.

Ideally, it is always best to place an animal in the home of their adopters as soon as possible after they come into our foster program. Once they have been with a foster family for a while, they feel like "this is the one." Sadly, they can regress once adopted. They have to re-acclimate and readjust to new people and new surroundings, which is stressful for the animal. I was worried this would happen to Ryder when or if I found him a home.

I knew it might take a long time to find a great home for this sweet dog and was pleasantly surprised when a couple contacted me about meeting him. Nancy and Glenn had seen him on the Pet Paw-see website and wanted to meet Ryder. They lived in another city, Helena, about 100 miles away but were willing to come to Great Falls. I kept my fingers crossed that he would show well. Despite me describing his issues with life, they still wanted to "maybe" adopt him. Our meeting went well, and I offered to do a Pawsibility with them and Ryder. (Pawsibility is our process where we allow an animal to have a trial period in a home before finalizing the adoption.) This works out well with our dogs, since many do not put their best paw forward at Petco but will relax in a home setting. In addition, it takes the pressure off the potential adopters, since they do not have to make a decision on the spot. I like this practice because I want people to understand the lifelong commitment that adopting an animal entails before they take one home. I never want anyone to make a split-second decision, only to regret it later. When that happens, the animal pays the ultimate price and often loses their new home. They become even more confused and untrusting. It becomes a vicious cycle, which many times ends with the animal being put down because they are "unadoptable," or in the case of many of our volunteers, the animal stays with us and once-again, we become a "Foster Failure."

The following weekend I drove Ryder to his potential new home to begin his Pawsiblity trial run with Nancy and Glenn. He loved exploring their yard and was curious about the horses in the adjacent pasture. But he was not curious enough to actually get nose to nose with his new friends. To Ryder these were very large, scary animals so he kept his distance and just sniffed the wind. Actually, the horses were friendly and wanted to meet this handsome dog, so they trotted over to make his acquaintance. They had been around dogs before and Ryder was not a threat to them.

Things seemed to go well, and I eventually left him hoping everything would work out. This was a wonderful home, with a secure fenced yard and a doggie door into the garage where he could warm himself next to a pellet stove during the cold months while his people were away. (Otherwise, he lived in the house.) It looked and sounded like heaven for this anxious dog. I prayed he would work out and that Nancy and Glenn would feel he was worth the trouble because I knew he would be trouble. He was! Ryder was a bit of a difficult dog. Luckily, both Nancy and Glenn seemed committed to working with him. We kept in touch a lot during those first few Pawsibility weeks. (I never put a time limit on a Pawsibility. I had one Collie in a Pawsibility for over a month to make sure he did not go after chickens. He didn't and was finally adopted.) Some great outcomes just take a bit longer, but we are happy to wait until they do.

After having Ryder in their home for about two weeks, Nancy and Glenn were getting ready to leave on vacation. We had planned for me to dog-sit Ryder while they were away. I knew it was a "go" when it got time for them to leave the dog with me and Nancy started to tear up. She already missed Ryder. That was when I knew he had found his *furrever* home. I texted them often while they were gone so they wouldn't worry. When they returned, I was excited to see how much they missed Ryder. He was glad to see them too, which was a bonus. We eventually did the adoption paperwork to make it official; Ryder had a home. This was a relief to me because often those of us in rescue end up keeping the especially hard-to-place dogs and cats. Our houses are full of them. Moreover, while I loved Ryder, I wanted a quieter home for him with lots of one-on-one attention. In this particular home, it would be two-on-one, which was even better. He had two of his very own people to love just him. In my home it would have been one-on-???. (That number changes often and can be overwhelming to anyone not in rescue!) Ryder was a hard case from the start but sometimes the hard cases surprise me the most by finding great people with great homes.

I like to keep in touch with my former foster kids but do not want to be a pain to the adopters and appear as if I am stalking them. I am always available if needed. Often times the adopters like to send photos and stories to us about their new friends, and we really appreciate this. These photos and stories help us feel good about helping an animal we loved to find their *furrever* home. This also helps us continue with our mission. Some people keep in contact with us and some don't, so we play it by ear. Happily, I got many emails with stories on how great Ryder was doing and was pleased to hear he had adjusted to his new environment.

About a year after taking Ryder into my home, I got call from the same rescue group about another Collie in need of help. The gal said he was a purebred Collie, but by this time I was doubtful about her knowledge of this breed. She meant well and I wanted to help, so I agreed to take him in. My first thought on meeting this dog was "I think there is more Collie in ME than in this DOG." I figured maybe a Collie crossed his path at one time, but this dog was far from a purebred Collie and maybe any Collie at all. However, I took him home anyway. He had come from the exact same area, found running stray, was young, thin, and very skittish. He immediately reminded me of Ryder. Personality-wise, they were twins! Another dog with no confidence, no manners (he liked to pee on the walls and jump on the counters, too), and scared of his own shadow. Could these two dogs be related? The same mother with different fathers? Possibly! This was Ryder in a different coat. Besides their coat differences, they appeared so similar that I had to come up with another "R" name for him. I named him Remy! He got the usual vet care and came to live with me until I could find him a great home.

His coat was not as bad as Ryder's was, so I was able to bathe and groom him myself and once finished he looked very handsome. Petco was another experience that left us both frazzled. He was a handful and jumped at every noise in the store. People scared him, cats scared him, and even the mechanical door at the front of the store scared him. Similar to Ryder, I felt I had another impossible-to-place dog in my home. While at my house, he lived in the same kennel as Ryder and seemed to adjust, but he was still extremely nervous of anything and everything new in his world. Aside from his many phobias, he was sweet and wanted to please, so I was not going to give up on him.

It was August and the Humane Society of Cascade County (HSCC) was holding a large adoption event for several shelters and rescues in the general area. It was being held at a park where we had plenty of shade, kiddie pools for the dogs, some fun events, and LOTS of dogs along with a few brave cats.

I had kept in touch with Nancy and Glenn over the past year. When I told them about the event, they said they would stop by for a visit. It was fair time in Great Falls, and they had planned on being in town and going to the fair. However, they said they would first come to the park to say hi to me. I told them I had another foster dog but never expected them to be interested in him. Holy cow, they fell in love with Remy! I told them to go home and think about it. Ryder was doing really well by this point, and they felt he needed a friend. I knew both dogs would be a challenge, but they insisted, and I NEVER turn away a great home.

I drove Remy to their house the following weekend to meet Ryder. After an introductory walk, the dogs seemed to hit it off well. Ryder appeared to have gained a lot of confidence and enjoyed showing Remy the yard and his toys. I left that day, again keeping my fingers crossed that it would work out. It did and I was overjoyed! I pray for this kind of home for all my dogs. After a Pawsibility trial period, they adopted Remy and signed both dogs up for doggie obedience classes. They knew this dynamic doggie duo was only going to work if they got professional help. The classes helped the dogs gain confidence as well as learn manners. I keep in touch with Nancy and Glenn and continue to hear of their boys' progress. It seems that each dog has helped the other navigate this scary world to become cherished members of a family. Since his adoption several years ago, the word from Nancy and Glenn is that both boys are happy, healthy, and inseparable. So maybe R&R actually ARE brothers! 🐾🐾

Cotton was one of the sweetest and most sociable bunnies ever to share his life with me. He was a rescued bunny and was given up when his owner felt she had no time for him. He looked just like a Seal-Point Siamese cat. Cotton had chocolate ears, nose, feet, and tail over a cream-colored body. He liked to follow me around his outdoor habitat asking to be picked up for a cuddle or two. He also loved his guinea pig friends and was a foster dad to a litter of tuxedo kittens. Cotton spent hours playing and snuggling with his "kitten babies." This precious bunny broke my heart the day he passed of old age.

A family discovered their two female hamsters were actually a male and a female. Not good! This resulted in MANY baby hamsters that needed homes. The babies were brought to Petco for possible adoption where I took in Molly & Polly. They were two delightful little hamster sisters who lived their lives in my menagerie. I loved these little sweeties and thoroughly enjoyed their funny antics for years.

Small animals often find themselves homeless and are in need of a safe place with people who can care for them. The small animals I have been lucky to own have given me many hours of laughter and I never regret adopting them.

Chapter 15

Foster Failures Anonymous

I think everyone in rescue has been a Foster Failure at one time or another and can relate to this story.*

I am starting a self-help group in the animal rescue community called Foster Failures Anonymous. I know the first meeting will be standing room only. The meetings will begin like this:

"Hi, my name is_____ (fill in your name) and I am a cat/dog/horse/pot belly pig/bird/lizard Foster Failure."

As with other similar self-help groups, everyone attending the meeting would say "Hi_____ (fill in your name again.)"

Every person I work with in animal rescue could be a poster child for failed fostering. We take in animals with good intentions knowing that we will find them a perfect *furrever* home. However, sometimes that *furrever* home does not materialize quickly. In addition, by the time it does, the cat or dog has snuggled its way into our heart. So, we ultimately end up adding the critter to our own growing fur family. Nevertheless, if we are reasonable, we understand that we cannot continue to keep all of our foster animals and that some would do better in a quieter environment. Begrudgingly, we adopt some to good homes.

Fostering is very rewarding, but it is very challenging. Saying goodbye to an animal that you have nurtured and loved, knowing that you may never see him or her again is extremely hard. We have people contact our group about fostering, and the first thing we tell them is how difficult it is to say goodbye. I have met many people who think they want to foster until they actually do and then have to give up the animal. You can see the panic in their face when someone inquires about their foster pet. At that point, many foster parents decide they have to keep the dog or cat and can't foster any more. I've heard some say they didn't realize it would be that hard. We hate to lose them as foster moms and dads but completely understand.

My good friend and fellow animal-rescuer Jo Anne and I were talking with a gal recently about a Blue Heeler she had taken into her home. She wanted us to help her find the dog a good home, but not until she had taken the dog through obedience classes to give her the best chance possible. We left her, looked at each other, and said, "Foster Failure." Sure enough, one weekend she came up to us at Petco and confessed "I'm a Foster Failure; I just can't give her up . . . ." It's nothing to be ashamed of. It shows that we care for these wonderful critters and grow attached to them. If you are in animal rescue and don't fall in love, then you really need to find another type of volunteer work.

My criterion for adopting out my foster kids is simple. I want the animal to go to a better home than they have with me. I have a good home and truly love my foster pets. But with a full-time job, lots of rescue work, and many to care for, there is not a lot of time for one-on-one interaction. Knowing the animals will be getting one, two, or more people in a family to spoil them rotten is what gives me the strength to let them go.

I recently fostered two very tiny puppies found abandoned at about fourteen days old. They came to work with me for two weeks and I bottle-fed them many times through the day and night until they could eat on their own. I was heavily invested in their future welfare. Everyone reminded me how hard it was going to be to let the puppies go. However, while it was hard, they each went to homes with two adults and another dog. Those were perfect placements for the puppies. I still get to see them occasionally, and I have made friends with their wonderful human adopters.

We recently had a couple join our group of Pet Paw-see volunteers. Gemma and Adam were hard workers and wanted to try their hand at fostering. They took in one adult kitty named Newman and shortly after, they took in a kitten, Cascade, who had a badly broken femur. The kitties bonded with each other as well with their foster people, and all of us secretly hoped Gemma and Adam would adopt them both. Adopting two kitties is a lot to ask for, so we just waited to see if either of the cats would find homes during our Petco adoption events. That was until Gemma and Adam left for two weeks to visit relatives over the holidays. Immediately upon returning home, they adopted both kitties! Gemma told us they didn't realize they would miss the cats so much while they were on vacation. They said they couldn't imagine handing them off to strangers and maybe never seeing them again. We gave them a hard time for being "Foster Failures" but were all very happy these two kitties wouldn't be broken up. Besides, this meant Adam and Gemma were finally initiated into our growing club of Foster Failures. We immediately gave them the location and dates of the Foster Failure Anonymous meetings.

Right now, I am fostering a beautiful Alaskan Malamute. I have had her in my home for over ten months and I keep telling people that if I don't find her a home within a year, she is mine. Meka thinks she's home already and has fit very well into my pack. She runs with me five mornings each week and loves her kiddie pool. Unfortunately, she is an escape artist, and I am afraid she will get out of most yards. Meka was finally adopted and lived with a family for a few weeks. But she kept sneaking out of their yard. One day she almost got herself killed playing tag with a truck, so Meka boomeranged back to me. I think she planned that because she has never once gotten out of my (her) yard.

Sorry, but I have to cut this short. There's a meeting in a few minutes and I do not want to be late. I will proudly stand up and say, "Hi, my name is Debi, and I am a Foster Failure!" We have all heard it said that acknowledging there is a problem is the first step to recovery. I'm not sure if that applies here! 🐾🐾

Many years before I was involved in animal rescue, I became very frustrated and depressed over the numerous animals in my home with a variety of health issues, many of which were life threatening. My Cocker Spaniel, Duster, had epilepsy, which eventually led to his dying young. I had a cat with feline leukemia long before there was any hope these cats could have quality lives. My other dog Blackie had several aliments and was on a first-name basis with my vet and his family. (Despite this, he lived to an old age.) I also had a dog with severe allergies and another kitty with mouth cancer. I was upset that most of my beloved pets had serious health problems. All I wanted was to deal with spay/neuter surgeries and annual vaccines, not diseases that I couldn't pronounce.

It really bothered me that I always seemed to have a dog or cat in crisis. I dearly loved them all and only wanted my furry kids to have a good long life with me. My attitude towards these "sick" animals changed one day when I heard a soft voice tell me "I save the special ones for you." I felt at that moment that God was whispering in my ear. He knew the "less than perfect" animals would receive love and care in my home, so He entrusted them to me.

Since that time, I welcome the special needs animals even knowing that some will dig deep into my checkbook, and cost me sleep, sanity and will eventually break my heart. I hate to say that that's ok, but maybe it is. I feel as though they were placed in my path for a reason and if God trusted them with me, then I know that He will give me the means and the strength to care for them.

– Chapter 16 –
Mousy

I n rescue, you always have to be ready to punt!

The Pet Paw-see volunteers were in Petco one Saturday in August doing adoptions when two young boys came in with a box. We expected to find a tiny puppy or kitten in the box but instead, there was a newly born baby mouse. It was about half the length of my little finger, helpless and blind. The boys said a dog had killed its mother and asked us to help the tiny creature. Being an animal rescue group, we couldn't tell them to just put it back out where they found it. So, we took the tiny mouse into the back room, got some kitten formula, and tried to feed it. That sounded easier that it was, more milk got on the mouse's head than in her mouth. Everyone started to look around thinking, "Now what do we do?" I said I would take her home but expected her to pass away during the night. I made a soft bed for her, with a rice sock for warmth, and tried throughout the night to feed her with an eyedropper. I didn't feel as though I was having much success, but she was still alive in the morning, so I continued to try getting her to eat. The eyedropper was too big and tended to drown her in formula, so I used my finger instead. I would dip it in the milk and put it next to her mouth where she learned to lick it off. So much for the first day!

I had to be back to work on Monday and knew she would not make it through the long workday without food. After debating what to do, I decided to take the baby mouse to my office. Now I know what a mom goes through packing for her newborn before she goes out. I needed enough formula for several feedings, the eyedropper (I was still hoping to get this to work as a way to get some food into this little creature), rice sock, small box, and some soft blanket material. Once at work I settled the mouse in my desk drawer after microwaving her rice sock. I did not feel good about warming the rice sock directly in the microwave, so I put it into a plastic food container. I also didn't want to explain to any of my co-workers what I was doing with a warm rice sock. (The container disguised the contents as my lunch.) About every two to three hours, I would take the little mouse with her formula into the basement restroom for her feeding. (The main restroom was for several users but the one in the basement was for single use so I wouldn't freak people out with my new office pet.) After a few awkward days, both the mouse and I got into a routine. I would pack the formula, cleaning cloth, and the mouse into my pocket to go to the restroom for her feeding. She learned to eat very well by licking the milk off my finger. When she had had enough, I would then clean her face and body with a warm cloth, heat the sock, and settle her back into her box in my desk drawer until the next meal.

This went on for about two weeks until she started to eat on her own. By this time, her eyes were open, and her coat was getting thicker. I knew it was time to leave her home when one day at work she started squeaking in her little box while a co-worker was in my office. I just turned the radio on louder and pretended it was my chair making the noise.

It was wonderful when I did not have to feed her several times a day and could finally leave her at home. The problem was she was totally acclimated to me and had no fear of humans so I knew she wouldn't make it out in the cold, cruel mouse world. If I let her go in my yard, the dogs, hawks, or neighbor cats would get her. That would have broken my heart. I had really started to enjoy this little creature and after all this work, I did not want to see her become a snack. So, I did the only thing I could, I made her a comfy home in a 45-gallon aquarium with toys, a small animal hut, wood branches for climbing, and everything a young mouse would enjoy. She rearranged her new home to suit herself by digging tunnels in the wood-chip bedding and burying her food in case there was ever a famine in the land. Mousy even had a wheel for exercise and seemed very content. One of her favorite treats was grapes. When I dropped one into her cage, she would pounce on it and run around with it in her mouth before diving into her hut to eat this delicacy.

My rescue friends couldn't wait to hear the latest story about Mousy. She seemed to enjoy the daily treats and affection from her foster mom, and I enjoyed having her as part of my menagerie. When I put my hand in her aquarium home, she would run over to it and climb on to get her meal. That was until she was a few months old. One day as I put my hand in the tank, she launched from her perch, bit into my hand, and hung on. She was telling me to stay out of her territory. Wow, did that hurt my feelings! Here was this small critter who I had hand-raised from only a few hours old and she had turned on me with a vengeance. From then on, I had to wear a glove when I cleaned her cage or fed her. She never tolerated me on her turf again.

I had to laugh when a good friend and fellow volunteer, Dawn, bought her a small stuffed mouse as a housewarming gift. Mousy LOVED it! She grabbed the stuffed mouse, took it into her underground lair and ripped it to shreds. In only a few hours, the toy was unrecognizable. Mousy was the queen of her territory, and I learned to watch but not touch. Even stuffed toys were a threat to her kingdom.

I was very sad when after four and a half years, she finally passed away of old age. In the last few months of her life, she had started feeling her years; I could actually put my hand in her tank without a glove. Her coat was getting rough and she moved slowly. I don't know how long wild mice live, but I know that her life was likely much longer than most. She has been gone for several years but I still look at her picture and think back to the funny little creature put in my path asking for help. I would do it again in a minute and am grateful that her life was trusted to me for this short time. 🐱

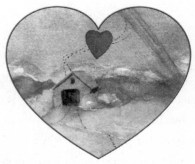

*P*epsi and his two siblings were found in a Pepsi Cola warehouse. The workers noticed the kittens and called Les, the founder of the Pet Paw-see for help. The kittens were likely born to a feral kitty who hoped this building was a safe haven for her babies. But with fork lifts moving large pallets of products, it was anything but safe for this furry family. Momma cat was nowhere to be seen but I would guess she watched as her precious family was taken away.

One call from Les and I took in this long-hair tuxedo baby. Taming Pepsi was easy. After only a few hours, he became a very affectionate house kitty. Pepsi had the cutest little chirp; he never meowed. He was a shy kitty but adjusted well to life in a busy house with dogs and other cats.

Even though he had a "feral" beginning, he appeared to be content and enjoyed a happy life with me for many years. I had the pleasure of his company until he left me last year to be with his friends at the Rainbow Bridge.

Chapter 17

The Siamese Collies

Winston and Diego, two of the Camp Collie dogs, inspired this story. Both Winston and Diego were smooth, tri-colored Collies who looked alike and became best buddies. When they were together, they seemed joined at the hip. I wrote this while I was dog-sitting Diego when his family was away on vacation. Mr. Winnie lived with me and my furry family in a small community called Vaughn. A good friend who had also worked at Camp Collie adopted Diego.

The Siamese Collies from Vaughn
Love to play on the lawn
They'd wrestle and fight
All the day and at night
And keep me up until dawn!

The Siamese Collies gave chase
To the cats at a breathtaking pace
They ran under tables, through doors
And up trees
Thinking, oh my how I love a good race!

The Siamese Collies did smile
When on my bed for a while
They ripped up my quilt
Those smiles changed to guilt
When my yelling was heard for a mile!

The Siamese Collies thought it funny
To stand and bark at the bunny
They hoped and they prayed
She'd come out to play
But, her look said, "In your dreams honey!"

The Siamese Collies said "Mother
If in trouble was likely the other
That did the bad deed
Wasn't me who had peed."
Isn't it nice having a brother!

The Siamese Collies would sleep
On the couch sweetly dreaming,
And counting their sheep.
I'm sweating, man, is it just me?
Yelling it's "Hotter than Hell" turn up the AC! 🐱🐱

oby was a feral kitten that I prepped for surgery during my first spay/neuter clinic. Once the vet tech anesthetized the cats for surgery, my job was to help shave. While shaving him I noticed a large abscess on one of his back legs. The wound was open, dirty, and exposed down to the bone. The vet neutered him, cleaned and sewed up his injury as best he could but there was very little skin in the area to properly suture it closed.

If this kitten was returned to his colony, we knew he would likely not make it. The chances were his wound would re-open and become infected. The only option for this kitten was to find someone to care for him. So, I took him home with me. While I thought he was a bit too old to domesticate—he was about five months old—Toby didn't know that and tamed down within days, becoming a content, happy house-kitty.

Toby was a flame red, long-haired cat who had the unfortunate tendency to become badly matted. He was so mellow throughout his life that he never minded letting me brush him. When his coat got too matted for brushing, he even let me take the dog grooming clippers to his coat to shave the impossible areas.

Toby aged into a loving, old Tomcat that wanted only to cuddle with his buddy Merlin. The two cats were inseparable and most often were found intertwined sleeping or grooming each other on the couch. Toby and Merlin left me for the Bridge only months apart. I know they are both enjoying the afterlife resting on a cloud together and telling stories of their time on earth.

– Chapter 18 –
Bizy

Rescue is never boring!

The Pet Paw-see rescue got a call one day about a dog that appeared to be in very bad condition seen running way out in the country. A landowner spotted the dog in a very rural area of Montana acting lost and scared. The people who called us felt sorry for the poor animal and left food out but were not able to catch her.

Jo Anne, one of our volunteers, and I drove to the location with our large dog trap, showed the people how to set it, and told them to call us if they caught the dog. The next morning, I got a call that a very frightened dog was in the trap. I drove out to the site and found a thin, beat up-looking German Short Haired Pointer (GSP). Her feet were sore from many days of running over rough, hard ground and her coat appeared to have been sun-bleached from being out in the elements for so long. According to the family who contacted us, she had been running across miles of ranch land over the course of several weeks. It is extremely lucky that no one had shot her since ranchers do not typically allow unknown dogs around their livestock.

While she was terrified in the trap, she appeared to be friendly, so I got her on a leash and she jumped into my pickup, happy to go for a ride. First stop for us was to a vet to scan her for a microchip.

Remarkably, she had one. It took a few calls to locate the microchip company, but they found the name and number of the owner and my contact info was passed along to them. A short while later I got a call from the original owner of the dog; a gal named Rae. She was a breeder located about 100 miles from my place and was very concerned about the dog. She was extremely angry that one of her puppies had been so badly treated. Rae told me that when selling a puppy her agreement includes a clause that she is to have the dog returned to her if the new owner does not want him or her anymore. I assured her the dog was safe and would get care, although it appeared as though aside from a rough-looking coat, all she needed was some good food and a bath. While I do not generally like breeders, this was one of the few responsible ones. Her concern seemed to be for her dogs rather than just making money. Rae said she would take this dog back and make sure she was healthy before re-homing her. She did not intend to sell her again. Rae also offered to pay for any vet expenses that our rescue group had incurred.

Rae shared with me that she made numerous calls to the person who bought the dog as a puppy, with no response. She also located the owner on Facebook and sent him a message about us finding the dog. By this time, it was evident that the owner didn't want the dog anymore and had dumped her in the country. Rae and I had several discussions over the following week about how the dog was doing and she agree to meet me in Great Falls the next weekend. I enjoyed the week I cared for this sweet girl and could see that she was a smart, sociable, energetic dog.

In the meantime, unbeknownst to me, a couple who volunteers with the Pet Paw-see had been in contact with Rae hoping to buy a GSP puppy. Steve and Lynn loved pointers and planned to get a puppy from Rae's next litter. They were heartbroken over recently losing their old pointer to illness. As their dog became ill and it was obvious that she would pass soon, Steve and Lynn had researched Rae's breeding facility and put down a deposit for a puppy. Through the rescue grapevine, they heard about this particular pointer. (I remember thinking about Steve and Lynn as potential adopters after I trapped the dog, knowing about their love for GSPs. However, by this time Rae had been located and was planning to take the dog back.) Steve and Lynn immediately called Rae to ask about the pointer I had trapped and drove to her home to meet the dog.

It was a match made in heaven! Both Steve and Lynn fell in love with this beautiful but ragged dog and asked if they could use their deposit for her instead. Rae returned their fee and gave them the dog, now named Bizy. Rae knew she would have no trouble finding someone to take one of her not-yet-born puppies and just wanted to see Bizy in a loving home.

When I see Steve or Lynn all they can talk about is how much they love Miss Bizy and how spoiled she has gotten! When I see Bizy she looks very happy. Her coat has returned to its stunning liver and white color and she has filled out from the skin and bones appearance when I first saw her. Bizy loves to go out bird hunting with Steve and even if they don't get any birds, they both still have a great time. It is wonderful to know that Bizy enjoys the life of a treasured member of their family. This is the happy ending we work so hard to achieve and it gives all of us in rescue the needed strength to continue.

have fostered quite a few adult kitty siblings for the Pet Paw-see. If the cats are inseparable, we try to find families who are willing to adopt both animals.

Tuffy and Dixie were an inseparable pair of elderly kitties who came to live with me. Sadly, their owner decided to give them away when his new girlfriend told him it was her or the cats. This pair of sweet old kitties had belonged to the young man and his former wife. His new girlfriend found that to be intolerable and wanted them out! (She wanted nothing of his ex-wife in the home.) We suggested he get rid of his lady-friend instead, but he did not care for our suggestion.

Tuffy and Dixie came to live with me as my foster kids. They were with me for almost a year when a lovely couple saw them on our website and had to adopt them. They are happily living out their golden years in their new and furrever home. We have also heard that their former owner greatly regrets his decision!

Roommates Terrance and Sable lived with me until they both found great homes. Sable found a home with a family but was quickly returned through no fault of her own. She then ended up in our Senior for Senior Program. Terrance went to a great couple in the eastern part of our state.

Siblings Rascal and Calliope came to live in my home when their owner, Father Bob, became ill with cancer and did not know if he would be able to care for them. We had hoped he would feel well enough after treatment to take them back, but that was not the case. After several years with me, I sadly said goodbye to both kitties. I got a lot of comfort knowing Father Bob was happily greeting them at the Rainbow Bridge as they passed from this life to the next!

– Chapter 19 –
Barn Cat Barnie

When I met Barnie, I didn't know that adult feral cats could not be tamed and Barnie didn't know that people could be nice. We were both in for a pleasant surprise.

Years ago, I was renting a small mobile home on a ranch in Bozeman, Montana, and noticed two feral cats hanging around the ou buildings, so of course I started to feed them. Not wanting them to breed, I was able to trap the cats to have them altered. After their surgeries, I kept food out but never tried to approach them. They really didn't seem that intent on getting to know me better, so I left them alone. While they had lots of places to get out of the weather, I often found them sleeping in my Cocker Spaniel's doghouse. Regular food and shelter was all they asked for and I was happy to make their lives a bit better.

I named them Brownie and Barnie. They were very wary of my dog, Cappi, although Cappi never tried to chase them. He was used to cats and really wasn't interested in running after them. I often saw the two kitties sunning themselves on a fence post or resting in a barn, but they always kept their distance. I talked to them when I brought them their food and over time, they learned to come out when I called them for dinner. Brownie never came near me, but I was excited to see Barnie allow the distance between us to become less and less. Despite this, I never tried to approach or touch her. She got to a point where she would follow me around the yard as I did chores, while always staying a safe distance from me. Surprisingly, the distance started to shrink until one day she was standing right in front of me. I slowly put my hand down while she walked right up to it and started to rub against it and purr. It was an amazing sight to see this feral cat enjoy affection with Cappi standing right next to me the entire time. I was so excited that she finally trusted us after months of watching. From this day forward, she happily came to me when she saw me. She grew to love her daily belly rubs and scratches and I enjoyed her company.

After about a year, I had the opportunity to move to another city in Montana for a job and was heartbroken to have to leave her behind. I had a friend who agreed to leave food for her in one of the barns, but I was sick at the thought of abandoning my sweet kitty friend. I had to be settled in my new job first and couldn't take her to live with me until I bought a house. I promised Barnie that I would come back to Bozeman for her once I found a place of my own. That took several months and reports from my friend were not that great. She rarely, if ever, saw Barnie although the food was often gone.

Once I was able to purchase a house in a small rural community, I thought often of going back to find Barnie to bring her home to live with us. I didn't know how she would acclimate to being a house cat but wanted her even if she chose to live her life outdoors. So, one cold weekend before winter finally settled in, Cappi and I drove the long distance back to my former home in Bozeman to look for Barnie. I had asked my friend to set some humane traps in the barn for the afternoon I would be back. I was very heartbroken when I got to the ranch and the traps were empty. She hadn't seen Barnie in several months and I wasn't too hopeful about finding her. Searching around the barns and outbuildings resulted in no Barnie sightings. About ready to leave and wanting to try one more time to find her, I walked towards some of the buildings calling her name and heard a familiar meow coming to me from inside a barn. Barnie came out running right up to us, telling me her sad tale, and wondering where we had been for so long. She remembered me even after many months of being gone. I was overjoyed and quickly scooped her into a carrier. I couldn't believe this once feral cat remembered the bond we had formed. I was ecstatic on the long ride while I told Barnie all about her new home.

She had never been in a house before and I wondered if she would be terrified, but Barnie adjusted nicely. Barnie was still a wild animal that knew only the outdoors, so I didn't want to confine her inside but wanted her to know she had a safe place to live. I would let her outside hoping she would stay around and quickly realized she didn't want to be an outside cat, which was fine with me. She loved her sunny window ledges and soft bed; having a warm, comfy home and regular meals suited her. Barnie quickly turned into a spoiled domestic house kitty, which suited both of us.

Barnie lived many years with me until the very sad day when I had to bid my former feral friend goodbye. I held her paw and told her what a special cat she was, thanking her for sharing her life with me. Even though she has been gone for a long time, I am still amazed at how this once unwanted feral kitty gave me the priceless gift of her trust. 🐱🐾

*G*age was a big black Labrador Retriever who had been in a total of nine homes and shelters (those are the ones I could count, there may have been others). I couldn't figure out why he bounced from home to home because he was very friendly, affectionate, and well-mannered. He was just LARGE and exuberant. Gage lived to please his person. Nothing could spoil his cheerful demeanor.

After about one month, I was able to adopt him to a nice family. Sadly, he came back to the Pet Paw-see after less than a year in this home. The people who had adopted Gage didn't seem sad to see him leave, they just wanted him gone. I never figured out why and that always bothered me. Here was this great dog with no bad habits and no one wanted to commit to him. I took a little comfort knowing they didn't just dump him at a shelter or sell him on Craig's List, they called the Pet Paw-see knowing that we always take our animals back.

It took a few more weeks but a very sweet gal named Brittany saw him on the Pet Paw-see's website. I was so impressed when she told me about her previous dog who she had recently lost to illness. Knowing her dog wasn't going to last much longer, she started a Bucket List for him and tried to give him lots of adventures before he passed. It was evident how much she loved and cared for her animals.

Brittany's entire family came out to meet Gage and me one afternoon at Petco. It was instant love between Gage and Brittany. I was so excited to finally find this fabulous dog a furrever home. He deserved so much more than he had received from humans but that never seemed to spoil his attitude. Gage knew someday someone would come along and fall in love with him and it happened!

— Chapter 20 —

Dys-Lexi

*L*exi taught me never to give up on a lost cause. Her memory
has helped me never to give up on other difficult dogs who
have crossed my path. Buddy should be very thankful to Lexi!

Bernice had been at our local shelter for a long time with no interest.
I love the herding/working breeds, and when I heard of an Aussie mix
in need of a home. I told the shelter manager that if no one wanted
her, I would foster her. Well, no one wanted her, so she ended up
coming to live with me. I remember the words of the kennel worker
when I picked her up that afternoon, "She is sweet but a wild child.
Good luck." I should have realized after hearing that what a handful
she would be. She was a large Aussie mix with a beautiful marbled gray
and white coat, a goofy grin, and NO MANNERS! Bernice, renamed
Lexi, was a very sociable, happy-go-lucky dog who needed someone
to rein her in and teach her how to be civilized prior to her adoption.
I had hoped that someone would be me.

The night I brought her home, I had the luxury of actually
cooking myself a dinner that consisted of more than one food item,
which I put on a plate, rather than eating out of the pot. I also took the
opportunity to sit at the table and enjoy my rare sit-down meal. That
was until I heard someone coming up my gravel driveway. I went to

my front porch to see who it was and in the few seconds I was gone, my dinner was gone too. I came back to this large dog standing with all four feet on top of the table enjoying MY dinner and watching me out the window. I wasn't used to that kind of flagrantly bad dog behavior. My dogs would never have thought standing on the table eating MY dinner was on their list of allowable things to do.

Lexi didn't act like she was doing anything out of the ordinary. She acted like this was an acceptable everyday occurrence. She was very happy to see me come back inside and was perfectly willing to share with me any of the leftovers on the plate. Unfortunately, there was nothing left on the plate. I don't know if she learned anything, but I sure did. Never leave food within jumping distance of Lexi. She was a canine vacuum cleaner and never passed up any opportunity to grab a snack.

I soon realized that she was also an escape artist. I have a four-foot chain link fence that she sailed over as if she was running the high hurdles at a track meet. I never let dogs run or roam out of my yard, as it is dangerous for many reasons. I am also completely against chaining or tying dogs up. I think it makes them frustrated and aggressive, aside from being cruel. However, I had no idea what to do about Lexi's bad jumping habit. Lexi couldn't be out in the yard for more than a few minutes before she was over the fence. She would play with the other dogs, hear the call of the wild and in an instant, she was gone. I always got in my truck to chase her down which she thought was tons of fun. She would run next to the truck for a while and then hop in. If I couldn't find her, she would always manage to find her way home. This was a game for her, but one that I needed to end. Luckily, she would not jump my six-foot kennel fence so I knew I could leave her there and she was safe anytime I was away from home.

Typically, I would let her out on a long 30-foot lead to play before leaving her in the kennel while I got ready for work. Early one morning she got away from me, spotted a skunk on the other side of the fence and had to get it. Over the fence she went after the skunk who let her have a full dose of spray at close range. There is nothing worse than a heavy-coated dog with skunk spray running down her face and chest. Even she knew she was in trouble and came back to me immediately after her unholy baptism.

I didn't know what to do with her but had to let her back into the yard. What I really wanted was to let her run to her heart's content and maybe never come back. I was thoroughly sick of her exploits and lack of obedience, everything smelled like skunk, and I had to get to work. By now, the garage smelled as bad as she did, and the smell was starting to infiltrate my house. I didn't want to leave her with my other dogs. (One dog covered with *Eau De Skunk* was awful, but several dogs would be more than I could tolerate.) Not having many choices, I put her in the back of my pickup and took her to work with me. Bad idea! All day long at the office, I wondered if I smelled like skunk. My nostrils burned with the rancid smell and even though I never touched her, I felt like it was on my clothes and in my hair. Lexi stayed in the back of my pickup all day and to my horror, the parking lot reeked of dead skunk when I left for home later that afternoon.

By this time, I really could have shot her. Instead, we went home, and I attempted to scrub the smell off her coat in the outside kiddie pool. I had researched recipes for getting rid of skunk on dogs, and while it helped a bit, it was only a bit. Now I had a wet dog who still smelled like skunk. The odor hadn't been eliminated, it only changed from an acute acrid smell to a chronic, it's never-gonna-go-away smell.

Lexi knew she was in the doghouse after this and tried her best to behave, kind of. She still jumped the fence whenever my guard was down. The smell eventually dissipated although even months after her skunking, I could still smell it. As you can guess, she didn't come in the house for a very long time. In addition, it is impossible to try to adopt a dog who smells like roadkill. She was enough of a challenge without this added feature.

While I was still trying to find her a permanent home, Lexi grew on me and eventually became a part of my household of motley dogs and cats. Despite her pushing me to the brink, I sort of liked her. Then one day something amazing happened. She had taken off over the fence as usual and decided in her tiny dyslexic Aussie brain that maybe my home was not such a bad place after all when I saw her jump over the fence and BACK into her yard. That was the very last time she jumped the fence, but it had taken her a year to make this breakthrough. Finally, she was content. Lexi had found her *furrever* home.

Lexi calmed down after some time and learned a *few* manners. She loved everyone she met and was truly a happy girl, but she was still a large dog who would knock people down in her exuberance to greet them. Lexi eventually learned to walk nicely on a leash, come, sit, and stay and was very proud when I told her she was a good dog. She just wanted to please her person but had no idea that most of what she did frustrated people and made her seem like a lost cause. That is likely how she ended up at the shelter. I am sure her former owners threw their hands up at this out-of-control mutt. She needed someone who saw her worth and would make the effort to bring out the best in her. How she chose me, I will never know.

She will never know how close I came to giving up on her. Lexi pushed my buttons and my patience further than any dog I had ever taken in. I am glad we finally became friends. For a while, I doubted I could ever like her, never-mind fall in love with her. However, I did grow to love and enjoy this large, wild child and I miss her like crazy now that she is gone. Her smiling photos throughout my house remind me of this wonderful dog who just needed a little time to decide that we were meant to be in each other's lives.

I miss you *Dys*-Lexi! 🐱🐶

L addie & Callie were housemates when their owner passed away and they ended up at a shelter in western Montana. Both were older Collies as well as best friends who deserved to live out their lives together, but it is hard enough finding a good home for one older dog never mind two. The shelter manager realized they were showing signs of stress while living in the shelter environment and asked me if I could take them in. We found a driver willing to take the dogs to my part of the state, which is how these two Collies became my foster kids. It really didn't take much time to find them a home together. A sweet lady, Karen, from the southeast corner of Montana saw them on the Pet Paw-see website and knew they were meant to live with her. She had Collies in the past and was more than happy to give both dogs a furrever home.

Her home was about 500 miles away, a day's drive from Great Falls. Karen had gotten into town very late at night, so I planned to meet her the next morning in the parking lot of the hotel where she was staying. I will never forget the look on her face the minute she set eyes on the dogs. I was walking the two dogs when she raced out of her hotel room and embraced both Collies She didn't even say hi to me, she was so excited at meeting her new companions. I knew immediately this was the purrfect home for these special kids. With my heart breaking, I hugged them both goodbye and watched as they left in the arms of their new person.

— Chapter 21 —
Another Mouse Story

*J*ust a fun little story that I had to write about!

I typically get up once a night to let my dogs outside to pee. I try to make it quick so that I don't fully wake up and can get back to sleep easily. One night while taking them through the garage to the back yard, I heard a metal-on-metal screeching sound coming from inside my garage. Without my contacts in, I had no idea what was making the noise. On closer inspection, I saw a small, wild mouse running on an old hamster wheel that was sitting on a shelf in my garage. It was a strange sight, but I was anxious to get back to bed before I woke up completely, so I hurried the dogs into the house and went back to sleep.

When I got up later that morning to get ready for work, I remembered what I had seen but really thought it was a dream; wild mice do not play with toys. I forgot about it until a few nights later when it happened again. I woke up to let the dogs out, and a wild mouse was running on the wheel. This time I quietly walked over to watch and, sure enough, the mouse was running like mad until he saw me and took off. I knew domestic mice and hamsters loved running on wheels but never heard of a wild animal playing on one. This continued all through the summer. Most nights, and even sometimes during the day, I would stand very still and watch a wild field mouse playing on the wheel. Sometimes more than one mouse at a time would wrestle for their new toy or they would run in tandem. I oiled it to keep the screeching down and enjoyed my garage friends for the summer months. Finally, winter came, and the mice were gone but I left the wheel on the shelf for them in case they returned. The mice never returned the following summer, so I eventually threw the wheel out, as it was very dirty. Sometimes I think of them when I am organizing and cleaning the garage and smile to think that even a wild field mouse understood the purpose of this simple toy and took some time out of his busy day to play. 🐾🐾

*T*hrough tears, as I hold a treasured animal for the last time, I always thank them for being in my life, however short that time was. Each animal, foster or my own, is special. I feel my life was enriched by knowing them. Hopefully, they understand how special they have been to me.

My heart and my head are usually doing battle, wanting to give him or her a little more time but knowing that letting them go is the compassionate thing to do. I often ask myself if I am keeping them alive for me or for them. If the answer if for me, I know it is time to say farewell.

Many times after saying goodbye to a precious pet as they pass from this world, I envision them happily running up the Rainbow Bridge to be reunited with their friends from earth. They have no more pain, their coats and ears are flying in the wind, and they are excited to be whole again. This is especially true if the animal was old and had been sick or had medical issues.

I know in my heart that I will see them all again one day. As they are racing up the Rainbow Bridge, I tell them to save a space for me in the clover. It will be a wild and noisy welcome when we are all reunited. We will have a lot of catching up to do!

— Chapter 22 —

Half & Half

Most animals know when they have found a safe haven. Half & Half came back to her safe haven when she needed help.

I never turn away any animal who comes to my house, even stray or community (feral) cats. I have a feeding station, heated water dish, and comfy cat houses for them. I want them to feel they are safe with me. I never try to touch the cats, and after a while they don't run like mad when they see me. If I am outside, they will just move away until I am gone and then come back to their beds or food when I leave.

Half & Half was a unique tuxedo kitty with half her nose black and the other half white. She was a typical stray cat gone feral who would stop by to eat every night at my feeding station and then hang out on the porch in one of the many kitty baskets. Half & Half knew she was safe at my place. I never knew her story or where she came from but one day she was gone. It saddened me because I love my community cats and try to give them some of the comforts of a caring home. They are trapped, altered, and vaccinated as well as given any other medical care needed. I figured she moved on, was killed by a predator (coyotes and great horned owls are common around my house and a cat makes a nice meal for them), or was hit by a vehicle. Sometimes they wander, especially the un-neutered males, but she was spayed and seemed content.

It was about two years since I had last seen her when she showed up at my door again. It was as if she had never left and was happily eating food when I spotted her. I was overjoyed! Half & Half was back. She looked the same although much thinner and ragged. I was able to trap her again and brought her to my vet. He called me later that day and said she tested positive for both feline leukemia virus (FeLV) and feline immunodeficiency virus (FIV). (FeLV is an untreatable virus that suppresses a cat's immune system and is the most common cause of cancer in cats. In a cat with FeLV, the number of white blood cells is either too high or too low. FIV is similar to FeLV since the cat's immune system is also suppressed making it vulnerable to infection and disease from bacteria or viruses that normally would not be harmful to a non-FIV animal.) The vet wanted to know if he should put her down. I told him no, I would give her whatever quality time I could before letting her go.

She came home with me and stayed inside in one of my cat rooms. Half & Half seemed to know that I wouldn't hurt her and for the last few weeks of her life, she let me touch and love her. Maybe she had been someone's pet kitty at one time and had to learn to survive after losing her home. Half & Half lived about six weeks with me until I realized she was fading. I brought her to my vet for the last time and held her until she was gone. I was glad to have been able to give her those last few weeks of comfort but was angry that she had to die. Both of those feline diseases are preventable. A cat living outside often contracts either or both of them from mingling with or being bitten by other infected cats. My guess is that she knew she was sick and found her way back to the place where she felt safe. I am so grateful she did. She gave me the only thing she could by coming back to my house, the amazing gift of her trust. Thank you Half & Half you make me want to work harder to help stray and community cats. 🐾🐾

Catios are wonderful outdoor hangouts for kitties that keep them safe from predators, vehicles, and other dangers. They can enjoy the world around them and watch the birds while being completely safe. My catio is nothing fancy but it gives my kitties a chance to be outside in the warmer months. Some of the volunteers in our group have beautiful catios where their cats can lounge and take in the scenery. They are often equipped with cat trees, kitty condos, and sleeping baskets. I also plant a large plastic litter box with cat grass so they can munch to their hearts content. My friend, Lisa, has a catnip garden in hers. She places a wire mesh over the top of the catnip plants to allow them to grow to a certain height. Once they reach that height, the cats can eat away, while the plants under the mesh stay intact.

My catio is constructed of two by fours and chicken wire with a gate, but yours can be as elaborate as your creativity and checkbook allow. There is a cat window from my basement to the catio. This lets them come and go as they please. I close it during the cold weather months and keep it open when it's warm outside.

Many people believe that it is cruel to keep your cat indoors and lots of kitties love being outside. This is an inexpensive way to give your cat the best of the outdoors while keeping them safe.

— Chapter 23 —

Grey Ghost

I *feel that each animal who crosses my path is a gift from God!*

Grey Ghost was one of many cats who found his way to the feeding station on my porch. There is always a large dish of food and fresh water (heated water bowl in the winter) for kitties. I also have several comfy houses for the feral and stray cats who decide it's not too bad of a place to hang out. Grey Ghost showed up last summer and would come back every few weeks to visit. I often watched him out the window and when he saw me staring at him, he would just move calmly down the stairs until I left. He never seemed scared of me, just wary. He would stop by for a day or two to eat or sleep in my kitty baskets and then I wouldn't see him for a while. (He reminded me of a ghost. He was here one minute and gone the next, like a vapor. The kitty seemed to fade away; I never saw him come or leave, thus his name.) Disappearing for days at a time is typical, as he wasn't neutered and was probably out romancing the un-spayed f males in my rural community. Little did he know that his days of being Romeo were soon to end!

When fall came and the days and nights got colder, I saw him more often and decided to trap him. When attempting to trap an animal, I usually tie the traps open, cover them with a sheet or large towel, and place a bowl of wet food near the entrance. This lets the animal eat the food easily while getting used to the trap. (The covering helps them to remain calm and not thrash around in the trap and hurt themselves when caught.) Over time, the cats get accustomed to being around the trap until I eventually move the food dish to the pressure plate in the back of the trap, set it, and keeping my fingers crossed, catch him or her.

It took a while, but I finally caught this handsome boy, and he was mad! I had a feeling that he really wasn't feral because even the tamest cat tends to get angry when caught in a trap. I brought him to the vet for the surgery and vaccines and was saddened when the vet called me to say he tested positive for Feline Immunodeficiency Virus (FIV). This is similar to Human Immunodeficiency Virus (HIV) in people. It is transmitted via cat bites. Males fighting other males over females is usually the way it is passed to other cats. The vet said this boy was a good weight (he loved the canned food at the feeding station at my house) and despite the bad diagnosis, he appeared to be healthy. He had broken teeth and a damaged eye from fighting, but the vet thought he could possibly see some light out of it. It didn't seem to hinder him at all. I told the vet I would take Grey Ghost home with me, rather than have him put down. (I would only have put him down if he was suffering, in pain, and couldn't be helped.)

The first few days at my house were a definite adjustment for this poor kitty. I still didn't think he was feral even though I couldn't get near him. I kept him inside my house in a wire cage until he healed from his neuter surgery. When I felt he was feeling better I let him out into my large cat room. He liked to sit in the window to watch the birds but never really acted as if he wanted to go outside. If he were feral, he would have been throwing himself against the windows to get out. Grey Ghost was warm, well fed, and content; why go outside where it was getting a lot colder and snowy. When I tried to pet him, he would hiss but never lash out at me with his claws, so I figured he had been someone's pet kitty at one time. (A feral cat would never let anyone get near enough to touch him.) The Ghost lost his home at some point in his life and had to learn to survive on the streets where humans were not nice to him. I was a human he didn't know or trust.

My goal was to give him the space and time to learn that I wouldn't hurt him. As often as possible, I would gently run my hand over his back. After a while, he allowed this but only for a few seconds before he would walk away. I never went after him and eventually I was able to pet him for longer and longer amounts of time. He didn't seem thrilled at the attention but tolerated me. It was so exciting when while I was petting him one day, I finally heard him purr. It was even more exciting when he started to rub up against me. Finally, after months of trying, we were friends.

Now when I walk into his cat room, he chirps his funny little meow, telling me to "Hurry over here and give me love". When I come up to him, he buries his head into my side and can't get enough affection. Then the engine goes into high gear while he revs up his purr motor. It is the best "Thank You" I could ask for. I promised him that he would always have a safe home with me and that I would do whatever it took to keep him healthy. Discussions with my vet as well as internet searches showed me that FIV is not the death sentence I had always thought it was. Many cats who test positive for FIV go on to live normal lives. I hope I can give "The Ghost" a great home for a LONG time. He certainly has been a gift in my life! 🐱🐱

I went outside one very cold night in February and saw a tiny, crying, nearly frozen puppy asking for help. I was horrified that someone could leave a puppy out in the freezing temperatures and quickly took this little guy inside to warm him up and give him some food. His coat was very sparse, and he was extremely emaciated. The poor puppy wolfed down three bowls of food before he stopped to breathe. He ate as if he was starved, which he likely was.

The puppy, now named Dylan, was too young to have wandered away from his home. It was likely someone dumped him near my house. Dylan found me long before I was involved with animal rescue. Not wanting to keep him (I already had three dogs and felt that was enough) I couldn't stand the thought of bringing him to our shelter. After trying to find him a home on my own, I gave up and he ended up living his thirteen plus years with me.

Dylan loved his toys, especially his tennis balls, and went crazy when he knew we were going for a swim. I think he was part fish! For most of his life he was one of my running partners and he LOVED riding in his truck. Nothing made Dylan happier than spending time with his person. He was a real momma's dog. It has been four years since I said goodbye to one of my best pals and it still hurts to know Dylan is not in my life anymore.

— Chapter 24 —

Buddy

*B**uddy is lucky that Lexi came before him; otherwise, I may have thrown in the towel on this very difficult Cocker Spaniel.*

I wasn't sure if I even wanted to write about Buddy. I took him into my home to foster and had a very difficult time forming any kind of bond with him. Buddy was actually the only dog who I have had that I really didn't like very much at first, never mind love. Typically, I fall in love with all the animals who cross my path and it's painful to let them go. With Buddy, I couldn't wait to get him adopted and out of my life.

He came to our group from another local rescue that couldn't handle him. Buddy was a three-year-old Cocker Spaniel owned by a couple with two young children. While the family was driving their car from California to Montana Buddy bit one of the kids. He likely had had enough of the two young children while packed in a car for four days and snapped when things didn't go his way. After this incident, his owners surrendered him to a small rescue group in Conrad, Montana. A short time later, Buddy came to live with me as my Pet Paw-see foster dog. I agreed to foster him knowing that adoption to a family with children was out of the question.

Buddy was a beautiful black dog and I felt I could find him a good home despite his background. He was okay with me, and did fine with my other dogs, but I could see he had a hair-trigger temper. There wasn't much warning from him if he didn't like something. Unfortunately, this was not a great marketing feature for a dog hoping to find a good home.

After a short time, I found a lovely couple without kids as potential adoptive parents. They knew his background and history of biting. Despite his bad press they wanted to take a chance on him, so I agreed. I kept in constant contact with them for the week they had him. Yes, he only lasted one week. He liked the man but was growly with his wife. Whenever the wife went near her hubby, Buddy would show his teeth. Not very good for a positive relationship with both of his new humans. He obviously never learned to share his people. After only one week, they called and said they couldn't keep Buddy. The gal was afraid of him, and I couldn't blame her.

I reluctantly took him back and continued to try to find him a good home. That was until he lunged at me one day while I was working with him on manners. I like to practice taking toys or other "high value" objects out of their mouths so the dog will know who the pack leader in the family is. This training helps in the event the dog had something dangerous in his or her mouth. I would like to be able to get it out quickly while still keeping all my fingers. I will give them the toy, chewy bone, or other goodie and then ask them for it while gently taking it from them. The dog receives praise for giving me the object and then eventually gets to keep it to chew on or play with. It usually works fine, but not this time. We tried it once and he willingly gave me the toy. The second time he charged at me, bit me badly, and then cooled down acting as if nothing happened. I seriously considered putting him down at that point. I did not need an aggressive dog who went postal over nothing and with no warning. No matter what my decision was, I knew he was un-adoptable to a family, so I was stuck with him. I couldn't adopt him out and then live with the knowledge that he had the potential to hurt someone badly. With Buddy, it would be a question of when, not if. I knew he would eventually bite again.

Buddy ignores the other dogs and the cats at my house. None of my other animals want to play with him. I think they know there is something not quite right with him, but he doesn't seem to mind their snubs. He is happy to hang out by himself. He loves to race around the yard until he is tired and then just sleeps in the grass. Despite his bad attitude, Buddy knows many obedience commands and is great on a leash. While taking a treat from my hands he is extremely gentle and never snaps to get the food like other dogs I have had. He also loves to cuddle, which surprises me since I didn't think he even liked me. Aside from being unpredictable, he is a perfect dog.

Although I have come close a few times, I don't want to give up on Buddy. If something happens in his world that he doesn't like, he goes nuts. After that, he is back to his typical happy self. It is as if his evil twin comes out for a minute or two and then the "Good Buddy" emerges. He has two VERY different personalities. I spoke with several dog trainers for suggestions in working with him, but nothing seemed to help. We even thought that he might have a brain tumor causing him to turn on a dime. No one had ever seen anything like this dog's very quick temper especially when he gives no warning.

Grooming Buddy was hell. I like my Cockers to be short-coated and clean smelling in the warmer months. However, finding someone who could groom him was tough. My vet told me she would knock him out as if for surgery and then totally shave him if needed. I didn't care if he was pretty; I just wanted him to be clean and comfortable. I was about ready to take her up on her offer when I found a groomer, Corine, who was also an experienced dog trainer. I talked to her at length before dropping him off the first time and waited by the phone for the dreaded call that he had bitten her. Sadly, she called me later that day and said she could hardly get anything done on him. He was snarling and biting her through the muzzle and eventually she had to quit. I took him home and was getting desperate because he was matted and smelled terrible. For his next attempt at grooming, I had a veterinarian who operated out of his mobile van stop by the pet salon to give him a valium shot to mellow him a bit. (I never asked for the gory details when I heard that the veterinarian told Corine "you had better work fast." I am sure Buddy was less than pleasant while getting his knock out shot.) Again, I got a call that the shot only lasted a short while, so there was not much progress made. The groomer was able to get a bit more of his coat clipped, but still no bath.

Corine knew I was at the end of my rope, but her experience with dogs didn't let her quit on him. She did some research and found a halter collar that she wanted to try. The strap went around his nose so when he turned towards her to bite, it would tighten, and he couldn't open his mouth. Fearfully, I took him back for my third attempt at spiffing him up. When I stopped by to pick him up later that day, Corine was so excited that she was able to complete his clip and bath and still had all her fingers! She took her time and when things got a little heated, she left him alone to cool down. Whatever she did worked and since then, each grooming adventure has gotten much easier. Corine comes to my house now to groom him and the last time he didn't even have to wear the halter collar except when she tried to clip his front feet. That was the only time he growled and tried to bite. When she comes over now, Buddy is actually relaxed and happy to see her. The progress she made with this dog is truly amazing.

We talked a lot about what was causing his postal moments. Corine thought abuse in his previous life caused his issues with people. He seemed to be always on edge, waiting for a kick in the butt or a smack to his head. As self-preservation, he was ready at all times to attack first and ask forgiveness later. Unfortunately, in other circumstances he would have been put down or taken out and shot. Putting down an animal that is not old, sick, or suffering would be difficult and while I have never had to do it, the thought was always in the back of my mind in those early days with Buddy.

Buddy has lived with me for four years now and is a new dog. He has been one of my running partners since I took him into my home, and I think this has helped us bond. He is wonderful on a leash while some of my others can be challenging. I think the daily run helps him to relax and dispel some of the monsters from his previous life. He still has his moments when demons from his past rise up, but they are few and far between. I still have my moments when I want to kill him because he is headstrong and can be a little jerk. I have learned a lot about difficult dogs from Buddy and I know he will continue to teach me. However, Buddy is my dog now and I can say that I love him (most of the time) and am glad that he is in my life (most of the time). 🐾🐕

Callie was a kitten I adopted from the shelter long before I was involved with animal rescue. She was born with deformed back legs. One leg only had the back half of her paw, the front toes were missing. The second leg was missing from the elbow joint down. She just had a stub at the end of her short leg that she used for balance.

Callie was otherwise healthy. She was a gorgeous, long-coated, dilute calico that didn't let her physical issues keep her from enjoying life. Callie had to be careful when jumping down from something so that she didn't hit her stump and she couldn't run or climb very well, but it didn't seem to matter much to her.

Callie was content to sit in the window and watch the birds all day long and she loved attention. She was a quiet, gentle kitty who thought her life was purrfect. I was heartbroken when she developed kidney failure at about ten and left me. Despite her only having two normal feet, she left MANY paw prints across my heart when she passed.

— Chapter 25 —
Goldie Oldies

Some of my favorite and most beloved animals have come to me during their final days and have been a blessing in my life.

I think the most fulfilling types of rescue I have experienced have been fostering or adopting senior pets. There is nothing like giving an older animal a safe place to live out their golden years. I have had the pleasure of taking in many older animals, and while these animals never live as long as a new puppy or kitten, their gratitude is overwhelming. They tell me every day how thankful they are to be with me, their *furrever* person. I have had senior dogs amble up to me, put their head on my arm, and stare into my eyes. I know they are trying to convey their appreciation for giving them some extra time in a loving home.

Many people shy away from adopting an older or senior pet stating that the animal won't be around all that long and they can't bear the eventual loss. That is true, as is the need for more vet care and expenses. But they are so worth the extra trouble. Senior pets are often quieter and easier to have in a home. They are typically housebroken. They only want a soft bed to lay on and to spend time with their people. They don't need to play for hours to get rid of excess young dog or cat energy and they don't tend to chew up your stuff. Typically, their teeth are so worn down they want to save any chewing for their food.

I have had the blessing of taking in numerous older dogs and cats over my years of rescue. Many times, I understand they won't live more than a year or two with me, but some have surprised me. Jake was one of those wonderful surprises. I adopted him from the shelter as a senior dog. His former owners had given his age at 13 on the shelter's surrender form. I took him into my home expecting a year, maybe two, of his company. Instead, he gave me seven wonderful years and at the ripe old age of 20, said goodbye to my pack and me. Until the very end, he was quite active and tried his best to keep up with the others. He didn't need much, just help getting onto his bed and some meds to keep him comfortable. I feel so lucky to have been able to give him the gift of those last years. He gave me far more.

Oscar was an old senior cat when I took him in. He had lived with his family for over 17 years when they moved out of the country. They didn't think he would survive the long trip or the new location and had decided the kindest thing to do was to put him down. I couldn't let them do that, so I took him into my home. Oscar fit in as if he had lived with me his entire life. He was such a friendly and loving kitty as well as being an easy keeper. He didn't fight with the others, used his box, and was content to watch life from his kitty bed. Oscar lived with me until he was almost 20 years old.

His previous mom, Jan, happened to be in town visiting and we were supposed to meet for dinner when I called her to tell her that Oscar was failing. We met at the vet and she was able to hold her beloved old friend for one last time before he passed over the Rainbow Bridge. His purrs told us how happy he was to see his mom and how thankful he was for a little extra time with me. Oscar is missed by two families and while I didn't have him long enough, the time we had together was special. I am thankful he gave me his company for the last months of his life.

Another super senior who I invited into my home was Magic. He was an old, ragged Great Pyrenees cross who had languished at the local shelter hoping to find a home for his last days. He was also deaf which made him even more unadoptable. Magic came to live with me, and I hoped I could give him a few more years, but from the looks of him, I doubted it would be that long.

It looked like he had had a rough life and I wanted to shower him with all the comforts I could. He didn't ask for much. Magic only wanted food, a soft place to sleep, and lots of love. Well he got that and more and thanked me often. At night, I would settle him on his dog bed with a blanket wrapped around his thin frame. He would almost purr his thanks. I doubt he ever had that kind of comfort in his life.

Magic liked to amble around the yard on his long legs and come to rest near me while I worked. He just seemed to like my company; I know I enjoyed his. Magic was one of the sweetest dogs I had ever taken in and I often wondered what his story was. He never told me any of the details, but I got the impression that he had suffered neglect. Sadly, his large, loving heart gave out on him less than a year after I adopted him. I wished so much that I could have gotten him sooner and given him more time, but I knew he was thankful for those few months with me. A photo of him hangs in my office. His coat was no longer ragged, he had gained some weight, and his face lost that forlorn look. I will always remember this handsome proud dog.

Panda is a senior dog who also found her way into my life and my heart. A neighbor picked her up while she wandered the roads around her house. It was winter and little Panda was lost and confused. It turns out that her owner died in his driveway, likely from a heart attack. No one knew how long Panda had been outside in the bad weather before she was rescued and taken to a vet for care. She was deaf, had only one eye, very few teeth, and was unstable on her feet from old age. Panda was a tiny breed, Cocker mixed with some other small dog. Like Sally, she was a train wreck with little chance of adoption. But those are the ones I gravitate towards.

A friend in rescue asked me to look at Panda to see if there was any chance of finding her a home or if it was kinder to put her down. I fell in love with her the moment I saw her and knew she was worth saving. My heart wouldn't let me turn my back on this very pitiful little dog. I took her with me to foster until we could find the perfect *furrever* home for her last golden days. Happily, Panda found her *furrever* home. It was with me!

Shortly after I took her home with me, I noticed that Panda seemed to have some difficulty breathing. A visit to the vet and some x-rays showed a large tumor in her lungs. At that point, adopting her to a family was out of the question. She left the vet office with me that day and I promised her she would always be safe in my home.

Panda did quite well on medication, gained some weight, and her ragged coat grew out a bit. She needed to wear a sweater all the time and didn't like to spend much time outdoors but was content to hang out in her doggie bed and watch TV. She was happy and when she spotted me, she would amble over to me with her crooked gait. Panda loved cuddling and didn't mind being groomed. I tried to give her the love and attention she may not have had with her former owner. I would tuck her in her bed at night and tell her how special she was. Panda gave me her unconditional love for one year before it was evident that she was going downhill.

One sad morning she let me know she was tired of fighting. The tumor had grown and when she refused food, I knew her days were over. I held her close to me and my tears wet her coat as she crossed the Rainbow Bridge. She was with me a relatively short time, but my heart still broke as if we had spent a lifetime together. I have her ashes with all my other pets and think of her often. I rarely get a small dog; most of my rescues are large dogs, so Panda was special to me. She was able to spend a lot of time on my lap, which is something I greatly enjoyed, and I think she did too. Panda was a brave little soul. I mourn her loss but never regretted letting her leave her tiny paw prints across my heart. 🐾🐾

R iley was a middle-aged Cocker Spaniel when he came to live with me. He had been dumped at the shelter when his people couldn't keep him anymore. They wrote on the shelter's surrender form that they had no time for him. I can't imagine why since he was very quiet, well behaved, and easy to have around. Riley had no bad habits and only wanted to please his person

Soon after I adopted him, Riley had surgery to remove one eye. He was likely in pain from his badly damaged, blind eye and there was nothing that could be done to restore sight back in this eye. A few months later, he went blind suddenly in his remaining good eye. It made me cry to watch him struggle to find his way around our home. However, once he had adjusted to his total blindness, he got around just fine. All he needed to know was how to find the doggie door, his food, and the couch. He scored an A+ on all three.

Riley lived with me almost eight years and my heart was broken when it came time to say goodbye to this gentle, quiet, little soul. I will always see him in my mind wagging his cute stubby tail with a happy smile on his face. Rest easy my friend; I will see you again!

— Chapter 26 —
The Coyote Puppies

These puppies were the most loyal, well mannered, and friendly dogs I have had in my life of many dogs.

Years ago, I was involved in a large rescue effort and ended up taking six puppies into my home to foster. They were known as the "Coyote Puppies" since they looked like they could have had coyote in their family tree. Because of this "label," they were un-adoptable within the city limits (most city ordinances prohibit wolf and coyote hybrids within city limits). This was long before DNA testing was available. If it was, I would have tested them. The local animal control said they would have to put them down if found living in Great Falls. I don't live in the city and was happy to take them into my home. They were a wonderful, friendly litter of pups who looked mostly like Husky mixes, but they had some characteristics similar to their wild cousins. It didn't matter to me; they were puppies in need of a safe place, and I loved having them.

The night I got them home, I settled them in the garage with their food, bedding, and toys. They were pretty scared and just wanted to snuggle up to me for comfort. I remember sitting on their bed and being covered with their wet puppy kisses. The next morning, they were happy to see me and to explore their new yard. The garage has a doggie door into the backyard so they could get outside to play and then back inside for a nap. It was pretty well puppy-proofed, so I wasn't worried when I left for work. That was my first mistake. I had recently insulated the entire garage with batt insulation and when I got home there wasn't any of it left on the walls from about four feet down. They had ripped off every bit of insulation, shredded it, and then mixed it in their poop, which they had generously left throughout the garage. I had wrongly assumed they would go out to the yard to poop, but the puppies didn't get that memo. I had never seen such a mess, and boy, were they happy to show me their artwork. But, how mad can you get when six little puppies are all clamoring to give their mom kisses? I laughed as I took the garden hose to the mess and re-thought how to better puppy-proof this area. They eventually learned to use the back yard rather than the garage as the latrine and adjusted quickly to their foster home.

They were a fun pack of puppies who ate everything in their path like a bunch of locusts. I had never had this many puppies before and was shocked at how much they could consume. A 20-pound bag of puppy chow disappeared in a few days. They were little eating machines! I learned the painful fact that their favorite treat turned out to be corn on the cob. One day while working in my garden I saw a puppy grab an ear of corn off the stalk and hold the cob between his paws while he devoured it. They all figured out this neat trick and before long every ear of corn in my garden was gone. The only thing I regret was not taking pictures of them with their tasty treats. I don't know if I got any corn for myself that summer and didn't plant more again for years. After that learning experience, I stuck to veggies that were not as appealing to dogs.

I thought it would be easy to find homes for these very adorable little guys and gals, but I quickly learned how wrong I was. They could only be adopted to people who lived outside of city limits, which cut down the number of potential homes. Sadly, once people heard they might have coyote in them, no one wanted to adopt them. Despite this, I did find two wonderful homes relatively soon after I took them in. Both new owners fell in love with their pups and didn't care what they might be mixed with. It took almost a year to get the third puppy adopted. Elle Mae went to a wonderful family and was doing great until about ten months into her stay, when she killed some chickens. After this incident, she was no longer welcome in her home, so she came back to live with me. By this time, I had given up on finding homes for the other three puppies and resigned myself to the fact they would most likely live with me for life. This was ok as I loved them dearly and they felt like they were home. When Elle Mae came back, I just welcomed her and enjoyed my pack of four "Coyote Puppies".

The four puppies turned into four amazingly, loving, faithful dogs and I never regretted that I had kept them. They loved running with me, were well behaved, and listened better than many of the other dogs I have had in my home. Bugg Z, Elle Mae, Banjo, and Wiley Coyote were some of the smartest dogs I have ever had. There was the Alpha male, Bugg Z, Alpha female, Elle Mae, and the Omega dog, Wiley Coyote. Banjo fell somewhere in between them all.

I found it fascinating to observe them speak to each other using doggie body language. Watching them interact taught me a lot about dogs and pack mates. They were constantly aware of where and what their siblings were doing. They were always relating to each other especially when we went to their favorite place where I would let them all off leash to run. It was a gravel road with almost no traffic and acres of wild prairie. They would run like a pack of wild dogs, happy for the freedom and the feel of the wind in their ears. When they got tired, they would always come back to me for assurance that a warm bed and good food was waiting back home. Perish the thought that they would have to catch and kill for their dinner. They may have been coyote mixes, but they were spoiled domestic dogs at heart.

During one of these outdoor adventures, they actually scared up a wild coyote. My "coyotes" gave chase while the real coyote just casually loped away. I saw him look back at his pursuers and I know he was laughing about these well-fed, lazy housedogs trying to run him down. My dogs eventually turned back to me when they tired, realizing that wild coyote is likely a bit too stringy for their sophisticated palates.

Slowly over the years, I have had to say goodbye to my "Coyote Puppies." However, I was determined to find out what they had in their lineage before I lost the last dog. Wiley Coyote was the most "coyote looking" of the pack so I bought a DNA test kit and sent it in for analysis. (I specifically found a kit that tested for coyotes and wolves.) After almost thirteen years, I found out that their father was a purebred Samoyed and their mother was equal parts Siberian Husky, German Shepherd, Border Collie, and Samoyed. Not a bit of coyote anywhere, although they sure howled like their wild cousins. I was a little bit disappointed but glad to finally learn what they were. I still call them my pack of "Coyotes" and am glad I was able to give them a good life. I miss their love and companionship. 🐾🐾

Stormy, a purebred Boxer, abandoned at the home of a young man's elderly grandparents, was extremely thin with a dry coat and numerous fighting scars on her body. The elderly couple loved her but were too old to care for this special dog. Stormy was very strong, nervous, and needed a lot of exercise, which they couldn't give her.

Stormy was used as a breeding female by their grandson until the Pet Paw-see took her into our foster program. The grandson had bred her and sold her puppies for money to finance his drug habit. (He ended up in jail, which is why Stormy was with his grandparents.) Once we took in this sweet Boxer, she got medical attention, spayed, and put up for adoption. Stormy lived with me while I fattened her up, brushed her pitiful coat until it glowed, and showed her how much fun life could be.

Despite her earlier neglect, she quickly relaxed and revealed her silly side. Besides being a bit goofy, she was also very loving, gentle, and obedient. It didn't take long for her furerver people to find her. A couple that had owned Boxers in the past met her at a Petco adoption event and fell in love. She now lives with a great family who thinks she is the best dog in the world!

— Chapter 27 —

Dear Puppies

I wrote this after taking in the litter of "Coyote Puppies". They provided hours of laughter and gallons of tears!

Dear Puppies,

The large Collie in the back yard is not a giant squeaky toy. I know you like the way he squeals when you chew on him and yank out his hair, but quit mauling him. Winter is coming and he needs his coat!

Dear Puppies,

A good rule of thumb: all the stuff on the counters is mine, all the stuff on the floor is yours. Knocking stuff off the counters onto the floor does not make it yours!

Dear Puppies,

I love that you want to help me with my daily chores, but please let me clean out the litter box!

Dear Puppies,

Your leash and the cat's tail were not put on this earth for the same purpose! Quit pulling them!

🐾 Dear Puppies,

When you are done playing, please place your toys in the box marked "Puppy Toys" and not in the toilet. They don't flush very well!

🐾 Dear Puppies,

Instead of trying to think up cute names to fit your different personalities, I will just call you by the names you seem to respond to: Leave It!, Stop It!, and D#$@ It! Oh, and let's not forget, Be Qui It!

🐾 Dear Puppies,

Although cats look cute, soft, and cuddly, the kitty's claws are lethal weapons. However, looking at that piece of skin missing from your nose you may have figured that out by now!

🐾 Dear Puppies,

It's amazing how smart you guys are and how quickly you learn new stuff. I saw how fast you learned to rip the insulation off my garage walls. Did the Collie teach you that? And, how did you know that the stuffing in the dog bed looked so pretty when it was strewn across the back yard. (I think the Collie taught you that one too!) So why is the concept of sit/stay/shut up so hard for you guys to figure out!

🐾 Dear Puppies,

I know you are just trying to show affection but please keep your tongues in your own mouths. I know where they have been!

🐾 Dear Puppies,

I realize I am outnumbered, but I am bigger than you are, and I pay the bills so that makes me the boss! (That's ok with you guys, isn't it?)

🐾 Dear Puppies,

Thank you for the hours of silliness and joy you have brought into my life. I feel so blessed to have had you these past months. 🐱🐱

R udy, his mom, and three siblings were the second litter of kitties I took into my home to foster. Rudy was cream and white as a kitten while his mom and siblings were all black or black and white. Rudy's coat later turned into a beautiful chocolate and cream Siamese color.

Rudy was adopted out and, after almost a year, came back to the Pet Paw-see. Since Rudy was still a kitten at his adoption, he didn't have any manners and was bitey. He tended to use his person's legs as a scratching post, so he was returned to us.

Rudy lived with me until a lovely gentleman named John met and bonded with him. John adopted Rudy and renamed him Brandy. Brandy lived for years with his person until John moved to a retirement home. The rules of the facility allowed only de-clawed cats. John wouldn't de-claw his best friend and sadly asked the Pet Paw-see to take him back. Les, the president of our group, contacted the retirement home to see if they would waive this requirement, which they did. Brandy happily lives with his pal John who has joined our Senior for Senior Program.

P.S. The Siamese cat on the cover of the book is Brandy. John did the beautiful cover for me and was excited to include a rendering of his precious kitty.

— Chapter 28 —
Chocolate Ice Cream for Breakfast

Dogs are just like kids; they will always push the limits.

Not having kids, but having many friends who do, I often compare how similar human kids and dogs are. I think both dogs and kids go through the same life stages; dog's stages are just a little accelerated. Puppies are so cute it doesn't matter if they chew your furniture or shoes to bits. I don't think babies chew like puppies, but I know they do other things equally as mischievous. Every day is a new adventure for a dog especially when they are young. The problem is that with dogs, they never grow up; they seem to reach the developmental level of a three-year-old child and then quit maturing.

Unfortunately, some dogs NEVER mature. My Lab-Pitt mix, Baxter, is nine years old and I have only seen a few indications that he is starting to act his age. He has been a knucklehead for most of his life and still acts like a juvenile. He takes every chance he can to get into things he knows he shouldn't, such as jumping up on the counters to eat anything within his reach or climbing his six-foot-high-chain-link kennel fence. This cost him (rather me) two very expensive surgeries when he blew out his anterior cruciate ligament (ACL) trying to pretend he was the canine version of Houdini. He liked to balance on the top of his slick Igloo doghouse, shimmy up the kennel panels, and leap over the side to freedom. Unfortunately, the landing part of this stunt has resulted in two badly torn ACLs and one knee with shredded cartilage. Thanks, Bax!

Another dog who has never acted her age is Meka, my Alaskan Malamute. She is about ten years old and astonishes me with her puppylike antics. She still has the energy of a very young dog and when my guard is down, she will take advantage of any situation. Her favorite stunt is to hang back where I can't see her while I open my front door and then sprint into the great outdoors. Once outside where there is no fence to hold her back, she will be in the next county before I find my truck keys to hunt her down. Luckily, she LOVES her truck. When she spots me driving around looking for her, she will often race towards my open door to jump into my lap. I am not sure what fascinates her about the world outside my yard but there must be something there because she never passes up the opportunity to break out and run.

The exploits of my dogs make it difficult for me to leave home for an overnight stay except in an emergency. Luckily, that hasn't happened often. I don't like to board the dogs and I don't know many people brave enough to stay at my house. However, years ago, a crisis forced me to be away from home and leave my precious animal family. When that happened, I depended on my friends, those other crazy souls who have houses full of their own furry bodies to help me out.

I asked (begged) my good friend Jan to stay at my house once when I had to leave for a family emergency. When I came home, I asked how the dogs behaved. Of course, the dogs got away with murder, like kids with a baby sitter or a substitute schoolteacher. They didn't listen to her when she called them inside for the night; she told me they "flipped her the paw." I should have told her to shake the cookie jar. They have very selective hearing but can hear the cookie jar rattling a mile away. They got extra treats with dinner and got to sprawl on the couch while my friend had to watch TV sitting on a hard kitchen chair. I laughed and told her she shouldn't have let them get away with stuff like that. Dogs with a new person in charge smell fear and take full advantage of it. My dogs are opportunists and never let a chance for mischief go to waste. I could almost hear the dogs tell her "Really! It's true! Mom ALWAYS lets us have chocolate ice cream for breakfast."

*O*ne July morning many years ago, before I was actively involved in animal rescue, I was out for a jog when I noticed a convenience store roof on fire. I raced inside the store to warn the workers and then ran to the house next door to tell them of the danger. The wind was blowing the flames towards their roof and since it was early in the morning, I doubted they were awake yet.

While banging on their front door and yelling for the residents, I saw about ten to fifteen tiny kittens running around. When the owners answered the door, I told them about the fire and asked for a box or container to gather the babies. I knew the mommas were long gone but the kittens were too small to escape. We collected the kittens we could find, and the owners drove off with their dog and the kittens to safety. (The emergency crews got to the fire before it damaged their home.)

I was horrified at the number of babies and went back the next week to offer to spay their nine un-altered females. In the meantime, I adopted one of the kittens, Taffy, for myself. She was a part Siamese kitten with a diva attitude, but I loved her despite her tendency to be a bit snarky. Taffy lived many years with me until she passed of old age.

— Chapter 29 —

Maggie

Happy endings are priceless!

My late friend Gloria had a very good relationship with the manager of the local shelter and would often take dogs out who she felt she could adopt. She had a large network of potential adopters and worked hard to reduce the shelter's inhabitants. Gloria knew of an overweight but very sweet Sheltie named Maggie at the shelter who wasn't getting any interest. She asked me to foster her, which I gladly did. Maggie was a mess; her coat was dry and matted, and she needed to lose about 30 pounds. I took her home with me and bathed and groomed her to make her more presentable, but the weight loss would take time.

A vet check with bloodwork showed she had thyroid issues and had to go on medication. Thyroid meds are relatively inexpensive so we knew this would likely not pose a problem for potential adopters. She had to get that weight off and we crossed our fingers the meds and a good diet would help. Maggie was previously spayed, so she was updated on all her vaccines and was good to go to her new home, when we found one. Meanwhile she lived with me and my pack of hairy monsters and didn't seem to mind the chaos.

I had an idea for a perfect home for Maggie but wasn't able to reach my dear friend Bobbie to tell her about my newest foster dog and to see if she was interested in adopting her. I called her several times but never got through and couldn't leave a message as she had no voicemail.

Bobbie is a lovely retired lady who had adopted one of the very old Collies from Camp Collie. Gabby the Collie lived the life of leisure with Bobbie, and after only a few years in her new home, passed away of old age. Bobbie was crushed to lose her sweet girl. She asked us to keep an eye out for another Collie, but Collies are not a common dog in Montana. (The Camp Collie seizure probably doubled the number of Collies in the entire state!) I figured a Sheltie was similar to a small Collie and hoped that Maggie would be able to fill the void in Bobbie's heart. I knew Bobbie would fall in love with Maggie and was frustrated when I couldn't get in touch with her.

After trying for over a week to get a hold of Bobbie, I gave up and tried to find someone else who could give this dog a loving home. I don't remember why Maggie ended up at the shelter, but it was clear that she had been neglected. Despite that, she was a very friendly, amiable, middle-aged dog. She got along fine with my dogs and cats and enjoyed her temporary home with me.

Life went on until one day, out of the blue, I received a call from Bobbie. (She must have been reading my mind.) Before I could say anything, she started to cry about a dog at the shelter that she wanted to adopt. For some reason the shelter workers rejected her application, even though her veterinarian called to verify that Bobbie was a wonderful home. Bobbie was the type of home I would want for any dog or cat and I couldn't understand why she was turned down. She was an excellent, responsible pet owner who gave her dogs and cats anything needed to have a great life. Bobbie continued to tell me all about this dog until I clued in on the fact that she was talking about Maggie. I finally got a word in and asked her the name of the dog. She told me her name was Maggie. I still remember how excited I was to tell her, "I have Maggie. She's my foster dog." All I heard on the other end of the line were screams and happy tears. I told her the dog was hers any time she wanted to pick her up.

I had previously told Gloria about Bobbie and my hopes to adopt Maggie to her. Gloria was as ecstatic as I was over this match made in heaven. Bobbie was overwhelmed with joy on the day she took Maggie home. Maggie was fine with Bobbie's two cats and quickly relaxed with her new *furrever* family. She went for walks several times a day, ate a healthy diet, took her meds, and eventually the weight came off. Regular grooming made her coat shine and she knew she was a beautiful dog. I got to see Maggie often and could tell how happy she was with Bobbie in her new life. It was the perfect match!

After a few years, Gloria learned of another Sheltie at the shelter and immediately took the dog home with her. One call to Bobbie, and Emmie found her *furrever* home too. The two precious Shelties quickly became best friends and lived their final years with their wonderful person. Sadly, both passed away within three months of each other from old-age related ailments. Bobbie misses both girls, but true to form, she has given a third homeless Sheltie, Kate, a chance at a great life and loving home. 🐾🐾

When I first moved to Great Falls, I only had one cat and wanted a second one, so I went to the shelter to adopt the purrfect kitty. While I love kittens, I figured it was harder to find homes for adult cats, so I told myself not to even look at the babies. Sure! I sat in the cat room and decided I would let the kitties decide amongst themselves who would go home with me. Merlin, a handsome young adult tabby and white kitty, jumped onto my lap immediately and said, "Let's blow this pop stand."

As I walked to the front desk to fill out the adoption paperwork one of the workers pointed out a tiny dilute calico playing on a cat tree all the while telling me that the kitten really needed a "good" home. She mentioned something about the kitten having a club foot, but the kitty looked fine to me. Anyway, I wanted an adult cat and cuteness and special needs wasn't going to stop me from adopting Merlin. He was a love and was anxious to leave with me for his furrever home.

So, I did what anyone else would have done under the circumstances, I adopted both cats. Three cats in my home didn't seem to qualify me as a "Crazy Cat Lady". Not yet at least! The kitten was VERY cute, and she needed someone who would care for her with her limitations. That shelter worker had pegged me, correctly, as a sucker. So, I left that day with two kitties and never regretted this decision for a minute. Unbeknownst to me, this was just a prelude to my future vocation in animal rescue.

Merlin lived with me until his passing a few years ago at the golden age of eighteen. Callie, who I wrote about earlier, lived to about ten and passed of kidney failure. Both cats were loved and are missed.

— Chapter 30 —
Goodbye Dear Friend

Before I say goodbye to an animal, I always thank him or her for coming into my life. And to honor the pet's memory I will eventually take another homeless dog or cat into my home and my heart in memory of the one who has passed.

One of the hardest parts of rescue is losing an animal. Even if we have had them for only a short time, we still feel the loss and grieve. This is especially painful for us if the animal was sick, mistreated, or neglected. Our hope is to get our foster animals into *furrever* homes where they can be spoiled and live a long life with their new people. And if they end up living out their lives in our homes, we want them to have many happy years. It breaks our heart when that time is cut short.

Sometimes when I lose an animal people say, "It's easier for you since you have so many." I know they are not being heartless, and, in a way, there is some truth to that statement. When I say goodbye to a cherished animal, I go home and have others with which to share my sadness. I can bury my face in a furry body and cry tears into their coat. I know that if the pet I lost was a friend to another, that animal grieves too. It's painful to watch a dog or cat search for a lost friend not understanding why they are gone. We share the pain of their loss and are grateful for the time we had the animal in our lives. If you only have one animal, and you say goodbye, going home to an empty house without a wagging tail or purring kitty to greet you can be awful. I can't imagine that kind of emptiness.

Unfortunately, those of us who work in rescue face those losses too often. Since we have many, we lose many. In addition, the ones we keep in our homes are the unadoptable animals: those who are too sick, old, or emotionally damaged to adopt to a family. Many have had to suffer bad nutrition, abuse, and neglect, so their life spans are not as long as they should be. This finds us saying goodbye on a regular basis. Our hearts break hard and often.

A good friend of mine in rescue devotes most of her time to helping stray and injured cats and has often lost two or three kitties in one week. Since I have known her, I don't think she has gone one month without saying goodbye to a precious cat or kitten. She has voiced to me often that it is just too much pain to bear, but still she takes in the ones who wouldn't make it otherwise. For her, the losses continue, as does the pain. Each one she helps is special and despite the heartbreak, I know she will never quit.

When anyone who works in rescue takes an animal into their home, they also take them into their heart. I am always very excited to be able to make a difference in "just one more life." Each life is very precious to us; we feel honored with this trust. Those of us who have the same passion for helping animals know people in rescue who have lost foster animals mainly due to illness or injury and withdraw from doing this important work. Their hearts hurt. Sadly, we can all relate to the terrible pain of these losses. Some ask how we can allow ourselves to be attached so quickly and then mourn as though the animal was with us for years instead of just a few weeks. I don't know the answer but maybe it's what drew us into rescue in the first place. Our passion to help animals in need results in us feeling drawn to do all we can for the unfortunate ones. I know it takes me no time at all to feel love for a new animal who needs my help. Usually it happens the instant I set eyes on them.

I think those of us with a yearning for helping animals in distress accept this pain as a part of our work, but we never really get used to it. I think if we ever do, then it's time to take up a other cause. It hurts and we cry and tell ourselves "No more! I can't keep doing this." But then, another sad face asking for help crosses our path and we take one more in knowing there may be no other choices for this creature. I try to tell other animal rescue friends as they grieve that they have most likely given the animal the only affection he or she has ever known. If even for a short time, that animal has felt love and safety. I tell myself that too, and it helps, sometimes.

We often don't get the time to be able to grieve the same as others with one or two pets. So many times, I have come home from the vet after having lost an animal and am mobbed by the other animals in my care. There is not time to cry for long when you have a houseful of hungry critters who need feeding or walking. We don't get the luxury of being sad for too long. Our tears must be set aside so that we can care for the other animals especially the needy ones. Maybe that's a blessing. I know having a houseful to care for helps me to heal from my many losses.

One dog who still breaks my heart is a Collie I took in and only had for four days. I got a call from a shelter in the state who had a Collie for adoption. After the large Collie rescue in Montana, I fell in love with the breed and agreed to take in Collies needing help. I picked up Dakota one cold, rainy October afternoon from a volunteer who happened to be driving through Great Falls. The Collie was painfully thin, with a terribly ragged coat, and looked depressed. The shelter manager told me he had stopped eating and needed a foster home where he could get some TLC while he healed. I gladly took him into my house and immediately fell in love with this gentle dog.

He was pitiful to look at, but I felt I could help him recover from his former neglect. I have hand-fed many dogs in the past, but he wasn't interested in anything I offered him. Dakota would only eat a few bites and then walk away. His gait was also very wobbly, and he seemed to be extremely weak. So, I made an appointment with my vet to have him checked out the following Monday.

Despite his awful condition, he was affectionate and responded to love. He would wag his tail when I called him and liked to follow me around the yard. Dakota had a sweet temperament typical of the Collie breed. He seemed to like it when I gave him a warm bath and brushed out his rough-looking coat. By Monday, he had eaten very little and I was anxious to drop him off at the clinic. My heart sank when the vet finally called to tell me the awful news about Dakota; he had distemper, and the disease had caused irreparable brain damage, which was the reason he was unable to eat. The vet said he probably wanted food, but his badly damaged brain couldn't tell him how to eat and it would only get worse. By that time, his walking had deteriorated to that of a very drunk person due to the ravaging effects of the distemper virus. The vet told me that this was not curable, and the kindest thing would be to put him down. It didn't seem fair that this precious dog who had likely lived a tough life would never be able to live in a loving family. I held poor Dakota and told him how special he was while he crossed over the Rainbow Bridge and took my heart with him. How does this happen after knowing him for only four days? Even though I knew it wasn't true, I felt like I let Dakota down. It was such a helpless feeling to be unable to help this wonderful dog.

What made the loss of Dakota especially hard on me was that I had just lost one of my cherished dogs about a week before from cancer. While being treated for another ailment, the vet discovered that Bugg Z, one of my precious "coyote puppies," had cancer. The cancer had quickly progressed to his lungs. I rushed him to the vet one afternoon and the next day said goodbye to my old and loyal friend. Two losses in such a short amount of time made me question if I wanted to continue opening myself up to this kind of pain.

The loss of foster animals had happened to me years before with a mother cat and her seven kittens. I took in this precious little family and loved mom and her babies for about two weeks. Sophie was a great mother until one day I noticed she wouldn't let her babies nurse. Mom wasn't looking good so off she went to the vet. About the same time, all of her kittens started to look and act sick. A test told us mom and babies had distemper and were all failing fast. Again, the kindest action was to humanely put them down. I didn't know how to say goodbye to these eight little creatures who had stolen my heart.

Dakota, Sophie, and the babies ashes are all on a shelf with ashes from Bugg Z and my other beloved animals. Even though these were foster animals, they were still as loved as the animals I have adopted into my home. There really is no difference between any of them. They were all put in my path for a reason. I loved them for however long they shared their lives with me.

I have lost many over the years and while it is very hard to say goodbye to either a foster animal or my own pet, I know that the sad stories will never outweigh the wonderful outcomes in rescue. The pain we feel at their loss is the price we pay for the endless love we get from these precious creatures. I will never get used to the pain but if that's the price I have to pay, then I will continue to do what I love most. I know my other animal rescue friends feel the same since they continue to help even when it is a hardship. I think we are the lucky ones; we get to see miracles every time we see a hurt animal healed. That magic is what keeps us doing the work of animal rescue even through the terrible pain of saying goodbye. The look of gratitude in their eyes along with their wags and purrs give us the strength to continue to take on animals who need a safe haven. 🐾🐾

*D*uncan was one of the friendliest cats I have ever lived with. I opened my front door one cold January night and he nonchalantly walked into my house as if he lived here. I had never seen him before, yet he acted as if this was his home. I kept him for the night, not wanting to put him back out in the cold, but I did let him out the next morning. I figured he would find his way back to his own home. He didn't!

That first night he strolled into my bedroom and jumped on the bed while my dogs just looked at him funny. I looked at him funny too, thinking he was insane to do this with dogs he didn't know. He wasn't unsettled in the least. Duncan acted like he was happy to be home after a long trip.

I brought him to the Pet Paw-see vet for vaccines and neutering along with a health check. Turns out, he was previously neutered. Unfortunately, the small rural community where I live is often a dumping ground for unwanted cats and kittens. My guess is that Duncan was discarded near my home and saw the flashing neon sign over my front door welcoming cats from far and wide to stop in for a meal and a soft bed. (I don't really have neon sign at my front door but sometimes I envision an invisible message board at my driveway beckoning stray animals to my safe haven.)

This beautiful black kitty strolled nonchalantly into my house and my heart. Now eleven years later Duncan still thinks he lives here with me and I haven't told him any different!

— Chapter 31 —
Chili Dawg

I *took in a dog that I really didn't want and ended up with a friend for life.*

Over the years, I have taken in numerous fearful dogs. Once they get into my home with good food, kind words, and a comfy bed, they quickly warm up to me. Then there are the ones who are terrified that another human is going to hurt them or treat them badly again. They have never known a person who wasn't out to get them. Those are the challenging dogs. They only know fear and pain from abusive people.

I experienced one especially damaged dog several years ago. He and his two siblings were seen being dumped out of a vehicle as young puppies. The person drove off quickly but was "thoughtful" enough to toss a package of hot dogs out for the puppies. One poor puppy was immediately run over as the "owners" tried to make a quick getaway. The puppy was taken to a vet but was too badly injured and had to be put down. The other two puppies ran off and hid in a culvert where they apparently lived for weeks. Kind people tried to lure them out with food, but they had no trust for humans. I am thankful the local people didn't give up trying to help them and eventually got both puppies out of the culvert and into a foster home.

The story told to me was that the female puppy quickly adjusted and was friendly, but the male was too wary to allow anyone to go near him. It breaks my heart to think of how he learned at such a young age to fear people so completely. While in his foster home, the male puppy ran off and after several weeks was presumed to have died. This was in a very remote area of Montana, with a high likelihood of him becoming lunch for coyotes or other hungry animals. Luckily, he was found and brought back to live in his foster home. Shortly after his adventure, I got a call to foster him. The rescue gal assured me that he was a very nice and adoptable dog, just a little shy and scared. I didn't want another dog, since I had just taken in a young sick puppy from about the same remote area of Montana. However, I agreed to foster him, not knowing how messed up he really was and how much he feared people. I picked up what looked like about a four-month-old Shepherd mix, brought him to my home, and named him Chili Dawg.

Chili was a skinny, motley-looking dog with terror written all over his face. And he howled constantly out of pure panic. I quickly realized he was feral, not at all adoptable, and I was clueless on how to help him. If he was brought to a shelter he would have been immediately put down, since most shelter employees don't have the time or knowledge to tame a feral dog. By this time, I was angry that I had been misled and was now saddled with an unpredictable and somewhat dangerous dog. While he was small, about 25 pounds, he could still do serious damage to me and my other pets if he became upset. Despite this, I didn't want to give up on this pitiful puppy, so I tried to befriend him and at least fatten him up. Chili went crazy when I brought him inside and shrieked for hours. He was a very wild animal suddenly forced into a foreign environment, and he was terrified! I knew at his former foster home he had lived in a barn. When he came to live with me, he acted as if he had never been in a house.

Chili wouldn't let me near him no matter how gentle I was with him. He hid and cowered when I was around and was very head shy. He would take a cookie from my hand with his neck extended. But he was always ready to run at the first sign that I wanted to grab him. He learned to sit by watching the other dogs and would do it when asked. However, I still could never touch him. I found that if I sat down, he would come near but never close enough to allow me to handle him. He liked to sleep on my bed with my other dogs. Some nights I would feel him sniffing me as I slept. I would pretend to be asleep as he snuffled over my hair and face, but if I made any move, he would jump away. Poor Chili was curious but the mistreatment he suffered as a puppy wouldn't let him trust me.

After weeks of unsuccessfully trying to gain his confidence, I realized that he would have to decide to trust me and that nothing I did would make it happen more quickly. I knew I couldn't force him, so I left him alone. I never tried to corner him or touch him, and I spoke to him often. I made sure he got his food and had a safe place to sleep but never tried to handle him. I could get him to go outside and then herd him inside with the rest of the pack but didn't try to collar or leash him. Chili learned the routine and adjusted to it well as long as I didn't try to "get" him. I figured someone had beaten and kicked him as a young puppy, so he had never bonded with humans.

He didn't fight with my pack but never really fit in. He didn't know how to play; survival and food were all he cared about. I equated him to the poor skinny kid on the playground who has no social skills, never gets picked to play ball, and is bullied continuously. That was Chili! The other dogs left him completely alone; they seemed to sense that he wasn't totally right and wanted nothing to do with him.

After about one year living in my home, he would slowly approach me when I talked to him but never close enough to let me touch him. One part of him appeared to want the attention, but his fearful side wouldn't let him get too close. This went on into the second year. He would come to just within touching range of me and then back off. That continued until one day he decided I was ok.

The breakthrough came when he saw me grooming the other dogs in the back yard. One evening as I was brushing the coat of my Husky, Chili came around cautiously and allowed me to brush his back. I would gently brush a few strokes and then leave him alone. He must have liked it because he started coming over to me asking for more, but if I tried to hold him, he ran from me. After a few weeks, he relaxed, and I could brush him all over. He even pushed at my hand if I was brushing another dog. Chili was trying to tell me he wanted the attention. That was the turning point in our friendship. I don't know what changed in his mind; maybe he saw that the Huskies seemed to enjoy the brushing and he felt left out. After that day, he gave me his total trust and now at almost nine years old he is one of my best doggie buddies. Chili loves walking and running and comes immediately when I call him. His complete about-face was one of the most amazing experiences I have ever had with a dog. Almost overnight, actually, it took two years, he went from being a fearful feral dog that I couldn't touch to a dog who couldn't get enough belly rubs.

He now crowds out the other dogs for my time and for hugs. He had learned to walk very nicely on a leash and cuddles with me at night. Chili Dawg is a great example of how a traumatized dog can turn around with love and patience. I did very little to help him come around. All I did was give him a safe place to heal. He did all the hard work as he overcame his fears of me. (Despite feeling safe with me, he is still terrified of other people so when someone comes to the house, I typically leave him in his kennel.)

Occasionally Chili will play with my alpha female Malamute, Meka, although he seems unsure of how to act around her. He appears to need reassurance that his actions are okay. Chili is often surprised when one of the other dogs corrects him for his clumsy behavior. The best way to describe Chili's insecurities are similar to a person who doesn't feel comfortable in his own skin. Buddy, my Cocker Spaniel, picks up on Chili's apprehension and can be a little jerk. He seems to enjoy targeting poor Chili. Buddy can be pushy and very obnoxious, but to Chili's credit, he puts up with it and totally ignores the smaller dog. Chili is twice the Cocker's size and could easily clean Buddy's clock, but he rarely even acknowledges Buddy and walks away when Buddy is looking for a fight.

Chili will always be the poor self-conscious kid on the playground that wants to hang out with the cool kids. But the cool kids shun him for his complete lack of people skills or, in the case of canines, "doggie etiquette." My guess is that Chili, taken from his mother at a very early age, never learned "dog speak." ("Dog speak" is what I call the amazing ability of dogs to communicate with each other using body language. Mother dogs teach proper etiquette to their puppies so when they are weaned, they will be able to navigate their world.) All Chili cared about in his first weeks and months was surviving. He doesn't seem to understand canine body language. I think if he lived in the wild, he would have been an outcast, run out of the pack, and forced to live away from his dog family or even killed.

Despite Chili's lack of dog sense, I love him and am glad to have him in my life. Chili has taught me so much about dogs and their ability to forgive. He has bonded with me and is now a beautiful, happy member of my family who has given me the courage to take on another difficult dog case. 🐾🐾

An orange tabby cat named Miss Peaches was being carried into our shelter at the same time I was there to pick up a different cat found injured at the side of a road. Once again, Gloria intercepted and asked me to take Peaches; she said that she would find a place for the other kitty. The Pet Paw-see wasn't a non-profit rescue group yet, we didn't even have a name. We were just a bunch of people trying to help as many animals as possible and would often take animals from the shelter to find them homes.

I gladly took home this beautiful girl and introduced her to some tiny babies I was fostering. Peached ended up being a surrogate mom to my litter of three orange tabby kittens, Cheerios, Marmalade, and Sport, who we nicknamed the Orange Gang. Peaches protected and cared for those babies as though they were hers.

In the early days of our organization, Petco would let us bring animals into their store every other weekend for adoptions. This was our only avenue to place cats and dogs. Our rescue group was so new that we didn't have a website or many resources to find good homes. And the public didn't know who we were.

While we were able to find homes for the kittens, Peaches never left my house. That was ok because now at the mature age of about thirteen she is happy to be a permanent foster.

— Chapter 32 —
Phill the Pill

Sometimes even the seemingly unadoptable ones finally find their **furrever** homes!

Phill came into the Pet Paw-see's foster program about seven years ago. I forgot the circumstances of how he found his way into the Pet Paw-see, but I remember that he was a stray. Phill was a nice, friendly, youngish tuxedo kitty who appeared at first to be easy to adopt. He got along well with everyone at our weekly adoption events and the volunteers felt it wouldn't take long to find him a great home.

Phill was boarding at one of the vet clinics. Due to the lack of foster homes, the Pet Paw-see has to board many of our animals at local pet facilities and vet clinics until adopted. We pick them up each Saturday for the three hours we are at Petco or Pet Smart and then back they go. It's not ideal, but if we weren't able to board these animals, we would have to turn them away. Both Petco and Pet Smart have kitty habitats where we also keep about eight cats at each location. This gives the stores a "draw." The cats get a lot of exposure, and most cats quickly find their *furrever* homes. Both stores have play areas where the public can watch the cats and kittens interact and play with each other on the various cat trees. Our relationship with each of these businesses works great since the adopters usually buy out the store before leaving for home with their new pet. It's always fun to see a shopping cart piled high with cat trees, toys, food, and litter before the new mom or dad finalizes the adoption. It has been a win-win partnership for the two stores and for the Pet Paw-see rescue group.

Phill was one of our boarded cats and over time, he started to show signs of stress. He got snarly and hissed at the volunteers and customers instead of purring and acting friendly. And, he would often throw up his food. When a cat starts acting like that, we take him or her to the vet for a health check to see if they are sick or in pain. He was brought to the vet several times and the vet couldn't find anything physically wrong with him, even after a few rounds of bloodwork and x-rays. We had hoped the habitat at Petco would be more favorable to Phill than being boarded at a clinic, so he was moved into his own private suite. This did nothing to improve his behavior. He continued to get worse and the vet decided it was likely due to anxiety. We took him out of the Petco habitat and boarded him back at the vet clinic, hoping they would figure out what was going on with him. Phill got special food for his sensitive stomach but he still acted as though there was something terribly wrong. Finally, we stopped bringing him to our weekly adoption events hoping that time away would help him to relax. (At this time, our organization was in our infant stages and we were still learning a lot about cat behavioral issues.)

It got to a point where we thought we would lose him, so as a last resort, I took Phill to my home in the hopes that he would chill out and heal from whatever was stressing him out. I have a bedroom for foster cats and at that time, it was empty. He moved in and seemed to adjust well. (I never let my foster cats interact with my dogs or my resident kitties. I want them to have a quiet (?) space for themselves and not have to compete with the other animals or feel threatened by them.)

Phill did great in my home. He had his own sunny window, his cat bed, and cat tree as well as toys. He stopped vomiting and even gained a little weight. He finally looked like he was content so after fostering him for several months, I took him back to Petco for our Saturday events. He was even worse this time around. After about half an hour at Petco, Phill turned into a hissing, spitting kitty who no one wanted to pet never mind adopt. Phill was a pill! A volunteer had to stay in front of his cage at all times during the adoptions to make sure he didn't bite anyone, especially little kids who liked to stick their hands inside the cages to pet the cats. He was telling us that he hated being there and wanted me to take him home. It was evident that we couldn't subject Phill to this kind of stress anymore and we hoped that his handsome photo on our website would be enough to generate some interest for someone to take a chance and want to adopt him.

Poor misunderstood Phill continued to live with me and do well once we realized that his ailments were all stress related. I knew he was a nice boy who didn't put his best paw forward when meeting people. After a while, I resigned myself to the fact that Phill would likely live with me for the rest of his life. That was okay but if my house was where he was going to end up, I wanted him to mingle with the rest of my family. By this time, I had weaned him off the special diet to allow him to live with the general population and eat their food. I put a baby gate in front of his room, which allowed him to come out when he felt like socializing and go back in if he felt uneasy about the dogs. I was happy when I would find him hanging out with the other cats. He seemed to have no problems and no more stress issues. Finally, Phill appeared to be content. He rarely showed any aggression and never fought with the others. Phill even tolerated the dogs. Once he found my enclosed outdoor catio he was in kitty heaven. The catio has cat trees, sleeping baskets, and a doghouse for the kitties. I also plant a large tub with cat grass for them to enjoy and there are plenty of dead tree branches for scratching. I love my catio because the cats can watch the birds and smell the fresh air while being safe from predators and cars. Phill was finally comfortable, and I loved having him as part of my animal family.

Like most cats and dogs, Phill had a few annoying habits, one of them was hanging out on my kitchen range. I hated it and tried to keep him off (while I was home) but knew that once I left the house, he would be back up there. That was until one day when I came home from work and opened my front door to a house that felt unbearably warm with a smoky smell permeating the kitchen. It was winter so the windows were closed, and the house smelled like something was smoldering. With horror I realized that one of the burners on my stove was glowing red and the area around the burner was scorched. I am so grateful that I didn't have any dish cloths nearby or they would have caught on fire. I don't know how long the burner had been turned on, but it looked as though it may have been on for most of the day. I was sick to my stomach realizing this could have caused a house fire, killing all of my precious animals. I know, you ask, why should I blame this on Phill and not on another kitty? Phill would rub up against the knobs and I never imagined that his action could result in a catastrophe. From that point on I took extra precautions; the breaker to the stove was always turned off unless I wanted to cook something. It was a pain but a small price to pay when I think of what could have happened that day. I couldn't risk losing my pets and my house. I also began to keep a small spray bottle of water nearby and sprayed any cat who came close to the stove. Eventually all of my cats including "Phill the Pill" learned to keep off. A few wet faces were a great deterrent for my feline friends.

After that adventure, Phill continued to live the good life with me. His stress level was down, and he was really an easy, amiable cat. My volunteer friends and I figured that Phill had found his *furrever* home with me, but I still didn't want to take him off the Pet Paw-see website. I hoped that one day he would find his own family. That day finally happened when after two years of fostering Phill, a couple came into Petco inquiring about him. One of our fabulous volunteers, Andrew, was working in our cat habitat and told them all about Phill the Pill. They laughed and said despite his bad press, they still wanted to meet and possibly adopt him. This couple loved tuxedo cats and had another one at home named Radar. If Radar approved of a companion, they would adopt Phill.

We had our doubts, but this was a great potential home and we didn't want to pass on it. After filling out an application, I brought Phill over to their house to meet Radar. The meeting went ok and the couple agreed to try him out, so we did a Pawsibility. Occasionally, we will let people try out a difficult cat prior to an adoption. It gives people the chance to see if the cat will work for them. They are under no pressure to keep the cat and can return the animal to us at any time. Phill had a rough start during his trial run but with time and patience, he settled into his new home. Phill was with them for about a month during his Pawsibility and was ultimately adopted by Jim and Leslie. They have a beautiful home with lots of space to explore as well as a sun porch catio. I was thrilled that Phill would still be able to enjoy the outside while remaining safe.

Phill has been with his people for over three years now. When we see Jim or Leslie, they tell us how well he is doing. On his two-year adoption anniversary, they sent me a great text and photo of my old boy. I couldn't be happier for my former foster kitty. After almost losing Phill from anxiety-related ailments, he was finally in a home with two people who spoil him. This is one of the reasons we don't ever want to give up on an animal. Phill was worth the trouble. Our volunteers feel there is a home for every animal. It may just take a few years to find it! 🐱🐱

When I first moved to this part of Montana, I wanted to become more involved with helping homeless animals, so I joined the shelter fundraising group called Animal Crackers. Having a heart for the hard-to-place cats, I told the shelter manager that I would be happy to take in special-needs kitties.

One day the shelter manager called me to ask if I would be able to foster little Katie Kat. She had come into the shelter as a very tiny kitten with a huge abscess on her back, likely from a cat bite. Katie's owners had not provided her with any care and the open wound covered a good third of her little body. I told the manager that I wouldn't foster her, I would adopt her.

Katie Kat was a quiet amiable kitty that was happy to be a house cat. She probably came from the outside and wanted nothing more to do with the great outdoors. I told people that I could leave my front door open knowing she would never venture outside. Katie Kat was happiest on the couch or on the windowsill looking out at the world.

I lost Katie Kat from age-related illness at fifteen. Throughout her years with me, she was sweet, gentle, and thankful for the chance to live in a loving home. I am thankful I had her company for so long.

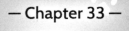

— Chapter 33 —
Kitty Warriors

Volunteers are the heart and soul of rescue!

Most animal rescue groups consist of a core group of dedicated people who have a passion for helping animals in need. Both the Pet Paw-see and Humane Society of Cascade County (HSCC) have many wonderful volunteers who are invaluable and tireless in helping animals. The work is endless and often thankless. Some of the especially hard-working people are those who are caretakers for feral cat colonies.

Since we live in an agricultural community, many cats are dumped out in the country and, if they are lucky, they end up living in colonies where a kind person tries to look after them. Some of the volunteers in both rescue groups spend countless hours feeding, caring for, and trapping these cats for Trap, Neuter and Release (TNR). Trapping takes a lot of time and effort, but we are lucky to have many people who know this is the only way to curb the cat overpopulation problem we have in our area. Many of the people who do this (I would love to mention their names but don't want to leave anyone out) are outside setting and checking traps in all kinds of weather and at all times of the day and night.

About a year ago, we learned of a local bar that had many cats living under the bar's deck. The business owner fed the cats but did not have them altered, so the litters of kittens were unending. Unfortunately, the only time to set traps at this location was after 2:00 a.m. when the bar's customers were gone. A couple of gals in the Pet Paw-see made it their mission to TNR the kitties after the bar closed down for the night. That's a lot to ask of anyone but these gals were willing to do it because they knew the animals needed help. Setting a trap in the wee hours of the morning, then waiting in your vehicle for an hour or more is no fun and takes dedication, to say the least. Happily, their efforts have paid off and they have been able to prevent more unwanted litters from being born. We took many of the kittens into our foster program and tamed them down for adoption. After the adults were altered, they were released back to their colony.

A few of our volunteers also have large colonies of cats for whom they provide food and water to every day of the year, even during our coldest months. They make sure there are adequate cat shelters with straw for the kitties and keep an eye on any animals who may need medical help. These caretakers come to know and love their community cats and grieve for the ones they lose to predation, illness, or vehicles. Most of these caregivers purchase food and supplies for the cats using their own money. Because of their hard work, many of these colonies are healthy and more importantly, not reproducing.

A number of our volunteers also help colonies where local residents are feeding the cats but don't have the money to alter them. These resident kitty caretakers are very appreciative of our help and very protective of their community cats. They alert us if they notice new cats, so that we can alter them. Some of these locations have fifty or more cats, which would be daunting for anyone to perform TNR without very substantial resources.

Because of our consistent efforts, there are several locations in our community where the colonies are stable. These cats are in good condition and not reproducing due to the hard work of a handful of

Kitty Warriors. We are lucky to have been able to obtain grants and donations for this work but without our committed and dedicated volunteers, these successes wouldn't have been possible. These are the unknown and unsung heroes of rescue. They don't do it for thanks from the public. These volunteers get their thanks knowing just one more cat is comfortable, safe, not reproducing, and has food in his belly. 🐱🐱

Kayla and her two sisters Emmie and Tessa were feral kittens when one of the Pet Paw-see volunteers found them and did her best to tame them. Being a bit older, they were a handful, but managed to become domesticated enough to live in a foster home. They would tolerate people but were still too wild to adopt to the public. At least in a foster home they would be loved and safe.

I had had some luck with older feral kittens over the years and tried with these girls. Over time, they all adjusted to me and even liked being petted. But they always had a "touch of wild" in them and never totally settled into domesticity.

Tessa, Emmie, and Kayla were almost identical tabbies. The only way I could tell them apart was a long stripe down the noses of two of the girls. Tessa had the darkest stripe, Kayla had a fainter stripe, and Emmie had no stripe.

Tessa crossed the Bridge years ago, but Emmie and Kayla are happy little house kitties with no interest in ever living outside and fending for themselves. They have grown accustomed to three square meals a day as well as lots of soft kitty beds.

— Chapter 34 —

Spay, Spay, Spay!

O ur spay/neuter program started in 2006 with four people. It has grown significantly and has seen wonderful results, altering over ten thousand animals to date!

The volunteers from two of the rescue groups in our county, Pet Paw-see and Humane Society of Cascade County (HSCC), work very well together. Many of the same people are active in both groups. While both organizations are involved in rescue as well as spay/neuter, the Pet Paw-see is primarily a rescue group and the HSCC is primarily a spay/neuter group.

The HSCC has made it their mission to organize a spay/neuter program for low-income residents in our county. The HSCC partners with a Montana spay/neuter group called Spay Montana, which travels around the state from March through October each year altering cats and dogs. Spay Montana supplies the vets and vet techs, surgical equipment, and medications. The host group provides the building and all other supplies for the clinic.

The program in our county started in 2006 with a five-day clinic. During that clinic, we spayed and neutered 1,236 animals. Since that first undertaking, we have had two clinics each year. During each of the two-day clinics we alter about 300 to 350 animals over the course of a weekend, which has resulted in thousands of dogs and cats being spayed or neutered in the past twelve plus years.

Despite these clinics, the cat population in our county seems to be an ongoing problem. Since our clinics were only held twice a year, it still appears as though too many cats missed this opportunity and continue to breed. Regardless of our efforts, we haven't been able to get a handle on the cat overpopulation problem. In 2015, the HSCC started a monthly cat clinic, which alters about thirty cats at a time. Our volunteers contact cat owners on Facebook and other social media sites who have unaltered cats or litters to give away. For those who bring their cats in for the service, the momma and babies are altered before they are re-homed to breed the next generation of unwanted animals. Many people who care for colonies of community cats also bring their animals in for the surgeries. When the small clinics are full, our volunteers arrange for any remaining cats to be brought to one of several vets who give us a reduced rate for the surgeries. Our aim is to make it very difficult for people NOT to alter their pets.

Most of the volunteers in the Pet Paw-see rescue group partner with the HSCC spay/neuter group to run both the large and small clinics. The small clinics are relatively easy. We have one vet, one vet tech, and a handful of volunteers. By contrast, it takes an amazing amount of people and months of preparation to organize the large clinics, although Pam and Judy, the two gals who coordinate these events, have the routine down to a science. They request donations, schedule the animals for surgery, and find enough volunteers to help at the clinics, among about a thousand other tasks they do to make them successful.

Between the two rescue groups, we have almost a hundred humane traps. These are loaned to people who have numerous community cats to trap. Prior to the clinics, they are shown how to feed the cats near the traps so that when the time comes, the cats won't have any qualms about going into them. Weeks before these clinics, some of the volunteers spend countless hours driving traps around the county to various locations and working with the cat guardians so the maximum number of cats will be trapped for our spay/neuter clinics.

The day before our big clinics requires a small army of human volunteers and a horse trailer to transport all the supplies to the site, unload, and set up. The surgeries take place in a large building at the county fairgrounds. We have stations for check-in and check-out, waiting areas, surgical prep, autoclave, recovery, and the surgery itself. The owners and their families are able to watch the surgery and talk to the vet during the procedure if they'd like. The vets are happy to talk about spay/neuter to the pet owners. For too many of the pet owners, this is the first time they have heard about the immense problem of pet overpopulation. (Not only do the owners get their animal altered, they also come away educated on the importance of not allowing their animals to breed.) After each surgery, the owner is encouraged to stay with their pet during recovery. The process runs like a huge MASH unit with dogs on one side of the building and cats on the other.

It is a great learning experience for the public. The sight of so many animals being altered is often an eye-opener for the pet owners who attend. Many of people who bring their animals into one of our clinics finally clue in to how important it is to spay and neuter their dogs and cats. Our hope is that they convey the message to others who in the past have thought, "It's only one litter and my female dog or cat should experience this. Anyway, it makes for a better animal . . ." We have all heard that line and remarkably, some pet-owners still believe it! NO, it is not a necessary "rite of passage" for our companion animals. Some people use the excuse they want their children to experience the "miracle of birth." A gal in our group tells them to Google a U-Tube video where they can watch a birth in living color. There is no need to bring animals into a world where they have no chance for a good life.

Just because our clinic is over, doesn't mean our work is done. If an animal has any surgery-related issues during the week or two following the clinic, we also provide aftercare at a local vet hospital. Sometimes an animal will rip out a stitch or have some problem days after the clinic vets are gone. The HSCC wants to make sure the cat or dog gets the appropriate help.

A large part of ensuring our clinics are a success is making sure the volunteers, vets, and techs are well fed. We are lucky to have access to a separate building at the fairgrounds with a commercial kitchen and dining area for our meals. It is wonderful to have a quiet place to sit down, relax, and eat a meal before going back to the surgery building. A group of hard-working ladies spend hours cooking breakfast, lunch, and dinner as well as fixing snacks for all of us over our two-day events.

Judy, one of the clinic organizers, starts baking and freezing goodies about two to three months ahead of each clinic to make sure we never run out of pastries, cookies, and coffee cakes. Several of the vets and volunteers put in their requests ahead of time for their favorite treats. (My favorite is her Apple Danish.) Hungry volunteers are not happy volunteers and we need to do all we can to make sure these people come back to help us year after year. Good food helps! Our clinics have become famous for how well we take care of everyone who attends.

Luckily, we have many local business owners who understand the need for this work and donate to our cause. We get all of our dirty bedding washed and dried for free from a laundry service. This typically comes to about 1,200 pounds of blankets, towels, and sheets for a two-day clinic. Additionally, several restaurants donate food for our meals. A few of the local hotels give free rooms for the numerous vets and vet techs who travel to Great Falls from all around Montana. A gas distributer in town donates all of the oxygen canisters for the anesthesia machines. An appliance store drops off and picks up a refrigerator for the weekend so that we can stock it with bottles of water for the volunteers. This is a lifesaver especially in the summer months. (Nothing tastes as good as an icy cold drink of water when you are running like mad and sweating bullets!) Without our generous donors, we would have to dig deeper into the HSCC's reserves to pay for these services. Every dollar we don't have to spend on items like hotel rooms and food, will alter one more cat or dog. This amounts to countless lives saved over the years we have been operating our clinics.

We are also very lucky to have a pre-release detention center in our city. The men and women in the pre-release center, known as "booters," have gotten into trouble with the law and are learning how to transition back into society to live productive lives. They are required to perform a certain number of hours of community service per week prior to their release. For years, we have utilized men and women from the pre-release center to assist us with our clinics. The word about how well we treat everyone at our spay/neuter clinics has gotten out and the booters at the detention center jump at the chance to help us.

At first, I was very reluctant to work with what are often times people who have spent time in prison for a variety of terrible offences. However, after being around them and seeing how happy they are to help with the animals, I now enjoy and look forward to working side-by-side with these people. These primarily young men are happy to assist us with the hard physical work and are appreciative of how we treat them like normal people, if only for a few days. We don't judge them, and we never ask what they have done, but many of them don't hesitate to tell us about their lives and their crimes. Their sad stories of neglect and abuse are often similar to those of the animals we rescue. Despite that, most of them are pretty upbeat and positive for their futures and love being out of the detention center for a while. Many of the booters love to talk to us about pets they had as kids and how they want to get a cat or dog when they get their act together.

Working with animals often brings out the best in people and it's obvious when watching the happy faces of the booters. It's funny to watch a big tough guy with tattoos all over his body sit on the ground with a scared dog to comfort or play with him. It's gratifying to know that as well as helping animals, maybe we have played a small part in helping someone get back on the right track. Animal rescue is all about giving homeless critters a second chance at a good life, so why not help a few humans do the same?

All of the clinic volunteers are grateful for the response and help from the community. Nevertheless, I think the best outcome of our clinics is that people who would have never considered spaying or neutering their pets now understand the vital need for this and have in turn, become champions for the cause. Many of these people give back by volunteering at our future clinics, or they will give blankets and other supplies that are in constant demand.

Our only source of income is from donations and from a popular spay-ghetti fundraiser dinner we put on each year. The HSCC asks for donations from the pet owners when we schedule them for surgery, but we tell them that even if they can't donate anything, we are still happy to alter their cat or dog. We never want anyone to be turned away because they don't have the money for the surgery.

I know that all of us in rescue understand the need for and encourage participation in spaying and neutering. I feel as though I am a walking, talking poster-girl for this work. I typically have a stack of business cards in my purse with the number to call for assistance. I hand them out to anyone who has a pet and needs help. I know the other people I work with feel the same and hand out cards like candy. We still have a long way to go but have seen improvements in the numbers of puppy litters and have even heard from our local animal shelter that the number of kitten litters seem to be fewer and fewer. Our hopes are that over time, we will see an end to the number of unwanted animals in our part of Montana. 🐾🐾

In the past, the local Petco would occasionally host a large adoption event for nearby shelters and rescues. These adoption weekends often brought in people from all over our part of the state and resulted in placing many dogs and cats. It was a lot of work but became very successful at placing animals in homes.

Taylor was another lost cause when she found her way to one of these large adoption events. This young Sheltie mix with one blue eye and one brown eye had been bounced from shelter to home to shelter way too many times. She had also been to several of these adoption events and never showed well. This little sweetie had the tendancy to be snippy at these large gatherings, likely because she was stressed from the noise, people, and all the activity. Not the best environment to show off our adoptables but we were trying hard to place animals and this is sometimes the only way.

When she had no takers after her second adoption weekend, Taylor went to live at a boarding kennel. The owners of the facility hoped to teach her some manners to make her more adoptable, but still she waited for her furrever home. After several months at the boarding facility, I took her home to live with me. She needed a home environment and I was very afraid that she would start to go downhill if kept in a kennel. Taylor has been a challenge but worth the work. She loves her daily runs and, while still a wild girl, is very sweet and has a heart to please her person.

— Chapter 35 —

Atlas

H *e was with us for too short a time.*

When Atlas came to me, he was one of the most pitiful dogs I
had ever seen. It was hard to look at him. A fellow Collie Rescue gal
from Oregon called me to say there was a stray Collie in a shelter in
southeast Montana, about 250 miles from my home. The shelter was
reaching out to Collie Rescue groups all around the Pacific Northwest
to help this poor boy. (A Collie Rescue group in Pennsylvania was even
trying to find someone near this Montana shelter to help the dog.)

The Collie was found running loose and ended up at the local
animal shelter where no one claimed him. The shelter employees
named him Atlas because of his size. He was about the tallest Collie
I had ever seen. While at the shelter, Atlas would only eat an occasional
hot dog and nothing else. It was obvious that he was just waiting to die.
After many phone calls, I arranged to meet a volunteer at the half-
way point between our two cities so that I could take the dog into
my home to help him. I was sickened when I first met him. Atlas
was nothing but a matted, tangled mass of hair on a skeleton of jutting
bones. But his wonderful personality showed through the sadness of
his awful appearance. I had brought some hot dogs for the three-hour
ride back to my home, but he wasn't interested in them. He curled up

in the front seat of my pickup and enjoyed our conversation wagging his tail the entire time. His deep brown eyes told me his sad story of neglect. I was in tears during the drive and determined to do everything possible to get him healthy again.

Knowing he had not eaten at the shelter, I wanted to have something tasty for him when I got him home. I had boiled a chicken and some veggies to make a sort of stew for him. I never knew a dog who would refuse chicken. Atlas took one sniff of the stew and turned his nose up. He wouldn't touch it, nor any of the dog food, cat food, or people food I put in front of him. He didn't appear to be in any pain; he just didn't want to eat. This panicked me. I knew from looking at him that he wouldn't be long for this earth if he didn't eat, but he showed no interest at all. Days after I took him in, he had eaten essentially nothing, and the vet didn't have much advice for getting him to eat. He just told me to keep trying. I was desperate enough to try to force-feed him. I would open his mouth, put a wonderful bit of food in, and hold his mouth closed, hoping he would swallow. He would patiently wait for me to remove my hand and then spit it out. Despite everything, his tail never stopped wagging. Atlas was a very agreeable, sweet dog with a goofy look on his face. It was impossible to get mad at him.

For about two weeks, I tried everything and anything to get him excited about food, but nothing seemed to work. Then he di covered peanut butter. I put a small dab on my finger and he actually licked it off and didn't spit it out. The relief I felt at finally getting something into his belly was overwhelming. I tried mixing peanut butter into his doggie kibble, but he wouldn't touch his bowl. Since I wasn't successful at getting him to eat from his bowl, I made small balls of peanut butter mixed with the kibble, opened his mouth, popped in a peanut butter ball, and held his mouth closed until he swallowed the food. This method worked; he was finally getting some of this sticky mess into him. If I could get him to eat a cup of this at a time, I was ecstatic. When he had finally had enough, he would spit the last mouthful out and I wouldn't push him anymore. I tried this pop and hold technique four to five times a day, anything to put some meat on his bones. He slowly gained a little weight and I felt that maybe he would actually make it.

Through all the hand feeding he never showed any impatience or anger towards me. Atlas was always friendly and gentle. After living with me for several weeks, I began the process of finding him a *furrever* home. Once he got a nice warm bath and brushing, he looked gorgeous! His dirty, dry coat was transformed into a shiny, soft mahogany. I knew someone would fall in love with him.

The Pet Paw-see rescue group has a weekly adoption event at the local Petco, and Atlas was a big hit with everyone who came into the store. When he was tired after a long day of meeting new friends, he just sprawled out on the floor of the store and took a nap. He loved the attention he got during these Saturday events and while everyone fell in love with this sociable Collie, no one wanted to adopt him.

Until...

We like to say that every animal has a special person who will eventually find him or her. After about a month of showing him to potential adopters, Atlas found his very own family. This lovely couple knew he had and would continue to have health issues, but they didn't care. One look at Atlas and they were in love and the feeling was mutual. He went to live with Gina and Clint and their rescued horses, chickens, geese, and kitties on their large property. They had had several Collies in the past, loved the breed, and wanted to give their love to this gentle Collie dog. Atlas was adopted and became the guardian of the chickens and geese but wasn't sure about the horses. He appeared to be fascinated yet afraid of them. Atlas loved the way they smelled and enjoyed watching them romping in their pasture. He would go out to the pasture with Clint every day when he fed the horses, which allowed Atlas to get to know then better. But I am not sure if they ever got to be best friends!

Gina and Clint worked magic with Atlas and renamed him Dudley. His new name fit his personality to a tee. He was a large, leggy, elegant Collie with a silly smile. Whenever I got the chance to see him, I could see how happy he was and how much he loved his new parents. They had him on a special diet and while he was still a picky eater, he gained weight and his coat glowed. I kept in close contact with them and got many great photos of him with his new friends.

Dudley was an older dog when found and adopted but I had hoped he could live with his family for a few good years. Sadly, that wasn't the case. He had lived in his new home for just over a year when Gina called me to say he was at the vet clinic, very sick, and failing fast. The vet told them there was nothing medically they could do to help Dudley, so his parents decided to let him go. Gina knew how special he was to me and asked if I wanted to say goodbye. I immediately left work and drove to the clinic. He was on oxygen and pain meds surrounded by the people who loved him most. The three of us held him and talked to him until he left us for his friends at the Rainbow Bridge.

It has been several years since Dudley passed and it still hurts to see his photos. Gina and Clint continue to mourn his loss but have opened their home and hearts to two more rescued Collies, Duke and Balloo. None of us had Dudley in our lives for very long but his memory will last forever! I know all of us are lucky to have met and loved this amazing soul. 🐾🐾

When I moved to Great Falls my Cocker Spaniel Cappi started having a very difficult time with my being away for most of the day while at work. He was showing signs of severe separation anxiety. Cappi would shake and pant when he knew I was leaving. I talked to my vet several times about the problem and he suggested I get a second dog. I didn't want to put Cappi on medication, so this sounded like a great idea. And besides, I really wanted another dog!

I called the shelter to ask if they had any Cockers or Cocker crosses. I love the breed and I wanted a dog who was about Cappi's size and temperament. They said there was one Cocker looking for a home, so I stopped by after work to meet her.

The little Cocker picked up as a stray, was happy but matted and needed a bath. I adopted this very nice girl and named her Sophie. I remember getting her to my home after her adoption and letting her loose in the back-yard. She ran full speed around the yard for quite a while as I watched and wondered what I had gotten myself into. Once she ran out of gas, she settled down and was a very nice dog. She had likely been cooped up in her kennel for a while and needed to stretch her legs.

Sophie was the perfect dog and was a great companion for Cappi. She was the best medicine for my sweet old boy, and I was so glad to see that he had stopped being anxious. Sophie gave me many wonderful years. She was a faithful friend to both Cappi and me and was mourned when she crossed the Bridge.

— Chapter 36 —
What's a CockaBeagaDor ?

I will always be grateful to my friend Gloria who took pity on this scared little dog. Harli enriched my life!

My friend and fellow animal-lover, Gloria, called me one day to say there was a very small, terrified Cocker Spaniel/Labrador cross at the shelter. She knew how much I loved Cockers and that I couldn't refuse to help. Gloria said that the dog was cowering in her kennel and shaking, too afraid to let anyone get near her. She was picked up as a stray. Their policy was that she had to be held seventy-two hours before she could be adopted. I told Gloria I would take her as a foster dog. I was leaving to visit my dad for a few days and planning to take her when I came back, if her owners had not yet claimed her.

That sounded like a good plan until Gloria called me the next day and said, "Forget it! That's the meanest dog I have ever seen." The kennel manager had taken almost forty-five minutes to drag the poor animal out of her kennel to the front room. She was biting, howling, and growling at anyone who came near her. No one had claimed her, so she was on the schedule to be euthanized after her stray time was over. That broke my heart. I told Gloria that Cockers can be snarky if scared and I doubted she was mean. The poor little dog was petrified. I begged her to talk with the shelter manager to allow me to take her home and give this dog a chance. Well Gloria did her magic and convinced the shelter manager to let me take her rather than put her down. She was transported to a local vet for her spay and shots and I was told to pick her up later that day. I raced to the vet clinic to get her before they closed and found a very docile, miniature yellow Lab with the head, ears and eyes of a Cocker Spaniel. She was just a puppy, less than one year and the look in her eyes told her story; she had been neglected and probably abused.

I put her into a wire crate with food, water, and a warm blanket to let her recover from her surgery and to hopefully relax in my house. She was the perfect little lady and I decided to name her "Harli." Gloria called me later that night to see how things were going. I told her Harli was fine. I will always remember what she said, "She's probably still doped up on the pain meds from the surgery. Watch out when they wear off." Despite her warning, I never felt the dog would be a problem. She seemed to trust me and even when the meds had worn off, she let me pet her. There was no fear or aggression, just mild curiosity. Harli was a timid, sensitive little dog who had been mistreated. I was so glad I was able to take her rather than know she was put down.

Finding a permanent home for her didn't work out, so I ended up keeping her. She turned out to be a funny, quiet little dog who loved to follow me around and ride in the truck. Harli looked like a Lab with a sweet Cocker face and she bayed like a Beagle. She was the funniest sight when she would stick her nose up in the air like a hound and bay. People would ask what breed she was, which is how she became the not-yet-AKC-recognized breed of "CockaBeagaDor." It fit her perfectly!

I have had Harli for over twelve years and she has been nothing but a wonderful faithful companion. Never once in those years has she shown me or anyone else any aggression. Harli loves to please me and holds her head up proudly when I tell her she is a good dog. She was my running partner for a long time, but she is now retired.

These days she is content to lay on her bed under my desk while I work. Her face is gray, and she walks slowly up and down the stairs, but she still enjoys sleeping in the grass on sunny days. Most of her teeth are gone but that doesn't keep her from enjoying her food. She is very gentle when taking treats or eating her glob of peanut butter with her meds each morning. I know I won't have her for too much longer, which is sad. But, I am grateful that her life was saved by a friend who took pity on this terrified and misunderstood dog. She was so worth the risk of allowing her into my home and my heart. I am just crazy about this little girl! 🐕🐾

Roo was an elderly dog who, one cold winter night, fell through the ice into the Missouri River. Luckily the Great Falls firefighters pulled him out, saving his life. The poor dog must have been in the cold water a while because he was hypothermic and in bad shape when he was fished out of the river. He was rushed to a vet who warmed him up and stabilized this sweet old guy, but no one claimed him. After that scary adventure, Roo ended up at the shelter for about two months and seemed to be extremely depressed. My friend Gloria was able to get him out of the shelter, into the Pet Paw-see foster program and place him for adoption.

Several months after his midnight swim, the local newspaper printed a story of Roo's heroic rescue along with his photo. A friend of Roo's owner read the story and recognized their precious old dog. His owners had searched for him but had eventually given up on ever finding Roo. (What a heartache not knowing what became of a beloved dog!) It was a very happy reunion when Roo's people came to claim him. The owners told us he was a Labrador-Shar Pei cross and that his real name was Boomer.

— Chapter 37 —
Little Man Barkley

L ittle Man Barkley didn't let his terrible past ruin his future.
  This precious little dog enjoyed every day in his furrever home.

In 2012 the Pet Paw-see rescue group was involved in the seizure of about thirty small-breed dogs taken from a garage in the middle of Great Falls, Montana. The dogs were most likely Lhasa Apso mixes, but it was pretty hard to tell since they were matted from one end to the other. They were filthy, covered with tangled dreadlocks and huddled together in one massive pack. It was a sickening sight. The owner relinquished them to animal control, and they turned the dogs over to our rescue group. The owner was apparently a "breeder," but his set-up fit the description of a puppy mill.

A local boarding kennel took care of the dogs for us while we figured out how to help them. Most of the dogs were completely unsocialized and acted like wild animals when anyone approached them. There were several old, sick, and blind dogs in the group; protected by the pack leaders. The only way they had survived was the safety of the pack. It appeared many of these dogs had lived their entire lives in a cold dark garage with no care, kindness, or positive human interaction.

Slowly, we took one dog at a time from the pack to be altered, shaved, bathed, and vaccinated. Once groomed they were cute little dogs who under better circumstances would have made wonderful companions. Some of them were friendly and able to be placed in temporary foster homes and then adopted, but many had no trust in humans. They would growl, snap, and lunge at all who came near them. It was heartbreaking and something that we rarely do, but the decision was made to humanely euthanize some of the dogs. There was little chance of socializing them and in reality, none of us knew how.

I remember being sick about putting any of the dogs down. I knew there was an old, blind dog in the mix, so I decided to take him into my home. The night I picked up this tiny little guy I fell head over heels in love with him. He was very friendly and cuddly although extremely thin, with sores all over his body from the filth he had lived in. He moved into my house with no fear of the other much larger dogs and settled in quickly. I named him Little Man Barkley.

Barkley had spunk despite his old age, lack of eyes (they had atrophied and shriveled up), and his tiny size of about five pounds. He relished being snuggled in warm blankets on his own soft bed. He also loved to eat and eventually put on a little weight. His blindness didn't stop him from exploring the yard and house and his greatest pleasure was rolling in the grass. Barkley couldn't get enough of it! He would roll on his back, kick his tiny legs up in the air, and smile. Barkley exuded pure joy at this simple act. I don't think he had known how wonderful grass felt and smelled. He took every opportunity to make up for a lifetime of missing out.

I tried to give him the chance to experience the things he had never had in his previous life of neglect. He loved to cuddle with me on my swing chair on warm summer evenings while I read. This sweet little man also liked bath time, maybe because I wrapped him up in a soft towel afterwards while he got a nice body massage. And, despite his terrible previous life, Barkley seemed to enjoy people, especially when anyone held and hugged him. He soaked up all the love he could get.

Dogs are amazing in that they can often forget their dreadful past and enjoy the here and now. Barkley was a great example of forgiveness and on moving forward with his life despite many terrible years.

Unfortunately, a lifetime of neglect and most likely no regular care from a veterinarian took its toll on my sweet little man. Many of his teeth, of the few that he had left, were badly infected and had to be removed. In addition to all his dental work and rounds of antibiotics, Barkley had a deadly bone infection in his jaw that would not respond to medication. After having him for only a year and a half, I saw that he couldn't eat and was losing weight. A vet visit determined that the infection was beyond help. Sadly, I decided my final gift of love was to let him go.

My sweet little man left my life as quickly as he had come into it. It has been several years since I said goodbye to Barkley, but his memory is still close to my heart. I was lucky that a friend had taken a short video of him rolling in the grass with his tiny legs in the air, smiling, and happy. When I watch it, I cry, and know that on the other side of the Rainbow Bridge is a sunny field of sweet-smelling grass where he is rolling to his heart's content. 🐾🐾

Black cats and dogs are often very hard to place and can sit in shelters and rescues for months before anyone sees their worth. They are passed over by the more attractive colorful animals. Chloe was just another black lab mix waiting at the shelter for her furrever home when I agreed to foster her. She eventually found a lovely family with her own kids as playmates.

Little Tucker, one more black lab mix puppy, was spotted outside, abandoned in a box waiting for someone to help him. The kind person who found him couldn't keep this sweet little guy but wanted him to be safe, so she called the Pet Paw-see for help. Tucker lived with me until finding a great couple who eventually adopted another one of our rescue dogs.

Tiny Raven Skye showed up on my doorstep several years ago. She was too small to have found her way to my house by herself. My guess is that someone "helped" her find my front porch. She was a very young black kitten with a badly damaged eye and a wee bit on the feral side. Wow, black-coated, half blind, and semi feral! Three strikes against her at only a few weeks old. Not a great way to begin her life.

But luckily for her, she ended up at the home of a Pet Paw-see foster mom. I took her to our vet where she got care but lost her eye. After recovering from her surgery, she came with me to Petco for our adoption events. It really didn't take too long to find her a purrfect home. She went to live with a family that fell in love with this special kitty. Last time we heard, she was doing great. 🐱🐱

— Chapter 38 —
Another Little Man

*C*ute and feisty comes in all shapes and sizes!

Then came along another "Little Man," no, not the same dog as Little Man Barkley. This Little Man was a tiny Chihuahua who came to the Pet Paw-see at about fourteen years old. He was nothing but bones with a shabby coat and at two and a half pounds, was the smallest dog I had ever seen. He had long spindly legs that looked more like the legs on a tiny baby fawn. They seemed too long for his little body and he walked as if he had still not figured out what to do with them.

His owner had passed away and Little Man ended up with the owner's son. This tiny dog didn't do well in a family with larger dogs and kids, so he was given to our rescue group to adopt out. Besides being very small and old, he was born with no bottom jawbones and had no teeth left in his little mouth. His lower boneless jaw just hung there so getting him to eat wasn't as easy as placing him in front of a bowl of dog crunchies. Despite this, he was a little doll and very feisty. Everyone who met Little Man fell in love with this adorable dog. A gal from our group, Jo Anne, took him in to foster and tried to find him a good home but his condition was so poor that no one wanted him. Happily, she decided to keep him (another Foster Failure).

Her first task was to find something he liked to eat so he would gain some weight. It had to be soft food and eaten off the end of her finger. She tried all kinds of dog, cat, and people food until she found a few things that he enjoyed. He couldn't chew and was only able to eat tiny bits of food at a time but once he liked something, he ate until he was full, which didn't take all that long. Jo Anne soon discovered that pancakes, minus the syrup, were one of his favorite meals so she made them for him at least once a week. Little Man had also tried tamales and told his mom to keep them on the menu. After getting regular nutrition, he ate four times a day, Little Man ballooned to a hefty three pounds and most of his bones were not as visible any longer. His coat, which was ragged with numerous bald patches likely due to poor nutrition, was also greatly improved.

Little Man didn't like to be walked on a leash; carrying him in a blanket was his transportation method of choice. While he liked to be kept warm, he wouldn't wear a sweater or coat. He found them beneath his dignity. He didn't want to be mistaken for a poodle, and besides, the clothes chafed his sensitive skin. So even through the cold Montana winters he would never let his person put any clothes on him. In fact, he wouldn't go outside when it was cold and used the indoor doggie pads to do his business.

It took two of us to give him a bath the first time. He wasn't afraid to let anyone know when he was unhappy and while his completely toothless mouth couldn't cause any damage, he still got upset and we didn't want to give him any undue strife. After the initial feel of the warm water and the soothing massage, he relaxed and loved it. We didn't want to push our luck by using the dryer on him, so we just wrapped him in a tea towel until he was dry. Another first for Little Man.

Little Man lived with a variety of foster dogs, a resident Labrador named Sage, and a cat. He was mostly indifferent to all of them as long as they followed HIS house rules and stayed away from HIS stuff.

He got first dibs on the sunny spot on the porch, he allowed no other animals in his carrier, and no one was to interrupt Mom during his mealtimes. If you understood these requirements, Little Man was happy to live in harmony with the other animals in his home. If anyone, human or beast, were dumb enough to challenge his rules, he would go after them with all the fury of his tiny body and toothless mouth. Little Man was a force to be reckoned with!

Little Man could apparently be goofy at times and liked to dance when his person came home to take care of his varied needs. He waited patiently until he heard the key in the lock and then did his silly version of the rumba for his mom. Even though he was ancient and fragile, he was still a happy little guy who felt so lucky to have found his final *furrever* person. Little Man knew he was loved and thanked Jo Anne every chance he got. I knew his mom was very happy she became a Foster Failure over him.

P.S. This precious Little Man crossed over the Rainbow Bridge during the editing of this book. While his feet were extremely tiny, he left large paw prints across my heart as well as across Jo Anne's heart. This sweet little Chihuahua is missed by his many fans! 🐾🐾

The Pet Paw-see has taken in many cats and kittens found along roadways while our volunteers have been going about their daily tasks. Naturally, we pick them up and if no owner is located, we take them into our adoption program. Trucker was one lucky little kitten when I saw him late one night "trucking" down a gravel road near my home. I scooped him up before the great horned owls who live in the area could get to him. He would have been a quick snack for these huge birds, and he was clueless to the danger.

Trucker was a silly kitten. He was a hit at our Petco adoption events with his goofy expressions and he seemed always to have his mouth open; telling all who would listen about his tough start in life. Trucker LOVED to talk! His antics and great personality made it easy to adopt this funny little guy.

Hobo Harry was another wayward kitty out for a stroll along a highway when a Pet Paw-see volunteer picked him up. No one claimed this gentle kitty, so he was put up for adoption and quickly found his furrever home. No more traveling the highways and byways of Montana for Trucker or Mr. Harry.

Chapter 39

Sophie & Sadie

I *felt so humble when the shelter asked me to help these two tiny puppies. They brought so much joy to my life and to the lives of their* **furrever** *families.*

It seems like every rescue always starts with a phone call. The story of Sophie and Sadie started with a call from our local shelter manager. Someone had brought in two tiny puppies whose eyes were just starting to open that day, which put them at around fourteen days old. They each weighed under two pounds but looked to be in "ok" condition. The puppies were found in a box in an alley with no momma in sight. They would need round-the-clock bottle-feeding and care and the shelter didn't have the personnel to feed them throughout the night. Well, if I can bottle-feed a mouse, then two puppies shouldn't be too much harder, so I picked them up after work and brought my two newest foster babies home.

The puppies weren't sure how to drink from a bottle at first but once they figured it out, I couldn't feed them fast enough. They ate constantly, which was fine on weekends, but what was I supposed to do with them during the workweek? They were too helpless to leave for nine or ten hours at a time. Therefore, I did the only thing I could. I found a nice soft carrier for them, filled it with blankets and off they went with me to work. Packing for a couple of growing puppies was like packing to go away for a week. I had to take extra blankets, washcloths and towels, puppy shampoo, LOTS of formula, and baby bottles. It took a few trips from my vehicle each day to get them and all the supplies into my office.

It was quite the ordeal to feed and keep them clean. If you didn't know, puppies poop about a hundred times a day and have no problems rolling in their "gifts" (puppy poop). This meant several baths in the restroom at work and then off to my truck with the dirty laundry. I didn't want my office to smell like a kennel, so I had to keep them and their bedding clean. These tiny babies also needed to eat often and weren't afraid to let me know if I was late giving them their bottles. Despite all this work, they were such cute roly-poly little puppies I couldn't help but fall in love with them.

For the first workweek, they couldn't walk yet so keeping them in a carrier under my office desk worked fine. As long as I gave them their bottles, they didn't make any noise and slept through most of the day. Once their eyes opened fully and they found their legs, things became a bit more interesting. The carrier quickly got too small and they wanted OUT! So they tended to make sweet little puppy noises to get my attention. Unfortunately, their sweet little puppy noises got louder and louder as the week went by and their carrier seemed to get smaller and smaller. I have a door to my office so I could shut out the squeaking, but noisy puppies are kind of hard to hide. And, once the word was out, there was a steady stream of visitors all day long to hold and play with them. It became the office secret that I was housing two puppies under my desk. (I guess it's better than a mouse!)

It was with great relief when they were finally able to eat on their own so that I could leave them home during the day. I had set up a large wire cage with toys, food, water, and blankets in my spare bedroom for them while I was gone for the day. When I got home each evening, it looked like the puppies fought a war in their large cage. The blankets and puppies were covered in food and their "gifts," the water bowls were turned over, and their toys were shredded. But there is nothing cuter than tiny puppies wagging their little tails in excitement that their mom is home so I really couldn't be mad at them. After a bath and more food, they played outside with supervision. This was the greatest adventure of their young lives. It was summer so they had free reign to chase bugs and each other in my fenced yard. Watching them run around on their unsteady legs was hysterical. After a tough day at work, they were the perfect remedy for stress. My other dogs were also fascinated at these very tiny creatures and loved to follow them around the yard, nudging them with their large noses.

It is amazing how quickly the puppies grew. One of the pups, Sadie, was spoken for before she was four weeks old, but she didn't go to her new home until about a month later, after she had gotten spayed. The other puppy, Sophie, took a little while longer to find her *furrever* home, but it was worth the wait. While I was in Petco buying formula after picking them up from the shelter, one of the Petco employees met the pups, snapped a picture, and sent the photo home to his wife. Jim knew he wanted one and was sure his wife Francie would too. Sadie and her sister had several play dates with Jim, Francie, and their dog Bailey, until she was old enough for adoption.

Sadie now called Snickers, gets to go on adventures with her new family. She has learned to run next to her person's bike, which helps to wear off a lot of her young dog energy. She has a swimming pool and tons of toys as well as her doggie companion, Bailey. I get to see her often, since her mom takes her into Petco to visit me during our adoption events.

During Sophie's first adoption event at Petco, she had three people furiously filling out applications for her. It was hard but I know I made the right choice in the family I picked. Mary and Rob fell in love with little Sophie at first sight and could not wait to bring her home. She gets to go camping and boating and has another dog to play with. She went to a home with an older dog, Rusty. Sadly, Rusty passed away from old age about a year after the couple adopted Sophie. But Sophie wasn't without a puppy buddy for too long. Fortunately, at that time, I had more foster puppies and Sophie's people adopted Tilly, who they renamed Sara. She was a puppy in one of the two litters I fostered in 2016 from the Indian reservation during the "Summer of the Puppies." I wonder if Sophie and Sara (Tilly) compare notes about how they both ended up in such a wonderful home! Each puppy went to a home with an older doggie friend to teach them about their new world as well as some resident, dog-friendly kitties. Sophie and Sadie (Snickers) hit the doggie lottery!

I am always touched and amazed at how many of my former foster kids remember me. Sadie goes crazy when she sees me, and the feeling is mutual. I think back to the day I got Sadie and Sophie, blind and hungry, left in a box as though they were someone's trash. It breaks my heart that anyone could do that to defenseless animals. I am glad I was able to give them a chance to grow up and live with people who will love them *furrever!* 🐾🐾

When the Pet Paw-see first started, we had few animals of our own so we would offer to take some from the shelter and adopt them at our weekly adoption events. (Unfortunately, that is not a problem now, there seems to be an unending supply of unwanted animals.)

Mikki was a little old grandma kitty who came from the shelter and gladly never went back. Her previous owner had her front paws de-clawed which made it very difficult for her to walk and use her litter box. Poor little Mikki was arthritic and had a hard time getting around but was very affectionate and loving. She didn't have many years left when she found us but lived those as a happy spoiled cat in her own home.

Chase, Allie, and Short Stop were three precious kittens who I fostered until all found great homes. They were originally brought to the shelter, transferred to the Pet Paw-see, and ended up living with me until they were old enough to adopt to furrever homes.

Many times when the Pet Paw-see has the room we take cats from the shelter and adopt them through our program. Several kitties that we've taken in have languished for months at the shelter with no interest. Once people see them at Petco or Pet Smart, they are quickly adopted. It's a shame that more people don't give the local shelters a chance. There are many wonderful, loving animals just waiting for the opportunity to shower their love on their new person.

— Chapter 40 —
From the Dawgs

I had to let my Dawgs write this story; otherwise, they said they would not help promote my book.

When my large dog family heard I was writing a book, which included stories about them, they insisted they also get a chance to write about life with me. Fair is fair! I was impressed with how they gathered under their favorite tree in the yard to go over their story ideas before telling me what to type. (I had to do the typing since they are all paws around a keyboard.) Baxter decided he was going to be the "spokes-dog," which immediately got Meka all riled up! Being an Alpha, Meka is a bit pushy and thought she would be the better representative for the pack. Occasionally, I had to step in to referee in order to prevent bloodshed. Well, after a couple of false starts, here goes, in their own words:

People are weird and our person is no exception. Each day before she leaves for work, she tells us to be good and be quiet. HELLO! We can't do both at the same time. Being quiet means that a bad guy could sneak onto our property, break into our house, and steal the good stuff. *(Note to Bax: After spending my paycheck on your food, treats, and vet bills, I have no money left to buy Good Stuff.)* Barking our heads off all day long is bound to scare away any would-be burglars. Doesn't she know that when we are making noise, we ARE being good! Good security for HER stuff! We have tried to get her to understand our reasons for barking, but she is very dense. We have heard this same complaint from our other dog friends. Why are humans so dumb?

We also don't understand why our person continues to believe we are deaf. She thinks that if she yells our names louder and louder it's because we couldn't hear her the first time. We did hear her. We just chose to ignore her unreasonable demands. It is very rude of her to expect us to drop the important stuff we are doing and come running at her beck and call. Most of us are NOT deaf and don't like to hear our names shrieked at the top of her lungs throughout the neighborhood. It makes us (her) look like we are uncivilized and more than a little wacky!

I keep trying to tell my Mom that my name is Baxter T. Brown, not "Get Down" or "Shut Up." My name has a lovely dignified ring to it, and I like it. (Not every dog has a middle initial or last name, so I figure it's because I am EXTRA special!) Why does she keep calling me other not-so-nice things when she should remember that she gave me the name "Baxter"? The other dogs in our pack feel the same way. We dogs prefer to be called by our given names, not a hodge-podge of ridiculous names such as Flea Bag, Worthless Mutt, D@#$ Dawg, and the like. Maybe she can't remember all of our names and is experiencing signs of early onset dementia. There are a lot of us, and it is reasonable to think she would occasionally mix us up. We have decided that unless we hear her call us by our very nice adoption-day names, we will no longer respond to her unreasonable commands. In addition, we would like our names to be spoken to us in gentle, sweet tones not roared at us like a bellowing buffalo! It's undignified! Sometimes a dawg has to practice "TOUGH LOVE!"

Despite it all, we know she is a good dawg-owner-person and she loves us. Therefore, we try to do what we can to make her life a bit easier by helping with the chores. I know one of her least favorite chores is scooping the cat's litter box. We have offered many times to help but she won't let us. None of us understand why not. Any one of us dawgs can clean the litter box as fast or faster than she can. Jump in, grab the nasty stuff, and out in no time! (Just imagine, if she let us do this chore, she could spend that extra time baking us homemade doggie cookies!)

One of the benefits of us helping is that she has no bag of disgusting kitty poop to haul to the trash. We know Mom is big on recycling. If she lets us help her this is one less item that will end up at the land-fill. But she refuses to let us help! It should be a win-win for her and our environment but being kind of dim-witted, our person doesn't see it from a dawg's perspective.

It's very strange but Mom seems to have a fixation with clean! All of us are astounded at how much she likes to run that loud, noisy machine with the sucking snake all over the house. It seems like almost every day she drags that contraption out of the closet because of a dog hair or two on the floor. What is wrong with dog hair? Us dawgs bathe a few times a year! We are clean! If we are ok with a little dog hair, she should be too. None of us ever freak out if we see a human hair on the ground. We have heard that some humans have something called Obsessive Compulsive Disorder (OCD) and will do things like wash their hands, check that the gate is closed, or the door is locked over and over again even when it makes no sense. Could our Mom have this OCD? This weird habit of constantly cleaning makes NO sense! Do you think we should get her some help? Maybe an intervention? We are certain they make drugs for her condition. Now we just have to figure out how to get them and if she will need the pills stuffed into a sausage or a bit of cheese.

One chore we all fight over is washing the dishes. A few of us have even jumped up on the counters (when she's not looking) to help Mom by licking the dishes clean as a whistle. Isn't that a nice surprise for her? The only thing we can't seem to manage is getting the dishes back into the cabinets once we wash them. (We need her help for that one.) Despite this, no matter how much we plead and beg, she still insists on washing them herself. So much for lessening the load on our person! She needs to learn to delegate the housework a bit better. Maybe then, she would have more time to play with us.

While we are on the subject of obsessive cleaning . . .

Another habit that has all of us dawgs confused is her obsession with bathing. Every day, day in and day out, even if she has not played in the mud, she climbs into that weird box she calls the shower and allows water to spray out of the ceiling onto her. And then she uses that awful-smelling stuff called soap. If Mom doesn't like what she smells like she could do what we do. She could find a nice dead animal on the side of the road and just roll around on it. We have tried many times to convince her that once she tries this, she will love it! Doesn't she see that look of utter joy on our faces while we throw ourselves to the ground and mash our bodies into a half-decayed critter? IT IS HEAVEN! And the best part is, that wonderful aroma stays with us for days! Sadly, our person is very hesitant to try any new things we suggest, and we can't seem to convince her otherwise. Maybe in time . . .

Mom's sleeping habits also seem contrary to us canine kids. In the wild, the pack will dog-pile on each other for warmth and security. We have tried that same logic with her, and she doesn't seem to appreciate our concern for her health and welfare. While she does allow us to sleep on the bed, she doesn't want us to sprawl on top of her and she won't share her pillow. Imagine! Mom lays down on her side of the bed and pushes us away. This seems very strange! We are offering our bodies to shield her from harm during the night. This way she can get the sleep needed to get up early and earn a living.

We have all heard her say that us dawgs cost her an arm and a leg so she will probably never be able to retire. Maybe if she gets more sleep, she will make more money and then be able to retire before she's dead! Letting us dawgs pile on top of her at night will allow her to sleep soundly without fear of attacks by the monsters that hide under the bed. Despite our interest in her health, she rejects our selfless benevolence *(Really Bax! Selfless benevolence! You could have just said thoughtfulness or caring.)* Sadly, we have learned that dawg logic does not equate to people logic, so we won't hold our breath waiting for her to see eye-to-eye with us dawgs. How humans have survived for so long with their odd behaviors baffle us. If our wild canine ancestors acted like this, our species would be extinct by now. Humans really are bizarre!!!

Our favorite pastime on a lazy Sunday afternoon is to hang out on the couch and watch TV. Mom has to operate the remote control since, as she stated earlier, we are all paws. Most of the time she picks "ok" stuff to watch. Actually, we don't really care what's on the TV; we just enjoy the nap. But what annoys us the most is sometimes she pushes us aside and tells us to get on the floor so that she can sit on OUR couch. Not once have we heard her ask, "Would you dawgs mind if I joined you?" "Do you dawgs care for some refreshments?" or "Don't bother moving. I can sit on the floor while you guys relax up there." You would think that after all we do for her, she would show us some consideration. But NO! Off the couch we go to make room for HER! We have often threatened to call the authorities over this harsh treatment but Meka chewed up the old cell phone and now Mom hides the new phone from us.

The biggest complaint we have about our person is her cooking habits. She forgets all about us when she is making a mouth-watering meal. Doesn't she know that we have very sensitive noses? To her the food on the stove smells tasty. To us the food smells like heaven just rained down and landed at our feet. It is hard to describe what a meal like Thanksgiving dinner smells like to a dog. We rarely, if ever, get a bite never mind a heaping plate full, unlike Mom and her silly guests. They fill up once, twice, and three times while we wait outside in the cold for the human's meal to end so that we can get a morsel or two of leftover turkey with our dry, boring doggie kibbles! Our pitiful whining from the backyard doesn't seem to get through to her cold hardened heart. This is abject cruelty! How do we get her to understand our pain? Should we just whine louder?

Our human certainly isn't perfect but what human is? Even though at times she drives us to chase our tails, she does some things we all really enjoy. Truth be told, life with our human is not all bad.

One of the best times of the day is our daily run. She gets us up early in the morning even in the coldest months and makes us go outside for exercise. This is our time to smell what the night creatures have been up to while the humans were sleeping. We live in a rural area with lots of intriguing critters rarely seen during the day. We get visits from coyotes, owls, bunnies, many deer, as well as a few skunks near our house. It's "Doggie Paradise" out there! Sadly, she only lets us explore this wonderland at the end of a leash. She never lets us run free like our wild friends. It's pretty embarrassing for big tough dawgs like us to come face-to-face with a coyote while being attached to a rope held by our MOM. I can't imagine what the coyotes must think about us! I'm sure they laugh their heads off at those wimpy domesticated cousins. We have even heard a few snickers from the coyotes about the wussy "pet" dogs who live in the neighborhood. (I guess we can take some comfort knowing the coyotes will never see us wearing cute little outfits, as some of our pathetic dog-friends are forced to wear!) How can we keep up our "street cred" as big mean protectors if the coyotes see us tethered to a weak little human? This is so not cool!

Another thing, while we are voicing our many complaints, we are not allowed to chase after the deer during our morning outings. They flaunt their bushy white tails in our faces as they quietly soar over the fences and Mom never lets us off our leashes to follow them. During our run this morning, the deer were especially taunting. They let us get so close to them and then suddenly dashed off leaving us forlorn. We told our Mom that we only wanted to sniff the deer and make friends with them. We would never hurt them. She doesn't seem to believe us. I wonder why? Have we ever lied to her before?

For that matter, the cute little bunnies we see on our morning runs are the bane of our existence! They like to gather in the long grass or hide behind bushes until we can almost reach out and touch them. Then they bolt in wild zig-zag fashion away to safety. Often there is more than one bunny racing willy-nilly in different directions, which drives us to madness! This also makes our person crazy since four or five leashed dogs going from an easy jog to Mach II in a few seconds tends to wreak havoc on her back and neck. Oh well, it's her fault. If she let us off our leashes, her body wouldn't suffer this kind of trauma. Dogs were born to chase and Mom's irrational need for control prevents us from fulfilling our natural canine instincts. She needs to learn to lighten up a bit!

We didn't mean to do it but the other day we made our Mom cry. Us dawgs are not very proud of what we did but what the heck, we did it anyway. We don't have a mean or malicious bone in our bodies, and we would never do anything purposely to make her sad, nevertheless sometimes we do. She needs to unde stand that dawgs just wanna have fun. But, when you come down to it, this incident was really all her fault. She left us alone in the house for what seemed like FOREVER. (It was really only about fifteen minutes but in Dawg-Time we thought she had finally moved out and left us as she often threatens she will.)

With no new dog toys in the house we had to be creative and come up with something to do to pass the time while Mom was gone. So, we thought we would play just a little bit with something that WAS new in our house; the BRAND NEW VINYL KITCHEN FLOOR. I (Baxter) didn't come up with the idea but it looked like a ton of fun, so I happily dove right in. One of our smaller pack-mates grabbed a hidden corner of the BRAND NEW VINYL KITCHEN FLOOR and started pulling. It was just a tiny corner, no big deal! Who knew about all the fun just waiting to be discovered under our very feet! What dawg doesn't love a game of tug-of-war?

It was madness and mayhem until we heard the door open and Mom walk in. She really didn't say anything for a while; the only sound we heard was gasping. At first, we thought she was having a heart attack and maybe we should dial 911 or start CPR. Then we realized she was just sobbing. She didn't try to kill us, at least not for a few minutes. Then all we heard was "Baaaaddddd Dawgs blah, blah, blah; That Flooring Cost Me A Mint blah, blah, blah; I'm Gonna Give You Worthless Mutts Away On Craig's List blah, blah, blah!" You get the picture. She was less than pleased with our antics. On the good dawg/ bad dawg scale of one to ten, this was a twenty-five! Eating a corner of the wall was only about a three compared to this incident. Even ripping out a screen while jumping through a window and chasing after a car only scored about a seven.

After she had calmed down a bit, Mom asked us, "Do you dawgs enjoy ruining my stuff and making me crazy?" Being dawgs we just gave her that dumb dawg look but in our minds we were thinking,

"What a stupid question! It's like asking, do dawgs love to go for rides in their truck?" Of course, we enjoyed ruining her stuff. It is much more fun than ruining our stuff. We know now that maybe we could have been better behaved and waited for her to come back inside before resorting to our imaginations for entertainment. We all know in our hearts that Mom loves us and always comes back. She would never leave us. On second thought, after this little faux pas she may decide to leave us! Oh well, dawgs will be dawgs!

Even though we have some very legitimate grievances about our person, we really love her and know she feels the same about us. She took all of us from awful conditions and gave us a loving safe home. We have tried to teach Mom stuff but have concluded that she is not at all trainable. Dawgs often hear the saying that "You can't teach an old dawg new tricks". I think the same applies to humans; can't teach them new tricks either! I guess all of us poor dawgs will have to adjust to life with our "Special" human. Even with all her faults and strange customs, it could be a lot worse!

Wilson and Windsor were a pair of handsome tuxedo kitties abandoned when their owners moved away during one of our very cold and snowy winters. A realtor told the Pet Paw-see about these poor kitties left behind. Their home was way out in the country along a narrow, unlit gravel road; the only light came from a few neighboring houses. Since it was near my place, I drove to the empty home but saw no cats, so I left food and blankets in the shed and hoped for the best. We had had a few feet of snow that week and since my truck was only two-wheel drive, I had a very difficult time maneuvering while trying to stay out of the roadside ditches.

I drove out there every night after work and finally saw that an animal had been eating the food. I also saw a few kitty tracks in the snow. That was a great sign! This was a very scary place with several old abandoned outbuildings; I didn't feel safe being out there alone. I was afraid of being stuck and someone finding my cold dead body when spring finally came.

One evening while I was rummaging through one of the sheds with my flashlight, I felt a person behind me and turned around to find a man standing there. I have rarely been as freaked out! I never heard him coming and knew if he had bad intentions, that screaming wouldn't have done any good. I was relieved when he said he was a neighbor and was wondering who I was. After telling him what I was doing, he told me about the cats and that he had also been leaving them food.

After many trips to the shed, I was finally able to catch both kitties. Wilson and Windsor were sweet, gentle boys who were glad to have found a warm, safe haven. It didn't take long to find them two wonderful homes.

– Chapter 41 –
Camp Collie—
Ten Years
Later

Jean, *the president of the AWCA and my dear friend asked me to write about Camp Collie on the 10-year anniversary of this animal rescue. Writing this article brought back memories I had forgotten about this amazing undertaking.*

Wow, hard to believe it was already 2012, ten years since the truck carrying the Collies, cats, and other dogs crossed the border into Montana. I found myself thinking about this milestone anniversary a lot this year as October 31 got closer and closer. I often pictured the animals waiting patiently in the filthy truck for someone to help them. That picture haunted me then and still does today. I thank God for giving the border patrol officers the courage to stop the truck, especially in the very remote location of Sweetgrass, Montana. (For those who are not aware, Sweetgrass is in the middle of "Nowhere", Montana.) I am sure the border patrol officer never envisioned the monumental task of caring for these animals; he just knew he had to do the right thing. Many thanks to these brave souls!

When Jean asked me to write on the 10-year anniversary of the rescue, many thoughts ran through my head on what to write about. All of us who helped in this rescue, whether by giving our time and sweat or by the many generous donations, lived a nine-month saga and heard the terrible stories about the conditions forced on these animals. I don't feel I need to re-tell this story. I thought it would be nice to focus on the good stuff that happened during this rescue.

I remember hearing of this seizure the first week of November 2002. It made me physically sick. It bothered me and no matter how much I tried, I couldn't get it out of my mind. I wanted to do something to help so I called the sheriff in Shelby and asked what they needed. I figured I could fill my truck with dog food and drive it up there. The gal I spoke with said they needed volunteers and money; they had plenty of dog food. I immediately crossed "volunteering" off my To Do List. It was too far to drive regularly, and I didn't want to get caught up in the emotions that working with these animals would surely entail. I know that we all have an inner voice, but mine was especially busy that week. It shouted long and loud, yelling at me to drive to Shelby to help the dogs and cats. Against my better judgment, I figured I would go up ONCE to volunteer. I honestly didn't think I could be of any help at all. My plan was to get in and out and rest in the fact that I had "helped" for a day.

The first time I drove through the fairground gates to the horse barns and saw dogs peering over the bottom half of the stall doors, I was hooked! They were skinny, matted, and filthy but they were dogs, and dogs tend to be happy even under the direst circumstances. The puppies were housed in several large horse stalls and it was "attack mode" when you dared to enter one of them. They just wanted to play and give kisses. They were in doggie heaven with all the attention showered on them by the volunteers. The adult dogs were a lot more wary of people, but most responded well to the kind attention of the volunteers. Some were beyond terrified so I left them alone and hoped they could recover from their trauma. That day, as I left for the long drive home, I knew I would be back, which I was, each weekend until the last dog and cat left Camp Collie, many months later.

This rescue has enriched my life in ways that are not easy to get down on paper. The memories include many heart-wrenching hours of worry over the animals and their ultimate fate. Besides that, I felt so lucky to be a small part of helping these dogs and cats. I met people from all walks of life and from all parts of the U.S. and Canada. We worked side by side in some very primitive conditions to help these animals and I never heard any complaining about the hard work. Many of these people became dear friends. This gave me the strength to continue. Even now, it makes me smile when I think of them. Sadly, while our paths don't cross often anymore, I feel lucky and blessed to have had these caring people in my life for even a short time.

There were special days at Camp Collie that I will never forget. One such memory was Thanksgiving Day. Several volunteers and I were invited to the home of an elderly lady for a complete turkey dinner. This lovely woman couldn't work with the dogs but wanted to help. My turkey dinner was eaten with total strangers in filthy clothes, but rarely have I felt so touched by such a generous gesture. Her meal warmed me long after I left that day.

Christmas Day 2002 was also especially heartwarming. I was at Camp Collie on Christmas Eve to help set up the food bowls and get ready for the next day. We figured there would only be a handful of volunteers to help on Christmas Day and we needed to get a head start on the chores. I got up early that morning and drove to Shelby fully expecting it would be a very long, hard day. Shortly after 8:00 a.m. the cars started pulling up with volunteers. There were so many people to help that we actually ran out of dogs to walk. At one time, I looked outside and there must have been 50 Collies walking in the beautiful Montana sunshine. All the dogs got out to walk and play at least twice that day. We cleaned all the kennels and every dog got a toy from a generous donor. It was an amazing Christmas. Once again, I was in awe of the people who were willing to give up their holiday to muck out kennels and show love to these animals.

Another special day was around Valentine's Day. I was at Camp Collie one Saturday in February and the long, cold days of endless cleaning and caring for the dogs had taken its toll on many volunteers. This had gone on for too long and the number of people able to help had diminished greatly. Some weekend days there were only a handful of us to care for the dogs. I remember feeling especially tired and disheartened one Saturday afternoon when there were only five of us to take care of almost 200 animals. That was until someone showed me a corkboard covered with encouraging messages, cards, and notes from people from all over the country. There were thanks, prayers, and wonderful letters of hope from animal-lovers who cared about the fate of these creatures. Someone had even sent a beautiful bouquet of flowers for the volunteers. At that point, I knew that while only a few people could actually be in Shelby, Montana doing the work, we had the love and strength of so many others. These simple gifts gave us all a giant boost and helped the tired volunteers continue with this work.

I will always fondly remember the day I met Jean, the president of the American Working Collie Association (AWCA). I had seen her going from cage to cage talking with each dog and petting each long Collie snout. She wasn't in a hurry. Her actions showed that she wanted to make sure each Collie knew he or she was very special. I didn't know who she was at first and besides it was extremely noisy in the barn, so conversations were impossible. I was on the way to my truck for the long drive home when someone asked me to meet Jean. At this point, I really knew nothing about the AWCA and their support for this rescue. I gladly met Jean and she told me of their involvement and concern for the animals and thanked me for caring for them, especially some of the special needs dogs. It was so wonderful knowing that things were going on behind the scenes to make sure these animals never went back to their former life. I truly had no idea that so many others cared about their fate.

There are so many other wonderful memories of my months caring for the dogs and cats at Camp Collie. I am lucky to have been able to keep in contact with many of these animals over the years since many people in Montana adopted the dogs and cats. There have been numerous "Collie Gatherings" where adopters and volunteers have gotten the chance to visit and watch the Collies interact with each other. Seeing these dogs and cats happy and living in loving homes made the long months of hard work worthwhile. One of the great things that came out of Camp Collie for me was I learned about this gentle intelligent breed. Except for growing up with "Lassie" on TV, I had never seen a Collie. This isn't a common breed in Montana. This Camp Collie experience has blessed me in so many ways and I am grateful that I listened to my inner voice that day and made the long drive to Shelby.

While most of the dogs and cats from this rescue have passed over the Rainbow Bridge, their memories will never leave us. I know it has forever changed the lives of many of the people who volunteered. 🐈🐕

*L*ibby Loo (Looie) was born in a puppy mill, sold at a pet store, and then ended up at the local animal shelter. Looie was a tiny Cocker Spaniel with a gorgeous, long, flowing red coat. When I met her at the shelter, I knew at first glance that she was coming home with me. I adopted her while I was looking for a companion for my two other Cockers. She fit in very well with Cappi and Sophie as well as the resident kitties.

Looie loved to go for rides in my truck and was my traveling companion for numerous trips around Montana. When I first adopted her, she would shake and quake every time she got into my truck. (I guess she was afraid that she was being dumped again.) After a short time, she realized that truck rides always meant lots of fun so she would excitedly jump into the front seat for a new adventure.

In almost every photo I have of Looie she has the tip of her tongue sticking out of her mouth. That pose seemed to indicate to me that she was content, either that or she just liked being goofy! Her delightful personality and funny mannerisms gave me many years of laughter. She was the best remedy for a lousy day.

Looie had a knack for acting silly; I think she knew that she made me laugh. Besides her funny sticking-her-tongue-out pose, the hair around her face was always in disarray no matter how often I brushed her. I called it the Wild Loo Doo. Being the smallest and cutest member of my pack, she often got away with murder. Looie lived with me until she passed of cancer. I still miss her terribly!

— Chapter 42 —
What is That Smell?

can laugh at this now but at the time it wasn't funny!

I was driving to work one summer day and I kept smelling cat. You know the smell I am talking about. I thought a cat had gotten into my pickup and peed on the seat or the carpet. Not good when the day was going to be in the 90s! Once I arrived at work, I went into the restroom and discovered to my horror that the smell was coming from my shirt. There was a large, round, wet pee stain on the front of my shirt. How and when it got there, I had no clue. I panicked because I had a meeting that morning and lived many miles from my office. I did the only thing I could think of at the moment. I took my shirt off and tried to wash the stain off in the sink. Anyone that has a cat knows that won't work and it didn't. Cat pee doesn't wash out easily. So, I put my wet shirt back on and drove to a nearby store in the hopes of buying a new shirt, but the store didn't open for another hour. Now I was really in a panic! An auditor was coming to my office to review one of my projects, and I couldn't cancel the appointment. I did the next best thing; I raced to my fellow cat rescuer friend, Leslie's, office for help. I knew she would understand my dilemma. Leslie is very experienced when it comes to cat pee!

I ran to her desk and asked if she had anything to wear. She gave me a scrub shirt that was so large that the "V" in the neck was open way too far down for appropriate office-wear. Oh boy, it was hospital green! Now I was just about in tears until she said, "Go to my house. I have some clothes on the line, maybe something will fit you." Luckily, her house was close by. I drove like a bat out of hell, ran into her backyard, and saw a lovely red top hanging on the clothesline. Quickly, I ripped off my shirt forgetting Les has neighbors who may not understand a partially naked woman stealing clothes off her line. I ducked into her garage to dress and was surprised that the shirt fit well, matched my slacks, and was only a little bit wet. Wow, things were looking up as I drove back to the office. It was still early, so I went into the restroom to comb my hair and make sure I didn't have the shirt on backwards or inside out. That is when I noticed that my slacks also had a large wet stain on them, and it wasn't from the damp shirt. Once again, I took them off, scrubbed the slacks in the sink, and realized my time and luck were up. I was going to have to wear them all day despite the cat aroma. That is where the rose body spray came in handy. I sprayed it all over my clothes, my hair, and my office. I can't say it eliminated the smell of cat pee, but it did add a layer of intrigue and if you didn't get too close, nothing seemed too out of place.

The poor auditor finally came to meet with me and must have thought I was nuts! I sat at the opposite end of a long conference table so that he wouldn't be treated to the smell of cat, handed him the information he needed and ran back to my office. In addition, I gave him my direct phone line so that he could call me with questions. This way I could hide at my desk and didn't have to be near him any more than necessary. I also avoided all contact with my co-workers. It was with a great sigh of relief when it was finally time to leave for home. To this day, I don't know how or when I got cat pee all over my clothes, but my adventure did provide a few laughs for those friends I dared to tell. The lesson I have learned from this is to NEVER ignore the smell of cat, dog, or other pet before leaving home. And always bring a spare change of clothes! 🐾🐱

*O*ur local Petco Store seems to be a great dumping ground for unwanted cats and dogs. Too many times over the years, the employees have come to work to find a box or carrier outside their front entryway. Mainly there are cats or kittens in the box but sometimes they find a puppy or two.

Several years ago, one of the employees opened a carrier left outside to find three adult cats happy to be free of their enclosure. That is how Dusty, Stripes, and Brownie came into the Pet Paw-see rescue program and into my foster home. All three were un-altered, but otherwise healthy and sociable kitties. This made them very easy to adopt.

They were sweet cats and deserved better than leaving them to an unknown fate in a shopping center. We guessed the owner didn't want to bring them to the shelter for fear they would be put down. He or she knew that Petco and the Pet Paw-see would take them in; we always do. It breaks my heart to think of how confused and scared they were while waiting for help.

Recently the Petco employees came to work to find another box outside their door. One of the workers noticed a cat climbing out of it. The poor confused kitty was standing by the front entryway waiting for someone with thumbs to open the door. Once the kitty got into the store, his sister jumped out of the box and took off down the sidewalk towards the movie theater. An employee captured her and brought her safely into the store for food and water. Salt and Pepper, two very scared tabbies, took a while to feel safe again. Happily, both adjusted and found wonderful homes.

— Chapter 43 —
Owned by a Beagle

f you have to be "owned" by any animal, a Beagle is the perfect dog for this. They never let you forget that we have to play by THEIR rules.

Most passionate dog lovers don't like to say they "own" a dog. Their dog is more like a member of the family rather than a possession like a TV or car. However, legally, we do "own" our dogs. The exception to that rule was my old sweet Beagle, Jake. Jake "owned" me and was not afraid to let me know every chance he got. He was thirteen years old when he was taken to (dumped at) the local shelter. His former owners said they had no time for him. Hard to believe that a thirteen-year-old dog was so much trouble that he lost his home at this senior time in his life. I heard of him being at the shelter and felt terrible especially since not many people adopt older dogs. I love old dogs and have been lucky to share my life with many during their golden years. For days, I couldn't get him off my mind. Since my current pack of misfits was at low census, I adopted him and hoped he would live at least a year, maybe two, with me.

He came to my house full of himself and stubborn as only a hound can be. I had never had a hound before, so this was a new experience. Jake would stand in front of me and bay at the top of his lungs when he wanted something. Being subjected to his very loud insistent bay was new to me. My dogs either bark, howl, or sing. I have never had a baying dog. Since getting Jake, I have spoken with other Beagle "owners" and they have all told me the same thing; Beagles are stubborn and can be hard to train. They demand to have their way! Often in frustration over his refusal to listen to me, I would tell him, "I will NEVER adopt another Beagle as long as I live." He would look at me with his soulful eyes and I could tell he didn't believe one word I said.

Jake easily settled into his new home with his new pack mates. He enjoyed riding in the truck and loved to stick his head out the window. Nothing was funnier than watching Jake's floppy ears flap in the wind with a goofy smile on his face as we traveled down the road. He also loved our long walks and ran on his old short legs to keep up with the younger members of his pack. One corner of the couch was his and none of the dogs could push him off. If one of my foolish pups tried, he wasn't afraid to tell them where to go even if the dog was bigger, younger, and stronger than Jake. I couldn't even push him off his spot. He was the BOSS!

You could say Jake was influential with his pack. Troublemaker that he was, he taught all of his pack mates BAD Beagle habits. The worst trick was how to open the lower cabinets in my kitchen. Jake used his long nose to open the cabinet door and get at the garbage can. In all my years of living with dogs, no other dog had ever done this. I could not seem to break Jake of this very bad habit. (I guess I should be happy that his talents didn't include opening the fridge. A good friend has to keep hers closed with a chain, otherwise her dog will open it and help herself.) Now all the dogs are great at this trick and even teach new dogs how to get into the cabinets. Thanks to Jake, the cats also learned this new very bad habit.

However, it was not all bad. Jake became one of my teaching dogs. The Pet Paw-see spends time in classrooms teaching the kids how to be kind to animals. Jake loved to get dressed up in his red bow tie and go to school. He especially loved the little pre-school class we attended each spring. He was so gentle with the kids, probably because they would feed him treats and give him hugs. Jake hobbled into his last class at the golden age of 19 and enjoyed the undivided attention and love he got from the kids. His back legs were arthritic, and I knew that he wouldn't be around for any more classes. He surprised me and lived to year 20. Old and unable to climb stairs, each day with him was a gift. I told him every night before we went to bed how lucky I was to have him for just one more day. I knew that his days were short in number and I cherished every minute I spent with him.

I watched Jake closely during his last winter. I would dress him in his doggie coat and carry him out into the yard, then bring him quickly back inside. He had no tolerance for the cold anymore and would shiver after only a few minutes outside. He spent most of his last days sleeping and dreaming. I knew Jake's time was running out, but I wanted him to tell me when he was too tired to go on. He was on pain meds for the arthritis in his back legs and as long as he had a good appetite, I felt like he still had quality of life. If I let him, Jake would eat until he exploded. However, slowly he started to be less and less interested in food, even special canned food and hamburger. On his last weekend, he refused to eat at all, and I knew it was time to say goodbye. I told him it was ok to leave us, and he seemed to understand and face his last hours with dignity. As I sadly drove him to the vet clinic for the last time, I assured him that I definitely would take in another homeless Beagle someday. That seemed to make him happy and gave him permission to leave me.

Quietly, quickly, Jake crossed the Rainbow Bridge as I held him and told him how much I loved him. I look forward to giving a good home to another needy Beagle. I know that if I listen closely when the next homeless Beagle crosses my path, I will hear Jake baying with happiness and excitement. Being "owned" by a Beagle for almost seven years was a blessing. I feel so lucky to have had this sweet, stubborn dog as such a special part of my life. Sleep well, old boy! 🐾

never know what I am going to find when I open my front door. I have opened it to a few neighbor dogs at the food dish and even a pair of skunks fighting over the kitty crunchies. (I didn't have my contacts in and at first glance thought they were tuxedo kitties. I slammed the door quickly, but they still sprayed my house.) One day I even had a large male peacock with a gorgeous plume of colorful tail feathers hanging out on my porch. (I was able to find his owner. He had gotten out of his bird pen and wandered off.) I get many deer who come up to the house for the apple trees and have had some livestock wander over to munch on a fresh patch of grass.

Most of the time I see new or resident community cats who have heard of the open-all-night kitty café. I think the kitty hotline has my home address on a neon sign; all are welcome, three hots and a cot! Not exactly, but there is always a food dish, heated water bowl, and warm dry cat condos.

When I see a new kitty at my feeding station, I try to determine if they are feral, tame, or just scared. Miss Eve was one of these kitties. She showed up on my doorstep on a cold New Year's Eve night many years ago and stayed. It was obvious she had been an owned cat. When no one claimed her, I made her part of my menagerie. Miss Eve was a sweet quiet kitty that was happy to have found a loving home. She never told me where she came from, but I am glad she found safety at my house.

— Chapter 44 —
Chester the Collie?

Chester's story makes our hearts hurt!

How can any decent human being dump a tiny, helpless puppy by the side of the road in the middle of a Montana winter? It never ceases to amaze and horrify me how anyone can be so cruel. Thank goodness for the kind person who found him and brought this sweet puppy to our local animal shelter. It was the first week of January and the weather had been in the single digits during the day and below zero at night. This tiny, four-week old puppy was sick, starved, frozen, and near death when rescued.

The shelter workers did their best to help this little guy. They took him to their vet several times to address his many health issues. Lack of good nutrition and terrible intestinal problems would have to be dealt with first. The vet saw that he had no use of his back legs and wasn't sure if he would ever be able to use them. He couldn't walk and would just drag himself along using his front legs. The employees knew the shelter environment wasn't the best place for this sick little puppy so I was called and asked if I would take him into my home.

The shelter manager knew I had a soft spot in my heart for Collies in need and this pup appeared Collie-like. I didn't hesitate and picked up this tiny, ailing puppy after work one evening. He was a little doll but in very poor condition. I hoped that I could give him a safe, warm place to gain strength and heal his pint-sized body. I named him Chester and while I doubted he was a purebred Collie, it didn't matter. When I met him, it was love at first sight! He was precious!

Chester was such a sweet little guy, but it took a lot of good food, medication, and time to get him to the point where I felt he would make it. Everything just poured out of him as soon as he ate, and he was so weak I wasn't sure if he would live. We bonded quickly during those first scary days. In the early weeks of caring for him, I would come home from work not knowing if he would still be alive. I didn't know how I would handle it if he died. This sweet puppy had a larger-than-life spirit and seemed very content in my home.

Chester would tumble across the floor to be by my side and loved all the attention I gave him. Finally, after a lot of TLC he started to look good and even began to walk better. His sparse coat and little body filled in and he had more energy. The vet concluded he had been so malnourished that he had lost the use of his back legs. Happily, they were gaining strength and after a few weeks, it looked as though he would be ok. It was such a relief to know this precious little puppy would most likely live a normal life.

The first time Chester went with me to Petco for an adoption event caused the usual "feeding frenzy". Everyone who saw him wanted to adopt this little cutie. Chester was still getting stronger and wouldn't be adopted until he was a bit healthier, but I wanted to start to show him to potential adopters. He was such an adorable, playful little guy that it would have been hard not to fall in love with him. His sad story sickened all who heard it. Many people inquired about adopting Chester but only one couple actually filled out an application for him, even though they knew it would be a while before they could take Chester home. Ken and Darcy were out killing time while their two middle-school daughters were busy at a get-together in town, so they stopped at Petco to visit our animals. They wouldn't leave Chester's cage and played with him for over an hour. I really liked them and knew if their application looked good, they would be able to adopt Chester. They were willing to wait for however long until he was ready to come to their home and wanted to surprise their daughters. We kept in touch via email and I let them know he would be theirs in a few weeks.

Meanwhile I thought of a fun way to do the adoption and Ken and Darcy both agreed to go along. I brought little Chester to their house one afternoon and rang the bell. I had asked Ken and Darcy to have their two girls answer the door, which they did. When they answered, I told the girls that I had found this tiny puppy wandering in the neighborhood and asked if he was theirs. They said no, they had never seen him before. So, I asked them if they wanted him. (Ken and Darcy were in the background laughing over our conversation.) They both looked at their parents and asked but Mom and Dad said "NO." I told the girls "It's ok, I will take him to the shelter where he will probably find a good home." The girls' pleading became desperate while both parents continued to say "NO!" I agreed and told the girls that a puppy is a lot of work and maybe I should just leave. When I thought both would break out in tears, I handed them little Chester. The looks on their faces were priceless as they turned to their Mom and Dad to beg one last time. At this point, it was impossible to pretend anymore. While trying not to laugh we all broke down and told the girls that Chester was their new puppy. After the hysteria settled a bit, we introduced Chester to his new pack-mate, Foxy. She took to her little friend and taught him all about their backyard and the other house inhabitants, the resident cats. Chester was used to the cats from my house, fit in well, and quickly adjusted to his new home.

It has been about four years since Chester's adoption and he has grown into a huge dog. There is absolutely no Collie in him, he looks more like a Great Dane with his long legs and streamlined body.

Chester had found his *furrever* home and the few times I have seen him since, he still remembers me. I will never forget him and still can't fathom why someone thought it was better to drop this helpless, little puppy out in the middle of nowhere rather than taking the time to bring him to a shelter or rescue group. It's probably a good thing I don't know that person; I would have a difficult time being civil. I would want to ask them how they would feel if they were alone, cold, hungry, and scared, left out on the side of a road to die. 🐾🐾

Charlie the Cat was a Pet Paw-see foster kitty who came into our program when he was a senior. He was a beautiful flame point Siamese who loved everyone he met and even tolerated dogs.

During our Saturday adoption events at Petco, we would place him on a chair near our cages where he could greet the public. He never wandered away or was afraid when a dog wanted to sniff him. Most customers were amazed that he would calmly sit on his cushion and not run off, no matter how busy things were around him.

The volunteers taught Charlie how to walk with a harness and leash. He seemed to enjoy walking around the store visiting the fish and birds while patiently waiting for his furrever person. Charlie became the Petco greeter, saying meow (hello) to all that entered the store!

After several months, Charlie went to live with one of our senior people in a retirement home. He did great in his home for many years until he developed heart failure. Saying goodbye to this wonderful cat was difficult for his senior person and broke the hearts of the volunteers who came to love this unflappable kitty. We all miss Charlie but cherish the memory of this remarkable boy.

— Chapter 45 —
The Leftovers

What do we do with the ones nobody wants?

I am sure every shelter and rescue group has animals who are passed over for adoption time and time again. Maybe the animal is too old, unattractive, or has the personality of Attila the Hun and no one is interested in taking a chance on him or her. We get a lot of those kitties in the Pet Paw-see; sometimes it seems as though about one quarter of our cats seem unadoptable. Mostly it's because they don't get along with other cats, dogs, adults, kids, or in the case of a cat named Ribbon, absolutely ANYTHING THAT BREATHES AIR!

Ribbon was a beautiful, longhaired gray-and-white kitty who hated everything and everybody. Period! She spent most of a year and a half with us housed at Petco in the cat habitat or boarding clinics. We couldn't put her in a foster home because she had zero tolerance for anything she didn't like, and her dislikes changed with the weather. We would try to show her to the public during our adoption events but after a short while, she became almost dangerous towards the Petco customers and us. She would hiss, spit, and lash out at anyone who tried to talk to her, never mind pet her. A volunteer had to be stationed in front of her cage at Petco at all times during our adoption events, since we didn't want to incur any lawsuits against our rescue group. She acted more feral than most of the feral cats we have cared for over the years. But she was never a feral cat!

Many people saw her and commented on how stunning she was as she posed sweetly on her cat tree in the kitty habitat. Some people inquired about adopting her. While we wanted to find her a *furrever* home, we were afraid of her hurting someone due to her occasional schizophrenic behavior. Ribbon was unpredictable and scary. Even at the vet clinic, she flew into a rage at the slightest touch by the vet or the tech. The vet had to knock her out to examine and vaccinate her. And, just forget about clipping her nails! None of us wanted to attempt that task. Despite her very hostile behavior, we all loved Ribby and wanted to find her a *furrever* home. She could never go to a home with kids and we were afraid she would beat the tar out of a small dog. Even a large dog would be fair game for our sweet Ribby. In a fight, I would put my money on this cat!

At the time, she was one of the most difficult cats in our program and we were at a loss over what to do with her. We never put animals down to make room for others. Only when they are in pain or suffering and our vet thinks they have no quality of life left will we consider euthanasia. Ribbon was a young, healthy girl and we wanted the best for her, but she wasn't cooperating. For over a year, we were busy adopting out other cats and kittens while poor Ribby just languished in her suite at Petco. She was like the leftover dinner that sits in the fridge until green fuzzy stuff starts to grow on it and eventually the container and contents are thrown out. We felt bad for her but her issues with life were beyond our experience and we didn't know how to help her. One of the girls talked about getting a kitty psychologist in to see what was going on with Ribbon that made her so hostile. What we really needed was Jackson Galaxy, the host of *My Cat from Hell,* to spend some time with her but central Montana is quite far off the beaten path for him.

Each week we tried to befriend Ribbon, and she seemed responsive to our attention for a short while. Regrettably, after a few minutes she would turn into "Psycho Kitty" and try to kill one of us. We even moved her to the Pet Smart habitat thinking the new environment would help mellow her out a bit. It didn't really help that much; she was still dangerous, and we knew she had the potential to hurt someone. (Cat bites are no fun. Some volunteers have ended up at the emergency room when their hands or other body parts become infected from a bite.)

Unbeknownst to us, a gal had been watching Ribbon and visiting her at both store habitats. Amazingly, Clarissa filled out an application on Ribbon even after listening to our fears. She really wanted to try out Ribby in her home. We did a Pawsibility and crossed our fingers while Ribbon went to her new and maybe *furrever* home. Although she had a rough first week in her "maybe *furrever* home," she eventually settled down a bit. After about a month, Clarissa and her boyfriend, Adam, told us that Ribby was doing great so they completed the paperwork to adopt her. It has been a few years now and Ribbon is still in her home. We keep in touch with Clarissa and Adam (they are now Pet Paw-see volunteers and foster parents) hoping this is the final home for this gorgeous but difficult cat. Just goes to show you that sometimes even the green fuzzy leftovers are still worth saving.

Another cat labeled a "leftover" is Shadow. He is the male version of Ribbon only a bit worse. He acts as if he "mainlines" catnip each morning to get his engine started and then it is full speed ahead all day long. Shadow came to us as a tiny kitten. We adopted Shadow and after only a short time, he came back into our program because he was too aggressive. Once we got him back, he never calmed down. He would stalk his fellow kitty friends in the habitat and attack them for no reason. His wild behavior made it impossible to allow him out to play with the other cats.

Shadow played by himself only when the other cats were safely in their suites. He was so rough with the habitat residents that most of the kitties were afraid of him. We humans were afraid of him too. If he was sitting on a cat tree while anyone was in the habitat, he thought nothing of swiping at us with claws out, showing no mercy. It seemed he didn't know how to be gentle. We certainly didn't want him to live his life in a cage, even though the habitat cages are pretty nice. He needed a home where he could run, leap, and tackle while not hurting his people or other animals. That hope was fading fast. He had been in our program for over a year when one of our volunteers, Lisa, said she would take him home with her on a trial run. She had a beautiful outdoor catio and we hoped this would give him a place to diffuse some of his aggression.

Lisa has her own cats, all rescues, and is our guru on kitty behavior. When anyone of us has a cat issue, we call Lisa. Once she got him into a carrier, Lisa took Shadow home and introduced him to her resident Alpha cat, Stanley. Stanley likes to be the top dog (or cat) in his world. We hoped he would be able to take Shadow down a few notches. It worked! Stanley has taught Shadow that he is no longer king of the world. He also learned how to play nice, at least "nice" for Shadow.

Shadow loved the catio, spent most of the time outside. The catio seemed to have helped him a lot. Lisa, who has said many times "I am NOT adopting Shadow", will likely keep him *furrever*. We are calling her an "Unwilling Foster Failure" since she had NO intention of giving him a permanent home. But sometimes life has a way of surprising us and those of us in rescue end up with another "leftover". Even though Shadow has done very well at Lisa's house, he is still not adoptable to a typical home. Lisa is afraid of the liability of finding him a real home. He is an accident waiting to happen. In the wrong situation, he would likely hurt someone and be put down. Reluctantly, she filled out the paperwork to adopt Shadow. He is now a very happy cat in his *furrever* home and to us, that spells success!

P.S. Shadow has been renamed Kylo.

One of the largest problems we have with "leftovers" are the number of black cats we get into our program. We often seem to have close to a dozen black or mainly black cats. To us they are beautiful, but most people pass right over them for the more colorful calicos, Siamese, or orange tabbies. And, we seem to go through streaks when all we get are black kitties. The volunteers always try to highlight their beauty, but most potential adopters don't seem to be interested. I watch people when they come into Petco and look down the row of cages at our cats. They seem to subconsciously walk right by the cages with black kitties. We try to "bling" them up a bit by putting fancy, colorful collars on them and sometimes it works, but have heard the same from other shelters and rescues, the black animals are the hardest to adopt. (I have heard about this same problem with black dogs, but I have been very lucky with the black dogs that I have fostered.)

Years ago, we had so many black cats that we advertised a black cat adoption event at Petco. We called the event "White Tie, Black Cat Adoption Day". Lisa (of the Shadow fame) crocheted white ties for each of the cats and we handed out sparkling non-alcoholic champagne to our guests. One of the volunteers printed cute signs for the cages with sayings on how wonderful black cats are but nothing seemed to help. We got NO adoptions that weekend, which was discouraging.

Even the longhaired black cats are passed over. We recently had a longhaired black cat who came into our program with horrible mats. Claire had to be completely shaved; the mats were too close to her skin to brush out, so the groomer gave her a very cute lion cut. She left the hair on her head, tip of her tail, and feet au naturel except for a good brushing. The groomer clipped the coat on her body very short. She looked spectacular and got a lot of attention. Sadly, it took her awful condition to result in her getting any notice at all. Besides that, she was a lovely kitty. Claire had everything going for her except the color of her coat. Adopting her should have been a no-brainer, but very few people are interested in black cats.

We always celebrate when we adopt out a black kitty. They get the short end of the stick through no fault of their own, just because of the color of their coat. It's not fair to these wonderful kitties but we will keep on trying to find homes for our precious "leftovers."

I rish, a large red male kitty, was one of several community cats who I fed and cared for at my house. These cats typically show up one day and decide that it's not a bad place to hang out. There is always food, fresh water, and a nice comfy cat condo for lounging. The best part is that no one bothers them or chases them off. They may be domestic or feral and, by chance, happen upon my house. Maybe the cat had been someone's pet at one time, was dumped, and has had to learn to survive. These cats often show up with scarred faces and nervous eyes waiting for a human to hurt them again.

I don't know where Irish came from or his story, but I started to notice that a new cat was hanging around my front porch. I never have a problem with newcomers and want them to feel safe. Irish was wary at first but over time, he learned that I wouldn't hurt him. I used to watch him as he ate and eventually he got used to me spying on him through the window. He would sleep in the cat baskets on the porch and only jumped up if I opened the front door. We even held conversations through the screen door; he seemed to accept the fact that I lived here too.

After many months of slowly interacting with Irish and gaining his trust, he was gone. It's been over a year since I have seen him and while I have had cats come back after time away, I am doubtful I will see him again. This special boy is missed, and I pray he has not come to any harm. I love my community cats and worry about them. Most are not tamable but if I can offer them a bit of comfort and safety, Even though he is gone, I feel as though I have helped one more unwanted animal live a better life. Maybe someday I will see you again big guy!

— Chapter 46 —
The Good Old Days

Hard to remember when life was so easy!

I was reminiscing recently about the good old days, when my pet family consisted of only one dog. Cappi was a very smart, well mannered Cocker Spaniel that I could take anywhere. He seemed able to read my mind and could understand an amazing number of words and commands. Cappi fit into my lifestyle effortlessly. I made very few adjustments for him even when I traveled. He was a very undemanding companion and friend and I loved the time we spent together.

I am now involved with animal rescue and have eight dogs, four of my own and four foster dogs. I can't believe how things have changed. It's funny though, the changes have been in small adjustments here and there until I stand back and wonder how they all happened. One of the lifestyle adjustments I've noticed is my cooking habits. I used to love to spend cold winter days baking bread or cookies. In the good old days, I used to set my kitchen timer to whatever the recipe recommended. For instance, if it said bake for 45 minutes, that's when I set the timer to go off. When it buzzed, I would remove a tray of cookies, a cake, or a loaf of bread. Now I set the timer for at least five minutes sooner than the recipe recommends. That's how long it takes me to negotiate around at least two fifty-pound Huskies, one seventy-pound Collie and a couple of Cocker Spaniels to get to the oven.

Although I have several other very nice rooms in my house, when I am cooking, the dogs feel the need to sprawl out under my feet on the kitchen floor. I used to trip over only one small Cocker Spaniel and he never caused me to burn anything. Now I really have to plan my meals around the dogs, literally. I actually cooked an entire Thanksgiving dinner several years ago with six dogs under my feet. They looked so sweet and innocent sleeping on the floor, but I know that their noses were on high alert waiting for me to trip and drop some food. Heaven forbid that I fell with a tray of cookies. It would be like dropping a pork chop into a tank of hungry piranhas. I know I would come up missing body parts!

My gift giving and receiving has also changed drastically since my single-dog days. I loved to pick out gifts for my friends that they would enjoy. Since my canine family has increased from one to eight dogs, I no longer give any gifts. After shelling out my paycheck for dog food and vet bills, I can't afford them. (My close friends understand!) The gifts I get from the friends I still have are nothing like those I used to get. I used to receive fun gifts like perfume, books, or clothes. They would come wrapped in pretty paper covered in flowers or butterflies. Now my friends give me dog food instead of perfume. Besides, it's never wrapped. It is kind of hard to wrap a fifty-pound bag of dog chow. However, if I do get a real gift it comes wrapped in paper covered with dogs. The butterflies and flowers are gone. Moreover, the attached cards always have a dog wishing me a Happy Birthday or a Merry Christmas.

It really saddened me recently when I realized the days of receiving "fun" gifts were long gone. I had my fears validated when a friend stopped at my office one afternoon in November to give me an early Christmas gift. I had been telling her how difficult it was scooping dog poop after work in the winter months since it is dark when I get home. She showed up with a very nice high-beam headlamp to make my nightly poop scooping easier. Of course, it came in a very pretty gift bag covered with, you guessed it, DOGS! I keep trying to figure out when my life changed from perfume and clothes to dog chow and poop retrieval devices. Oh well, it's the thought that counts, and I really appreciated that gift.

I remember hearing friends talk about their pre-children days and the things they no longer were able to do once they had kids. I can relate! In my single dog days, I loved to have people over to my house. I realized recently that I don't do that anymore. The only people I dare to have over are people with dogs and they have to have more than one dog. People with only one dog often stand in shock at the sight of eight boisterous dogs running at breakneck speeds around the yard, or worse, in their direction, to greet them with their giant, muddy paws. I do make the exception for a dear friend, Sue, who has only one dog, a sweet quiet German Shepherd. Nevertheless, she is very understanding and seems to love the chaos!

I still remember how I felt when I decided to adopt my third dog I really debated this decision and wondered if three was too many. At that time, I had two Cocker Spaniels. Cappi was getting very old and I had adopted another Cocker Spaniel named Sophie to keep him company. I was worried about how Sophie would feel when Cappi finally passed on, so I found my third Cocker, Libby Loo, at the shelter. I wondered what people would think if they came over and saw THREE dogs running around my house. Now I laugh when I think of those days. I no longer really care what people think about my large dog family. However, I tend to mumble something unintelligible when someone asks how many dogs I have. "A houseful" isn't really a number, which is a good thing. The truth is too scary! 🐾🐾

*O*ne very cold winter day the family who had adopted Chester called to tell me about a sad, thin dog they had found. The poor old guy was limping along a highway near their home and looked to be in very bad condition. When they got him to their house, he ate as if he was starving. The poor dog was so beat up that he could hardly walk.

Ken and Darcy asked me for help with this sweet old guy, so I raced up to their place in Power, Montana, to help. He looked like he had been on his own for quite a while, probably dumped. He was so weak that I had to carry him to my truck but assured them that he would get proper vet care. If no one claimed him, I knew he would find a safe place with our rescue group for whatever time he had left. In the meantime, we put up "found" posters, left his description at the shelter, and waited to see if anyone was searching for him.

Jo Anne, my friend and fellow rescuer, took him in to foster and named him Timber. He did great in her home and it was apparent that he was a well-trained dog. Even though we doubted that a dog this old was adoptable, Jo Anne still took him to Petco where he enjoyed riding around in a grocery cart greeting the customers. It looked like no one was going to claim him when one day out of the blue, Jo Anne got a call. Timber's owner had seen our "found" poster in a convenience store in Power. She was overjoyed that he was safe. Apparently, he had wandered off her ranch and walked about twelve miles to where he was found. Her fear was that coyotes or the weather had killed him. He was a sixteen-year-old Australian Kelpie and one of the best ranch dogs she had ever had; he could do the work of three other dogs in his younger days. He was retired from ranch work but was still very much loved. We were thrilled to have been able to unite this wonderful old dog with his person.

— Chapter 47 —
You Can't Pay Me Enough To Do This!

There has got to be a better way to spend my time off!

It is probably a good thing I am a volunteer and not paid, because I would never do some of the stuff I do for money, or if I did, I would want a LARGE raise. I don't know how it happened, but I became known as the "gal who will crawl under trailers to find kittens." We get many calls from trailer park residents who need our assistance helping litters of kittens spotted living under their homes. The homeowners see the mommas with babies and ask us to help them. For a while, I was the only one who would dare crawl under the trailers to retrieve kittens. Thankfully, we now have another crazy person, Andrew, a Pet Paw-see volunteer who will also do this dirty deed.

My first attempt at trailer spelunking was in my street clothes with a hand-held flashlight. BIG MISTAKE! It is typically very filthy under the trailers with everything from common trash, mud, spiders, as well as the occasional dead animal. Not pretty! Several years ago, we had gotten a call that a badly injured kitty lived under a trailer and we wanted to help her out. While crawling through a very dark and dusty place I found two mummified cats who had been dead a long time but neither fit the description of the cat we were trying to help. Begrudgingly, I crawled around to check out the four corners of the mobile home with no luck and finally had to get out. I remember coughing for days afterwards from all the dust and dirt I had inhaled. We had to come up with another plan or my health would suffer. This one was bad. Unfortunately, I would eventually crawl under worse trailers. This one was just a gentle warm-up for those that came later in my "career".

Well, this first trailer adventure earned me some unwanted fame, which is most likely one of the reasons I am still single. But, that's another story! While we had no luck with the kitty we were looking for that day, we did eventually capture her to give her medical help. She appeared to have had her two back legs caught in a trap (they are legal in Montana) and both were severely damaged. She couldn't use them and had to pull herself around using her front elbows. She is now a house kitty, no more pulling herself around trying to find food and shelter outside in the cold.

I never go under a trailer by myself. My greatest fear is to crawl under a trailer, get stuck, and have no one miss me. I always have a spotter, mainly my fellow cat-rescuer and friend, Les. Her job was to talk to me constantly to keep me from freaking out from claustrophobia. I am a little claustrophobic and some of these trailers have very little clearance between the ground and the trailer's underside. Les would stay outside and talk to me. It was very important that she keep me focused on the task ahead and not on my surroundings. All I heard from Les was what a wonderful, kind, brave, super-duper person I was and what an awesome job I was doing. Boy was this good for my self-esteem! Les missed her true calling in life; she should have been a motivational speaker. She is very encouraging mainly because, if I ran out screaming, she would have had to take my place.

I quickly learned to pack well for these "under the trailer" excursions. I grabbed a disposable haz-mat suit from my office, my respirator, gloves, hoodie, booties, and a headlamp. (I sometimes need these items for the work I do in my Day Job. They have come in very handy for my after-work exploits.) With the haz-mat suit and accessories I could stay a bit cleaner and wouldn't have to worry that I had spiders or other bugs on my clothes or in my hair while driving home. That's a big deal because while I don't hate spiders or bugs, I get the willies if I know they are crawling on me! Not safe for driving!

One of my next jaunts under a trailer was not too bad either. We got a call about a momma cat and three kittens, all of which we easily found and brought into our program. The owner of the trailer was very helpful and appreciative. The trailer had plenty of room to negotiate and I didn't see a single spider. It was also relatively clean and dry. I was able to grab one kitty at a time, crawl over to Les with each baby, and then dive back in for the next one. Piece of cake!

The trailer that still gives me nightmares, even though it was years ago, was located in a very run-down mobile home park. These trailers were falling apart with trash strewn about in their small yards. It was a sad place for humans and cats, and I just wanted to get in and out as fast as possible. In addition, it was early spring and the weather in Montana tends to be a bit bipolar. Mother Nature throws everything at you: rain, sleet, snow, and wind, often at the same time. Not the best of circumstances but we wanted the kittens we were told lived under the trailer. Les and I showed up at the trailer and asked the owner if he would remove a portion of the skirting so I could crawl under. He was less than helpful as we looked at the mess I would have to crawl through to get the kittens. He begrudgingly made a small opening for me amongst the mud, garbage, and dog poop and then went back inside where it was warm and dry. I almost lost my lunch knowing I had to get into that slop. Les was at her best encouraging me as I stooped down to belly crawl beneath the trailer. The last words I said to Les were something to the effect of "Don't tell me if you see any spiders or snakes or I will freak out". To her credit, she didn't tell me 'till weeks later what she saw crawling on me.

This trailer had little to no headroom; I was literally on my stomach with my back touching the flooring of the trailer as I pulled myself along with my arms. While I am not a big person, there was scarcely any room for me to maneuver. But, I was determined to help those kittens, if they were still there. I never did find them after crawling throughout the entire underside of the trailer. I eventually got out; soaking wet and covered in mud and dog poop. I felt that I should autoclave my entire body since I knew a shower would never remove all the filth I slithered through that day. Typically, I can throw my suit, gloves, and booties in the washer and they are good to go for the next excursion. Not this time. They went into the garbage. I didn't want whatever was on them to go into my washer. Happily, we were able to trap the kittens at another time and get them to a safe foster home. Even writing this makes me cringe as it brings back the memories of how disgusting I felt after that misadventure. "Gross" doesn't do it justice. This was a trailer from hell!

This past year I had the equally "pleasant" experience of going into two abandoned trailers where hoarders had accumulated numerous cats. Both residents had vacated the homes due to poor health. Our rescue group got a call from the trailer owners to help the animals before the trailers were hauled off site to be demolished. Surprisingly, the cats at the first trailer were very friendly and well fed. We were able to get them out of the trailer and into our foster program where they quickly found great homes. Being in that trailer was something I had never before experienced; mountains of cat feces, human trash, and urine-covered EVERYTHING. It made me wish I were back at the previous "Gross" trailer in the mud and other filth. (Not really, but time heals all wounds and dulls the memory.) I had never seen hoarding up close and personal, and this was a huge wake-up call.

We needed to set traps inside this first trailer to catch any remaining kitties before the trailer was hauled away for disposal. There was so much trash in the trailer where kitties could hide that we were afraid we would miss some. There was also little room on the floor to set a trap, never mind walk around. It took every ounce of strength in me to move the mountains of garbage and cat poop to make a flat surface for the traps. We did eventually get all of the kitties out of that trailer to a safe place and found them good homes through the Pet Paw-see.

The second trailer made the first one look like a picnic. It had been purchased sight unseen by someone who refurbishes and then sells the trailers. The buyer was appalled at the terrible condition of his new acquisition and asked the Pet Paw-see to remove the cats. But, the new owner wouldn't let anyone inside the trailer without a respirator. He didn't want to be sued if we got sick. I got a call from Les asking me if I would be willing to lend her my respirator. I told her it's like lending someone your underwear, it would be better if I just went in. I could hear the sigh of relief from her as she agreed to help me by staying outside and sending me warm wishes and encouraging words. So once again, I ended up donning my haz-mat suit and accessories for the trek into this trailer.

The description of what I saw in this trailer was beyond words. The windows had been broken out, so cats were coming and going freely. We had set traps outside but wanted to find animals left inside the trailer. I was looking for sick or injured cats who needed help. We had an idea of how many cats this lady owned and wanted to get all of them out and to a safe foster home. The junk in the trailer was piled so high that I had to crawl on top of it and move mountains of stuff around to search for cats. I never saw the floor; garbage covered every square foot. Even through my respirator, I gagged as I opened the refrigerator and cupboards to look for animals. The foul smell was so pervasive it almost knocked me over. When I was certain no injured cats were inside the trailer I gladly left, we set traps for the remaining ones outside. I also set a motion detection camera inside the trailer to see what was going on when no one was there. There was a good chance that a cat or two was hiding under the trash somewhere and we didn't want to miss it.

We ended up trapping and helping about a dozen cats from this trailer. All of the cats were tame and very friendly, which made them easy to adopt. Coincidentally, this trailer was across the road from the trailer from hell I had crawled under years before.

I started this story saying I would never do this for pay. There is not enough pay in the world for some types of work. When you are paid for nasty stuff like this, you tend to get annoyed at the little you feel you make versus the discomfort it entails. Volunteers have no expectation of monetary rewards, so we just grin and bear it! What does this say about us? 🐱🐱

Big Red was a stray Golden Retriever found in Sand Coulee, a small rural community east of Great Falls, Montana. The local people had been feeding him, but his obvious health issues were a deterrent to anyone wanting to keep him. Someone called the Pet Paw-see for help, so we took in this extremely overweight and mostly hairless dog.

A vet visit and bloodwork showed that he had a severe thyroid problem, but luckily, meds for this are inexpensive. Big Red had large hairless areas all over his body and his tail was completely bald. It looked like a long skinny rat-tail. His skin was also a mess with dry, scaly patches. His condition was so bad that the vet warned us his coat might never grow back.

Despite his awful appearance, he was a sweetheart of a dog, very affectionate and playful. He had a wonderful outgoing personality that made it impossible to not fall in love with him. His great personality convinced his new person to adopt him, even before his hair grew back. In his new home, he slowly lost the weight and his skin and coat improved greatly. Big Red's before and after pictures don't look like the same dog. It was an amazing transformation! Success stories like Big Red's give us the strength to take on the more challenging animals.

— Chapter 48 —
Kitten Sitter!

Animals will never cease to amaze me.

I have had various species of animals in my home, all of them rescues of some kind. This includes a few rescued bunnies. I enjoy them and their funny antics and am happy to help these sweet critters. But, up until recently I never put different species in the same living space with each other, aside from housing guinea pigs with a bunny or two. Bunnies and guinea pigs get along great. They can live together and will share the same food and shelter. During the warmer months, I have housed my rescued bunny and guinea pig outside in a large, secure, covered dog kennel with hideouts for sleeping and straw bales for sunning. However, they come inside during the colder weather. This year I happened to have a litter of foster kittens when the weather got too cold for my guinea pig, Twix, and my bunny, Boo, to live outside anymore. Twix went into a large aquarium but I hated to put the bunny in a cage so I let him loose in my foster cat room and watched to make sure there would be no issues. Boo is a very large bunny, three times as big as the tiny kittens were when they first met, and I was afraid he might hurt them. He was curious but very gentle and left them alone.

The kittens were more annoying to the bunny than Boo was to them. They wanted to chase him and bat at his floppy ears. He tolerated it and never got aggressive with them. Boo was a very good surrogate dad to the kittens and seemed to like his little friends. After a few days of watching, I realized that Boo loved the company. It was hysterical to watch the kittens and bunny chase each other through the cat tunnel and around the room. The kittens also loved to cuddle with their big friend. I would go into their room to find the bunny and kittens asleep together in their basket. Most often, the kittens were piled on top of Boo, but he didn't seem to mind. Their antics got even funnier when I bought a cat tree for the kitty babies. Boo thought the new toy was for him too. He would perch on the bottom level while his little friends jumped onto the top of the tower. Boo surprised me one day while I watched as he and his two little friends enjoyed a breakfast of kitten kibble. It was hysterical to see the three of them crunching away together at the food bowl. Amazingly, Boo seemed to like their food.

It was bittersweet when I was finally able to find homes for Boo's two little roommates. He seemed to be sad without his kittens, and since they have been gone, I haven't seen him run in the tunnel or sit on the cat tree. He hangs out in his basket and looks blue. Although, it is hard to see much expression in his face, he appears to be depressed without their company. It's not kitten season in Montana for another few months so Boo may have to be content with his guinea pig friend, Twix, for a roommate. (Twix lives in his own cage during the winter since he isn't box trained, while Boo is pretty good at using his litter box.) Although Twix was a great companion in the dog kennel, he doesn't like to run and play like a couple of rowdy kittens. I told Boo I would get more kittens for him to baby sit but sadly, he will have to wait until spring.

P.S. Since baby-sitting his first litter of kittens, Boo has had two more litters to co-foster with me. The last litter had two semi-feral kittens. I give him much of the credit for helping me tame them down and turn them into cuddly, purring, adoptable kitties. 🐱🐱

Daisy, a yellow lab, had lived in a shelter in a neighboring city for almost three years. She got lots of love from the shelter workers but needed her own home. She came to live with me for the short time it took to find her a furrever home. This was years ago, and my wish is that Daisy is now old and gray and being spoiled by her people. She deserved the good life!

Hunter was a sweet tabby that lived at a construction site on Malmstrom Air Force Base. Construction to build more base housing was underway and Hunter found his safe place in the contractor's job trailer. A military family that relocated to another air force base likely owned him. Sadly, Hunter was not included in the move. It appeared he was left behind and had to fend for himself.

The construction workers kept him supplied with cat crunchies and Hunter paid for his keep by performing rodent control duties. Unfortunately, once the project was over, Hunter was again out of a job and out of a home. One of the inspectors knew me and asked if we could take this very friendly cat into the Pet Paw-see foster program. It didn't take long to find this hard-working tabby a furrever home.

— Chapter 49 —
Thanks Foster Mom!

This is a thank you to all the Foster Moms (and Dads) out there.

Thanks, Foster Mom, for looking beyond my dirty, matted coat and seeing a beautiful animal in need of help.

Thanks, Foster Mom, for not being afraid of my unfriendly, cowering behavior. You know I'm not mean; I am just scared and yearning for love.

Thanks, Foster Mom, for taking a chance on me by bringing me into your home when no one else saw my worth.

Thanks, Foster Mom, for spending your hard-earned money at the vet to make me healthy. I wish I could tell you how great it is to feel good again.

Thanks, Foster Mom, for going without sleep to give me comfort when my past wakes me up in the night.

Thanks, Foster Mom, for taking time away from your other pets to be with me.

Thanks, Foster Mom, for your infinite patience. I know that I wasn't easy and screwed up often, but you loved me anyway.

Thanks, Foster Mom, for forgiving me when I ruined something of yours. I didn't do it to be bad; I just never learned manners or how to tell right from wrong.

Thanks, Foster Mom, after crying, "I can't do this anymore. It's just too hard and I'm tired," you took one look at me, allowed me into your life, and let me steal your heart, knowing that you couldn't turn your back on me.

Thanks, Foster Mom, I know that if you didn't have all of us rescues, you would have more money, more time, more sleep, and maybe even let friends come to visit at your house.

Thanks, Foster Mom, for the endless phone calls to potential adopters. You never gave up trying to find me the *purrfect* home.

Thanks, Foster Mom, for being my voice when no one would listen to mine.

And lastly, Thanks, Foster Mom, for your unselfish gift of tearfully watching your heart walk out the door as I left for my new life, happy in the arms of my *furrever* person. 🐾

U nfortunately, some people have to give up their pets when they go into a nursing home or retirement facility. The Pet Paw-see has taken in many cats and dogs from their elderly owners during these heart-breaking times. (It is very important to make arrangements for your pets before a crises or emergency forces a hasty decision.) Often family members are not able or willing to take in a pet and it ends up at the shelter, sad and confused.

Sparky's elderly owner had to move to a nursing home and her daughters were worried about what would happen to their mother's little dog. The Pet Paw-see took this precious Yorkie mix into our program and in no time at all she found a purrfect couple to call her own.

Gladly, some retirement and assisted-living facilities allow pets. Libby was one of my foster kitties until she went to live in a retirement home with a wonderful woman. Sometimes the gray tabbies are as hard to place as the black cats. People seem to overlook them. However, Libby's friendly personality easily won her a loving home.

Retirement homes or assisted living facilities are not ideal for every cat. But many mature, mellow kitties find the atmosphere just purrfect for their temperament. While an active kitten wouldn't work well, a more stable cat can give a lonely person a reason to get up in the morning. Many of our cats offer devotion and companionship to our elderly neighbors and in return get undivided attention and continuous love. We have seen the magic over and over again when we place a senior cat with a senior person. It gives us immense joy to know that our cat rescue program can bring happiness to someone that needs it in his or her golden years.

— Chapter 50 —

Is It Time?

Most pet-owners struggle with this question and the answer is always difficult!

When do we say goodbye? This is the hardest part of owning and loving an animal. I am struggling with this question as I write this story. Last week I had to put down one of my cherished old dogs. Riley was fifteen, blind, partially deaf, and I felt he was also suffering from a bit of dementia. While all those aliments are difficult, he was not in pain. He still enjoyed eating and loved to snuggle when I held him. I had to watch him closely when he went outside to make sure he didn't get too chilled. In his later months, Riley had trouble finding the doggie door, so I had to be there to pick him up and bring him inside to his warm couch. I would also stand near him while he ate so that none of the other dogs would push him away to snatch his food. Despite this, he still seemed to enjoy life. His tail wagged constantly when he was exploring his backyard and he responded to my voice. He didn't appear to be in any discomfort that I could see, and I wanted to give him as much time as possible with his pals and me. Sadly, when he started to refuse food, even his favorite foods, I knew the end was near.

What I hoped for was to have him whisper in my ear that he was too tired to continue and wanted to join his fellow pack-mates at the Rainbow Bridge, but he relied on me to make that very difficult decision for him. What a horrible decision to have to make for a dear pet! It doesn't matter if it's a cat, dog, bunny, horse, or parakeet. If the animal has spent time in our life and grabbed ahold of our heart, it will break when we have to say goodbye.

My wish is to know the exact moment when life becomes too much for my sweet pets and then quickly let them go. I don't want to be too hasty and rob them of more good days with me. And I never want them to suffer even one minute if I can ease the pain. Most often, it is a battle between my head and my heart. I always wish they would just fade away quietly in their sleep so I wouldn't have to make that heart-rending decision but that rarely, if ever happens. My head says they are failing, and I need to let them go but my heart can't stand the thought of taking that final drive to the vet's office and holding them till they breathe their last. Usually when I have said my farewell and they are gone, I know I have done the right thing, but it is NEVER easy. I had a vet tell me once, years ago, that letting them go is the final gift of love we can give to our beloved pets. I have repeated that many times to myself and to friends. The pain of their loss is the price we pay for a lifetime of their love and companionship. It's true, but when that pain is right in front of us and we are hugging them one last time, it seems too much for most of us to bear.

It's at that time, once we have said goodbye that I often wonder where the time has gone. How did eight, or ten, or fifteen years go by so quickly? Why didn't I cuddle that animal one more time and not be so quick to be frustrated with him for his transgressions? Why didn't I get down on the floor for one more hug and not worry that the carpet needed vacuuming, or the dishes needed to be washed? Why didn't I take the time for one more walk with her on a beautiful evening instead of wanting to kick back and read or watch TV? And it seems as though right after my final goodbye that I start to beat myself up. Maybe I didn't do enough or see his or her struggles. Why didn't I call this vet or try this treatment? I always feel as though in some way that I have failed my precious friend. I torment myself with those questions and don't know the answers. I know we all get so busy just trying to live life and sometimes forget about these amazing creatures that have chosen to spend their days with us. Our pets' lives seem to revolve around their people and they always seem grateful for any time bestowed on them. I only pray that I have given them the best that I have; they deserve it. They have certainly given me their best.

As I write this, my tears are covering the keyboard. The loss of Riley is very fresh in my heart, but even worse is that later today I have to drive another old dog to the vet for our final goodbye. Harli's heart is failing and the medications the vet tried haven't made an improvement. It's gotten to the point where it is more loving to let her go than keep her around to get worse and suffer. Sweet Harli has been my very special companion for almost thirteen years. I still struggle with the question of "Is it time?" but know in my heart that I am giving this precious friend the last gift I have. I am giving her my broken heart to hold while she crosses the Rainbow Bridge! 🐾🐾

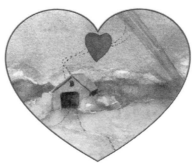

Kittens born to feral moms (community kitties) are tamable if they get lots of hands-on human attention while they are still small. The Pet Paw-see has taken in hundreds of feral kittens and successfully tamed them over the years. Adults are a lot harder to tame. Typically, we spay or neuter the adults and allow them to return to their colonies.

Tic Tac, Tigger, and Jessie were a litter of tiny babies the Pet Paw-see took in before we were a registered non-profit group. They were feral kittens but tamed down quickly with lots of love and human interaction. The kitties eventually found their furrever homes.

Precious mom Lily was dumped out in the country. Luckily, she found her way to a safe barn to have her kittens. The Pet Paw-see heard about their plight and this little family became my foster kids. Lily was semi-feral but with lots of love, she was tamed down. She may have been somebody's house or barn cat at one time but became very wary of humans. Her kittens were young enough to overcome their feral start in life and became domesticated easily. Eventually Lily, Blossom, Jett, and Danny Boy found furrever homes.

Sweet little Brodie and his family were my foster kids until they were old enough to be adopted. They were born to a feral mother but with lots of play time with me, their foster mom, they quickly tamed down and became lovable house kittens. Two of the kittens were adopted to the same person. Adopting two kittens at a time often works well because they tend to play together instead of hoping their adopted person is their personal play toy. But, sometimes it does double or triple the mayhem in their new home.

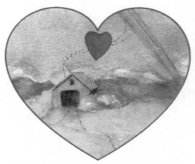

S adie Gray and her four kittens were my very first Pet Paw-see foster family. They found their way to our local animal shelter while we were still a very young rescue group, without a name or website and with no non-profit status. Since we had few animals of our own, we took them into our fledgling rescue program.

At that time, the Pet Paw-see Rescue Group had few options for showing our animals to the public. We relied on word-of-mouth to advertise our cats and dogs for adoption. Sadie's four kittens, Sugar, Spice, Peanut, and Espresso all found great homes, but no one wanted momma. I adopted her and after over twelve years, she still lives with me.

Three adorable tuxies were a trio of long-haired black and white kittens that ended up with me. When I took them in, they had been living in a chicken coop and eating next to their fowl friends. Not too good for young growing babies. The kittens were semi feral but young enough to tame down. I dropped all three at our vet clinic and told the receptionist that the three boys needed the usual kitten checkup, worming etc. The vet called me back a while later to tell me to "Keep my day job". The kittens were all females! Ok, so I am not great at telling the difference between very young male and female kittens!

Tuxie, Butler, and Checkers were named while I thought they were boys and I didn't want to rename them. Potential adopters laughed when I told them this story and fell in love with these three precious loving kittens. It took little time to place all three girls in great homes. 🐾

Chapter 51

Be Careful What I Wish For!

How I began my "career" in the crazy world of animal rescue.

My wonderful friend and first editor, Nancy, suggested I write a chapter on how I got started in my "career" of animal rescue. As I said in the beginning of PawPrints, I always had a burning desire to help animals in need, even from a very young age. Animals fascinated me and I felt deep compassion for them. Helping animals came naturally to me even though I had no clue how I could make any real difference. I always knew in my heart that "someday" I would dedicate more of my time and energy to making a difference for hurting animals on a larger scale than just baking a batch of brownies for a random bake sale or helping with a rummage sale for the local animal shelter. I knew deep down there was more out there for me to do, but I never knew how to put my "wishes" into action.

In 1998 I moved to Great Falls, Montana to start a new job. I didn't know anyone when I got to Great Falls and while I enjoyed the people at my new workplace, I didn't hang out with them; they were busy with their lives and families. My lifestyle at that time was low-key and a bit boring, but that was ok with me.

After buying and settling into my new house in Vaughn, a small community a few miles north of Great Falls, I heard about a volunteer group that raised money for the local animal shelter. I gladly joined it and helped at their fundraisers. It was fun and rewarding but I still wished there was more I could do.

For the first few years in my new home I spent most of my free time working around the house and enjoying my two Cocker Spaniels, Cappi and Sophie. The three of us also spent my days off exploring our new home in east central Montana. The dogs had a blast swimming in the nearby rivers and streams or hiking over hundreds of acres of prairie. I was used to living on the mountainous west side of the Continental Divide and had spent many years surrounded by forests. The east side consists of rolling hills with little forested areas. It was an adventure learning about this part of Montana with my two best doggie friends.

My "wishes" to help animals on a larger scale were realized when the Camp Collie saga began in November 2002. I read about the Collies and other animals confiscated at the Canadian/U.S. border and felt that I needed to do something. As I wrote earlier, I was very reluctant to drive an hour north to Shelby to care for them but the nagging voice in my head wouldn't let me forget about these animals. I am so glad that I finally decided to take the long drive to the Shelby Fairgrounds to help the cats and dogs held as evidence in that cruelty trial. It certainly changed my life and catapulted me into the "Crazy World of Animal Rescue."

When the nine months of caring for the Camp Collie dogs and cats ended, I was on fire to continue in animal rescue. I knew that I was born for this work. While it was very hard physically and emotionally, I loved seeing the great outcomes in the lives of the animals. Experiencing a victory when a previously abused or neglected animal found a loving *furrever* home gave me the strength to continue.

A year after Camp Collie was over there was another large puppy mill seizure in a nearby county. There were fewer dogs this time, about 100, but it was still a lot of work to care for them. (The Camp Collie seizure had about 178 dogs and 12 cats.) Each Saturday and Sunday I drove about two hours away to the temporary shelter and not surprisingly, fell in love with the dogs there. The confiscation of and care for these animals only lasted about three months. Due to lack of funds and little interest from the county government to prosecute, most of the dogs went back to their owners. Luckily, we were able to save some of the dogs the owners didn't want any more. I was fortunate to be able to take the six "Coyote Puppies" into my home for potential adoption, but was heartbroken that many dogs couldn't be helped. To this day, almost fifteen years later, I still grieve over this sad ending.

For a few months, I spent time trying to find homes for the coyote puppies but had very little luck. As I wrote earlier, they looked and acted as though they had wild coyote in their heritage, which made them unadoptable within city limits. Their lineage didn't matter to me; they brought me so much joy. After work each evening, I would sit with them as they clamored in my lap for attention. Their sweet kisses and silly antics made me laugh no matter how tough my day had been. Having these little cuties around was the perfect balm for my broken heart over the ones we had to leave behind.

During the many months of caring for the dogs and cats from both animal seizures, I met wonderful people who had passions similar to mine. They LOVED animals and were willing to jump in to help whenever needed. I kept in touch with many of my new friends and through them I learned about a large "M*A*S*H-style" spay/neuter clinic held in Helena, Montana, about a hundred miles away. After volunteering at a few of these clinics, I asked the organizers how to get a clinic started in our community. The head of the Spay Neuter Task Force, the group that hosted these clinics, put me in touch with several other "animal people" in Great Falls who had the same desire to end pet overpopulation.

Four of us formed a committee and began organizing our first spay/neuter clinic for low-income pet owners. We called our group Spay of the Falls. (Great Falls is located on the Missouri River near a series of natural waterfalls.) We received numerous monetary donations as well as donations of supplies and services from the community. One of the best surprises for me was the number of people that gave endless hours to make sure we were successful. Spay of the Falls teamed with a local animal foundation to share their non-profit status. (Teaming with a non-profit organization allowed the public to donate to our cause and claim the donations on their tax returns.) We were off and running!

It took about ten months and numerous meetings to organize our first clinic, but we were excited to be able to provide this service to people in our community that needed help. The response was overwhelmingly positive from pet owners and potential volunteers. It took a small army but after our first five-day clinic was over, we had altered 1,236 dogs and cats. I was completely hooked! Finally, I knew how I could help animals and really make a difference. This was what I was meant to do!

As I got more and more involved with helping to organize and work at the clinics, I became good friends with another gal on our spay/neuter committee, Leslie (Les). For many years, she had taken in injured and abandoned cats and kittens, got them medical care, and worked hard to find them good homes. She accomplished all of this using her own money while working three jobs to fund her passion. What a wonderful feeling it was to find a kindred spirit and a great friend.

An added dividend as a result of our clinics was that a handful of volunteers from the Spay of the Falls started taking in homeless animals to foster. We met often to brainstorm how to find homes for our foster cats and dogs and eventually founded the non-profit Pet Paw-see Animal Rescue Group. A handful of the volunteers from the newly formed Pet Paw-see were also from the Camp Collie rescue. Others heard about us through word-of-mouth and wanted to join our merry band of animal rescuers. While we had no physical location for potential adopters to meet our cats and dogs, we were lucky that our local Petco Store allowed us to show our animals on weekends. All of our adoptable animals lived in foster homes or were boarded at vet clinics or boarding facilities. On weekends, we brought them to Petco for adoption events.

The manager and employees of Petco were very accommodating to us as we took over their store with cats and dogs each weekend. (Pet Smart was not in Great Falls in the early days of the Pet Paw-see. They opened a store in our city about two years ago.) It took a small army of volunteers to transport tables, cages, blankets, toys, and other paraphernalia to and from Petco for our adoption events, but we were achieving great results. This was all the encouragement we needed. The hard work paid off. We had found an avenue to find good homes for homeless animals.

Everything we did in the first years of the Pet Paw-see was by the seat-of-our-pants. We also learned a lot about what Not To Do during that time and we are still learning. It started with the dreams and passions of a small group of people and has grown larger than we could have imagined. The Pet Paw-see is now a well-respected, non-profit animal rescue group in our city and in our state.

The other non-profit animal rescue group I work with is the Humane Society of Cascade County (HSCC). A group of people formed this non-profit organization in 1975, many years before I moved to this part of the state. While the HSCC does rescue work, the current mission of the board of directors is to attack the issue of cat and dog overpopulation in our county.

I became involved with the HSCC in 2014. In 2015, the non-profit foundation that was the partner with Spay of the Falls decided to go in a different direction and didn't want the responsibility of running the spay neuter clinics. Gladly, the HSCC took over the work of Spay of the Falls so this important service would continue. Since that time, we have held two large annual spay neuter clinics as well as monthly cat-only clinics. In between the clinics, we also schedule pets with local vets for these surgeries rather than "hope" they won't reproduce. Our view is that it is easier to spay or neuter a few cats or dogs now rather than MANY later at one of our clinics.

Being heavily involved in two active rescue groups can be exhausting but very rewarding at the same time. I have met the most wonderful people and made lifetime friends while doing something that I know God put in my heart to do. It is very exciting to know that addressing the huge problem of pet overpopulation in our county started with only a small handful of passionate people and is at a point where we are seeing good results. We still have a lot of work to do but are on the path to improving the quality of life for many cats and dogs.

I started out this chapter by saying, "Be Careful What I Wish For." Even when I feel overwhelmed in rescue, I believe my wish to help animals did come true. I wouldn't have wished for any other way to spend my life. ❧

Fender Bender or "Bennie" for short is my recent foster dog. He was found wandering on an Indian reservation in northern Montana and taken to a vet clinic in the hopes his parents would be found. They were found but didn't want him anymore. At first, I couldn't understand why his owners weren't ecstatic to get him back. Bennie is a sweet cuddly little Whippet mix with lovely melting brown eyes and a unique brindle coat. He LOVES people and wants to always be at my side.

Now I know better! Bennie is like a firecracker on steroids. He doesn't have a "slow" setting. He runs like a maniac whether in the house or in the yard and good luck to any human or animal in his path. Bennie will slam right into my dogs, me, or a wall without a second thought. Nothing seems to slow him down. While he is smaller than my resident mutts, his diminutive stature doesn't seem to deter him. My dogs have threatened to "clean his clock" but he takes no heed. Bennie is fearless!

If Bennie wants something, nothing and no one stands in his way. Bennie makes some of my more challenging canines look tame. In Bennie's world, cats must be chased, (the cat room has a baby gate to keep dogs out but that never stops Bennie, he sails over it) the kitchen table is a handy tool to assist him in viewing the outside world, and my couch . . . Well let's not go there, I am still mad about his latest adventure.

What worries me is how do I find him a good home while still warning a potential adoptive parent about his "quirks"? I don't want to scare anyone away but can't hand him over to an unsuspecting family. I will ponder how to balance raw hard truth while still promoting his good qualities. But I don't have time right now. I am on my way to the furniture store. I heard there was a great sale on couches.

— Chapter 52 —
Rescue, My Passion

I cannot imagine my life without rescue. The blessings have far outweighed the sadness and heartache.

As you can tell from my various stories, rescue is a lifestyle and my passion. It can be extremely heartbreaking while at the same time, incredibly rewarding. Rescue work is difficult because you see the incomprehensible. We see things that bring a person to their knees in tears and hurt our hearts. Often the worst characteristics in some people bring out the best quality in others. You see people rally to help the helpless and give, in countless, astounding ways, to assist animals in trouble. I have seen people bring blankets, dishes, food, and toys to mistreated, scared animals. I have seen people drive hundreds of miles to transport an animal to a safe haven and seen others go out in all kinds of weather to provide an animal with food and comfort.

Those of us who share this passion understand what I mean. It isn't just something you do on an occasional weekend or day off. It becomes a part of your person, a part of your being, a part of your soul. Those of us involved in rescue can often remember the point in our lives when helping animals went from baking some cookies or helping at a fund-raiser, to spending most of our free time actively working to make the lives of unwanted animals better. Some people watching from the sidelines would call it an obsession; I call it a passion.

Animal rescue to me means people helping animals as well as people helping people. It is a network of fellow animal-lovers who keep in contact often only through email. I have so many "rescue" friends with whom I share so much in common, but I have never met face-to-face, some to whom I have never even directly spoken. However, I know that if needed, they would jump to help me help an animal in need. All of us in rescue have a bank of email addresses and phone numbers of people who share this passion. I hope one day to actually meet my wonderful internet friends who lend their support. Som times the support is in the form of money or supplies (toys, blankets, food), but most of the time it is just an understanding ear. I have had the pleasure to meet some of these special friends in rescue and when I do, we chat like old friends. We share a common bond with others who have been through similar difficult situations. Meanwhile, you make a friend for life. We speak the same language and understand the same emotions. When I meet other people involved in animal rescue, we talk about how we manage our home and work lives with the stress of trying to help just one more. Likewise, we like to talk about the successes more than the difficulties. We all need to hear that the emotionally and physically exhausting work we are committed to REALLY IS MAKING A DIFFERENCE.

I often catch myself feeling frustrated and depressed because I sometimes believe my small contribution is really just a little drop in a very LARGE bucket. Then I look into the eyes of the last "drop in the bucket" who crossed my path and I know I AM making a difference. This gives me the fuel to continue even after I have cried many times, "I want my life back, I am done with rescue." I have heard that cry from other "animal rescuers" who have given far more than I have and yet they often find their way back to the world of rescue. It is in our blood; both a blessing and a curse.

A dear friend of mine who has been involved with rescue most of her adult life calls rescue "A Journey." She reminds me that we are all in different places on this journey. Some are "newbies," just starting out in rescue while others are more seasoned, having been involved for many years. It is often hard not to overwhelm people new to this work with how it changes a person and their life. The changes are mostly good but can still take a toll on your mental and physical health if you are not careful, not to mention your pocketbook.

If you have a family, this lifestyle can definitely take its toll. The time required to devote to the "cause" is one essential ingredient in making a difference in the lives of hurting animals. It is often a juggling act if the "rescuer" has a family who also need their time. Seeing families get involved with animal rescue is fairly rare but very inspirational. The Pet Paw-see has been lucky to have a few families jump into our world. It is so heartwarming to see mom, dad and the kids get involved in fostering cats and dogs. What a positive way to teach the next generation how to be kind to animals.

In order to keep their sanity, some volunteers get hardened by seeing animals in trouble. I pray that will never happen to me. If there ever comes a time when I can look into the sad eyes of a mistreated animal and not feel an ache in my heart, then I need to find some other way to spend my time. I truly don't think that I will ever get blasé about helping animals. It seems the longer I am involved in the world of animal rescue, the more passionate I am about doing as much as humanly possible to help animals during my time on earth.

My home has always been shared with animals and I can't imagine my life without them. In these chapters, I shared stories of some of the animals who have been with me on my life's journey. Some animals have been with me for years; others only a short time, but all have left their mark. There are animals I remember with laughter and joy as well as numerous tears. Many have left scars; some scars are visible (bite marks), but most are on my heart.

The tragic stories of incomprehensible maltreatment and those with unfortunate endings are always going to be part of being involved in rescue. Rescuers carry the spirit of the animals that have touched their lives throughout their days. These precious animals are never far from their thoughts and their constant prayer is that the animals they knew are being well cared for and loved. One of the hardest parts of rescue is to watch an animal that has captured your heart, spent day after day with you in your home, been nursed back to emotional and physical health, walk out the door to start a new life with a new adoptive family. But that's the story of rescue. We rescue animals so we can find them a *furrever* home, which usually means with someone other than us (except for an occasional "Foster Failure"). Before letting go I always hug them close to me and whisper in their ear, thanking them for being a part of my life. I feel genuinely blessed by each one.

I chose to write stories that can provide hope and inspiration to others who may be on their own journey called "Animal Rescue." Right now, I want to encourage others with the stories of the amazing animals who have crossed my path as well as the selfless people who continue to help them. The animals on my life's journey have made me a better person and have left countless ***PawPrints Across My Heart.*** 🐾

About the Author

Debi Pace lives in the small community of Vaughn, Montana, with her family of rescued critters.

When she is not working at her full-time job, she is active caring for her resident and foster dogs and cats. Many of the stories in this book were written during the Camp Collie rescue in 2002/2003 with the idea of compiling them into a future book. Unfortunately, the book idea took a back seat once the "rescue" bug bit. What started as baking cookies for the occasional shelter bake sale turned into a passion for helping animals by fostering, working at adoption events and helping to organize spay/neuter clinics. These took up most of her time and the book became a will do someday bucket list item.

As Debi got more involved in animal rescue she had little extra time to sit in front of a computer. But once started, the stories wrote themselves and in only a few months, PawPrints looked like it would become a reality. These stories sometimes heartbreaking, often funny and heartwarming will hopefully inspire others to go the extra mile to help an animal in need.

This is Debi's first book of what she anticipates will be other books on animal rescue. All the animals in this book left lasting paw prints across her heart. Her hopes are the readers of this book will identify with precious animals that have left large, tiny, muddy, and hairy paw prints across their hearts. Fifty percent of the proceeds from *PawPrints Across My Heart* will go towards animal rescue.